Urban Inequality in Finland

Edinburgh Studies in Urban Political Economy

Series Editor: Franklin Obeng-Odoom

In a world characterised by cities, their disproportionate share of problems as well as prospects, and the limitations of mainstream urban economics as a compass, the *Edinburgh Studies in Urban Political Economy* series strives to publish books that seek to better understand, and to address, such challenges. The Global South is of particular interest, but it is by no means the only focus. As an alternative political economy series, it emphasises social sustainability of urban transformations, encourages the use of transdisciplinary political-economic approaches to urban economics, and welcomes books that are both heterodox and pluralist in their economics. Books in the series strive to both engage and to transcend mainstream urban economics, in methodologies, values, and visions, while placing their insights at the disposal of the wider fields of urban studies and political economy.

Titles in the *Edinburgh Studies in Urban Political Economy* series include:

Published:

Open Access *Coal and Energy in South Africa: Considering a Just Transition*
Lochner Marais, Philippe Burger, Maléne Campbell, Deirdre van Rooyen and Stuart Paul Denoon-Stevens

Open Access *Marx's Theory of Land, Rent and Cities*
Don Munro

Open Access *Urban Inequality in Finland*
Mika Hyötyläinen

Forthcoming:

Spatial Agency and Occupation: Foreign Domestic Helpers in Hong Kong
Evelyn Kwok

Urban Inequality in Finland

Land, Housing and the Nordic Welfare State

Mika Hyötyläinen

EDINBURGH
University Press

Edinburgh University Press is one of the leading university presses in the UK. We publish academic books and journals in our selected subject areas across the humanities and social sciences, combining cutting-edge scholarship with high editorial and production values to produce academic works of lasting importance. For more information visit our website: edinburghuniversitypress.com

We are committed to making research available to a wide audience and are pleased to be publishing Platinum Open Access ebook editions of titles in this series.

Edinburgh University Press Ltd
13 Infirmary Street, Edinburgh EH1 1LT

First published in hardback by Edinburgh University Press 2024

Typeset in 11/13 Baskerville by
IDSUK (DataConnection) Ltd

A CIP record for this book is available from the British Library

ISBN 978 1 3995 0151 4 (hardback)
ISBN 978 1 3995 0152 1 (paperback)
ISBN 978 1 3995 9153 8 (webready PDF)
ISBN 978 1 3995 0154 5 (epub)

Contents

Chapters 2 and 4 are loosely based on articles which appeared in the Finnish journals *Sosiologia* (Hyötyläinen 2016) and *Yhteiskuntapolitiikka* (Hyötyläinen 2015) respectively. They have been significantly revised, amended and rewritten. Chapter 5 is rewritten and rearranged from Hyötyläinen and Haila (2018). And some of the research presented in Chapter 6 has been previously published in Hyötyläinen (2020).

Acknowledgements

My sincere thanks to series editor Franklin Obeng-Odoom. It is a privilege to contribute to the Edinburgh Studies in Urban Political Economy. Your comments and feedback greatly improved my original manuscript and helped turn it into a book.

I thank the excellent team at Edinburgh University Press, especially Beatriz Lopez, Sarah Foyle and Grace Balfour-Harle, who showed me great patience and worked with professionalism to see this project to the end.

Anne Haila, Robert Beauregard, Tom Slater, Sami Moiso, Özlem Celik, Callum Ward and Jani Vuolteenaho have all read and commented with precision on some major part of the research that underpins this book. I am deeply grateful for all the advice and criticism that helped sharpen my arguments.

Many thanks also to the anonymous reviewers of the book for their constructive responses.

Finally, thanks to my awesome colleagues and friends at the University of Helsinki and at the Institute of Housing and Urban Research, Uppsala University, for inspiring and supportive work environments over the years.

For Etti. Helsinki, May 2023.

Introduction

For a moment, public attention seemed to focus on the social and economic inequalities of our cities.[1] As cities across the world adapted to the COVID-19 pandemic, nurses, cashiers, people working in food industries, cleaners and delivery workers were called essential workers. While those of us in "less essential" work retreated to our home offices and virtual workspaces, many working-class people were threatened with punitive measures and ordered to brave the pandemic with their bodies, day after day, in public and in their physical places of work (Vegh Weis and Magnin 2021). Not that this was reflected in their pay checks; essential workers continued to toil on wages often insufficient to meet their essential needs (Ferreira 2021). As we stopped eating in restaurants and going to the movies, the CEOs of global corporate giants like streaming services and food delivery platforms enjoyed excessive salaries and bonuses while their employees' incomes saw little or no change.[2] Many lost their jobs altogether as small businesses had to close. And as unemployment soared, people in big cities especially began to fall behind on their rent and mortgage payments. Landlords raising rent or selling their investment properties during the pandemic put tenants at particular risk of eviction (Rogers and Power 2020). Marginalised groups everywhere, including LGBTQI+ people, sex workers, people who suffer from addictions, and those experiencing homelessness, were hit hardest by restrictions and penalties that exposed them to further discrimination and human rights abuses.[3]

Of course, these and many other inequalities were running rampant well before the virus did. Incomes and wealth, for instance, have always been highly unevenly distributed. According to the World Inequality Report (2022), global inequalities are as great today as they were at the peak of Western imperialism in the early 20th century. Today, the richest ten per cent of the global population takes home 52 per cent of global income, whereas the poorest half of the global population earns just 8.5 per cent of it. Global inequality has deepened over recent decades as wealth and assets are hoarded by a miniscule, powerful economic elite (Piketty 2013; Sayer 2015; Christophers 2023). Between 1995 and 2021, the top one per cent seized 38 per cent of the global increment in wealth, while the bottom 50 per cent captured merely two per cent. The richest ten per cent of the global population now own 76 per cent of all wealth (World Inequality Report 2022). And in 2020 just eight men held more wealth than the poorer half of the world's entire population (Politico 2020).

During our era of explosive global urbanisation, it is in cities everywhere that these income and wealth disparities are most evident (UN 2020). While the economies of the world's most prosperous cities are growing, hand in glove with urban economic growth go urban poverty and marginality (Holt 2018; Nijman and Wei 2020). Distributions of occupational opportunities, accessible health care and good schools in cities across the world are skewed in favour of high income and wealthy households. Houses in growing cities are treated increasingly as economic assets for the few and less as a social right for all (Madden and Marcuse 2016; Buller and Lawrence 2022). Just as the British industrial city of Friedrich Engels (1887) in the 19th century was segregated along class lines, and the American city of W.E.B. Du Bois (1903) in the 20th century was segregated along "the colour line", cities in the 21st century continue to be divided along class and racial lines. A vast and precarious urban working class, made up of racialised and systematically marginalised groups, is financially locked out of many of the improvements brought by the growth in urban economies, and spatially locked into distinct, disinvested, often peripheral urban territories (Gourzis et al. 2019; Wacquant 2008). International studies find urban inequalities to persist nearly everywhere (e.g. Arbaci 2019; Nijman and Wei 2020; Slater 2021; Smets and Salman 2008).

There is a place in the world that in the face of these global and urban inequalities is held by many as a beacon of hope. An international political and academic consensus among progressives is that Nordic countries and their cities are exceptionally equal arrangements (Kvist and Greve 2011). The international left and liberals in particular tend to hold Denmark, Finland, Iceland, Norway and Sweden in high regard for promoting social equality in things such as housing, education, well-being and health, and for maintaining economic equality measured in incomes and wealth.[4] And since Esping-Andersen's (1990) influential work on welfare state types over 30 years ago, there has been wide academic agreement that the Nordic countries and their social-democratic welfare states continue to be particularly equal socio-economic configurations (Fritzell et al. 2012; Kangas and Kvist 2019; Righard et al. 2015). The Nordics are widely acknowledged for building economic prosperity on a platform of free market capitalism yet preventing the harsh inequalities and uneven spatial development intrinsic to capitalism's globally dominant neoliberal mutation.

Finland, a Nordic welfare state with a population of five and a half million, has a stout reputation for preventing aggressive social and economic inequalities through extensive redistribution, progressive taxation, collective consumption and universal access to social services, pensions, health care and education. The materialisation of existing social and economic inequalities as spatial differentiation of urban populations was for long averted in Finnish cities through public control over the development of the built environment and consistent planning for the evenness of the urban fabric and inclusive allocation of residential space and public services. And Finland is often flaunted as an example of successful housing policy, characterised by its housing policy targets of tenure and social mixing and housing first initiatives. Recently Finland has made headlines for being among the few OECD countries with falling numbers of people who are experiencing homelessness (Boone et al. 2021).

While Finnish decision-makers are happy to advertise such successes on global forums, Finland has managed to keep up appearances in progressive narratives. Fuelling its continued fetishisation as a place of equality, happiness and harmony, are the kind of irksome lists placing Finns as the world's happiest nation,[5] and armchair analyses discussing what individual Finns do to keep happy.[6] Omitted from such accounts are any notions of how rich Nordic countries happily benefit from the international division of labour and global inequality. Meanwhile, research on the 'Nordic Model' often continues to praise the combination of welfare, equality, growth and export performance. The focus is keenly on institutional complementarities but blind to their many novel contradictions (Tranøyet al. 2020). At the same time, Finland and Finnish cities have also remained off the map of international critical social sciences, including urban studies, which have been more concerned with "the heartlands of global neoliberalism and financial capitalism" (Peck and Tickell 2002). Part of the reason certain countries and their cities remain veiled from research is also the parochial prevalence of studies on the anglophone context. But even a comparative study regarding 'Nordic perspectives on urban marginalization' (Righard et al. 2015), leaves out Finland from the analysis. This has created somewhat of a blind spot in international research on urban inequality as regards Finland.

Does this political and academic consensus regarding the Nordic welfare state, and Finland in particular, hold water? Are Nordic societies and cities today equal arrangements as many like to think? Or is there reason to believe that a Nordic welfare state endures more as a Shangri La, a fiction that plays a "cathartic role"[7] in international progressive narratives, which seek desperately to establish alternatives to neoliberal capitalism and its inequalities? This book, in part, engages with these questions in the specific context of Finnish cities and urban policies. Studying cities on the periphery of mainstream urban studies provides ample opportunities to gain new insights and to widen the scope of analyses in many respects. Analysing second and third tier cities, less spectacular and smaller cities, where issues of social equality are pressing but often more concealed, will help us understand and unpack the motley outcomes of the global urban process under capitalism (Chatterton 2010) and provide a deeper understanding of how that process unravels under the local institutional and state arrangements and the contradictions within those arrangements.

Class dismissed?

The short answer to the above questions is that socio-economic inequalities in the Nordics are still moderate compared to 'the heartlands of neoliberal capitalism'. However, they are increasingly pronounced for instance in Finland. The income and wealth gaps between the rich and the poor are widening (Fritzell, Bäckman and Ritakallio 2012; Stjernberg 2019). It is especially the rich whose incomes have taken a clear break from the rest in recent decades (Jäntti, Riihelä, Sullström and Tuomala 2010; Statistics Finland 2022). Capital income is crucial for explaining growing income differences in Finland (Blomgren et al. 2014). When capital income is included, the growth in income differences in Finland has been the greatest in all OECD countries during the past decade (OECD 2011; Statistics Finland 2013, 2022). According to recent data from Statistics Finland, the official national data registry, in 1995 the average annual income among the lowest-income tenth of the population was 8,900 euros, and it has increased in real terms by approximately 31 per cent from 1995 to 2021. Correspondingly, the average income of the highest-income tenth was 38,100 euros in 1995, from which it has increased in real terms by 103 per cent.[8] So, in 2021 the average annual income of the lowest income decile was approximately 11,703 euros, while for the highest income decile it was 6.6 times higher, or 77,389 euros.

The Gini coefficient, a standard measurement of income inequality receiving a value between zero and one, or alternatively 0 per cent and 100 per cent, zero meaning that everyone has the same income and one meaning that only one person has 100 per cent of all income, has grown from the mid-1990s by seven percentage points. It received the value 29.1 in 2021, which was also 1.4 percentage points up from 2020 (Statistics Finland 2021). Thomas Piketty has criticised the use of the Gini coefficient suggesting that it is "intended to sum up inequality in a single number, but it actually gives an overly optimistic, and difficult-to-interpret picture of what is really going on" (Piketty 2014, 344). The Gini illustrates overall inequality but does not tell us how bad a person's situation is if they belong to the bottom ten per cent, compared to those in the top one per cent (see discussion in Burnazoğlu 2023). Looking at the shares that people belong to, the average for disposable monetary income of the top one per cent of Finns grew in 2021 in real terms by 20 per cent from the year before. In comparison, for the lowest-income decile, average for real income remained unchanged and the income level of the four lowest-income deciles rose by just 0.3 per cent. Persons living in low-income households, households with low work intensity or households that experience severe material and social deprivation are considered being at risk of poverty or social exclusion. According to Statistics Finland, 16.3 per cent of the household population, or 894,000 persons, were at risk of poverty or social exclusion in 2021. The number of persons at risk grew by 117,000 from 2020. Although the COVID-19 pandemic played its part in this growth, a total of 421,600 persons were at long-term risk of poverty, meaning they were at risk of poverty in 2021 and in at least two of the three preceding years.[9]

Again, it is in urban areas that the greatest inequalities can be seen. Large cities, especially the capital city Helsinki, portray the greatest income inequality (Saikkonen et al. 2018). The prosperity brought by growth in urban economies is distributed unequally between and within Finnish cities (Karvonen and Kauppinen 2009; Saikkonen et al. 2018). Urban scholars have for decades mapped the socio-spatial segregation of households with different incomes, but also educational and ethnic backgrounds in Finnish cities. Segregation has been closely followed and has been reported to intensify over the better part of the past two decades. Research shows increasing differentiation again especially in the capital city of Helsinki and the wider Helsinki Metropolitan Area (HMA). This spatial differentiation has been meticulously mapped, geocoded and described and its possible detrimental consequences discussed (e.g. Kemppainen 2017; Kortteinen and Vaattovaara 2015; Saikkonen et al. 2018; Stjernberg 2019). Neighbourhoods have been compared on the basis of experiences of social disorder, and researchers have studied the relationships between neighbourhood background and educational attainment, health, employment and over-generational poverty.

Raising special concern amongst the public and decision-makers are the findings of so-called neighbourhood effects studies, which have looked at the correlations between low-income neighbourhoods and an array of social problems (e.g. Bernelius 2013; Kemppainen et al. 2014; Vilkama et al. 2013). Another major concern for researchers but also policymakers and politicians in Finland is how segregation might affect what researchers call 'social cohesion'. For example, Saikkonen et al. (2018, 48) write "Both low- and high-income households appear to be concentrating in cities, which aligns well with the findings of international research regarding urbanization [. . .]. Social cohesion could be threatened if groups living in very different social realities within and between cities are not acknowledged."[10] Analyses of urban inequality often call our attention to the differences between neighbourhoods, their residents, and the experiences of their weakened social cohesion and separation of 'social realities'. Segregation researcher Venla Bernelius (2020) suggests that what is more important than equality is that people from different backgrounds and social positions 'bump into each other'. Her worry is that the future horizons of the marginalized people and neighbourhoods are narrowed if they do not encounter the better off.

The experiences of inequalities are obviously complex. Related to such complexities, Kvist and Fritzell (2012, 5) write how in the Nordic context:

> the framing or vocabulary of social inequality is now significantly different from that of two or three decades ago. For example, both policy makers and researchers have adopted the discourses of exclusion, misrecognition, segregation, discrimination and inaccessibility – terms that were hardly known or used much more rarely

three decades ago. As a result of this shift, when people today speak of increasing inequalities, they may have in mind something different from or more complex than traditional class inequalities.

Indeed, the experiences of inequality are loaded with intersecting forms of discrimination and exclusion that make those experiences all the more complex and violent. One argument I defend in this book, however, is that for many mainstream commentators, policymakers and scholars, the vocabulary they adopt, claiming to address the nuances of inequalities, is not always informed purely by 'having something different in mind', but by a clear motivation to not speak of class. Very deliberately, class is dismissed from urban analyses as a central dynamic of inequality. The working class has in the long term been made "unfashionable, inscrutable, unnoticed if not invisible" (Wacquant 2008, 200). Studies of segregation, urban poverty, violence, and street crime for instance have replaced traditional research of working-class neighbourhoods in urban studies in general, as the "language of class has been supplanted by the tropes of the 'underclass' in the United States and 'exclusion' in Western Europe wherever working-class neighborhoods have undergone involution" (Ibid.). This supplanting of class is also true of Finnish urban research, as I will illustrate in the coming chapters.

Meanwhile, I argue that urban inequality is in very profound ways about class and class conflict. It is the omission of class exploitation from analyses that leads to paternalist suggestions that if the working-class only "bump into" the better off, they could see their horizons expand and work harder to improve their lot. At the same time this paternalism and class-blindness has allowed some European urban scholars to even worry over *too much* equality, fearing that it will be detrimental to urban economic growth and productivity, as individuals on an equal footing will be less motivated to work hard. Van Ham et al. (2021) for example are concerned that with too much social and economic equality, cities become less dynamic, less diverse, and dull places to live in, where widespread public interventions result in low levels of motivation to achieve and the economy lacks dynamism, leading to sluggish growth and low productivity. They perceive that extreme levels of equality will hence have negative consequences on individuals, cities and societies. The narratives about 'extreme equality' during the contemporary age of severe inequality and persistent urban poverty, as well as advancing marginalisation and uneven development, are not only preposterous but carry possibly severe implications. The suggestion that inequality should be embraced as it will somehow motivate individuals to work harder and boost urban economic growth does little else than fuel penalising workfare and austerity policies towards the already precarious and stigmatised working-class (Wacquant 2008). Coupled with this, class blindness tends to accompany the mainstream faith in urban growth as a cure to urban problems.

A political economy of urban land use and housing

Urban growth is often held to hold the answer to urban inequalities. Mainstream urban economists, celebrants of the 'urban age' and entrepreneurial city managers argue that urban inequality signals the triumph of cities, as it shows cities simply to attract both the poor and the wealthy with their opportunities and riches (for instance Glaeser 2011). Urbanisation is depicted as a rising tide that will lift all boats. Or, at least, the economic growth of a city is argued to eventually trickle down to all of its residents. Against the best convictions of neoclassical and mainstream urban economists and the fantasies of city managers, however, the fruits of urban growth fail miserably in trickling down to those on cities' lowest rungs (Holgersen and Baeten 2017). The tired, market-triumphalist truism about inequality being proof of an accomplished, attractive city does little else than justify the continued development of cities based on the dominance of a neoliberal market rationality of deregulation and privatisation, retrenchment of welfare services and implementation of policies that prioritise the needs of capital.

Critical, urban political economic analysis posits that it is exactly the prioritising of the needs of capital that is behind urban inequality. Although inequalities are perhaps most visible in cities, it is necessary to understand how growth-centred urban development under capitalism itself creates and exacerbates inequality. First, the production of capitalism's contemporary geography is characterised by aggressively uneven urban development as capital investments move through space in search of profitable opportunities to further accumulation (Smith 2008). It is the uneven development of and investment in the built environment that gives social and economic inequalities and class-struggles their spatial character, as cities are segregated into enclaves of wealth and prosperity on the one hand, and neighbourhoods for the working class and the marginalised on the other. And second, the continued project of accumulation by various forms of working-class exploitation, value extraction and dispossession of collective goods and resources as capitalism advances in its assortment of neoliberal and now rentier forms, means that overall global income is unevenly distributed and wealth becomes ever more concentrated in the hands of a tiny elite.

This second dynamic is also intricately linked to the way assets work for the world's wealthiest. One major asset class that has exploded in its importance as a store of wealth and source of yield on investments is real estate (Christophers 2020, 2023). The development of the built environment under contemporary capitalism is propelled onwards more by the need to realise gains on real estate and property assets and less by the needs of people who live in cities (Harvey 2010). There is a tendency to treat land and housing in cities as financial assets according to the rent they yield (Harvey 2006; Haila 1988). Following this, working-class neighbourhoods and households are constantly under assault from gentrification, displacement and housing dispossession as property owners look for ways to maximise rental yields. As Lilius and Hirvonen (2021) suggest within in the context of Nordic welfare states, Finland included, "housing has become increasingly commodified with access to housing becoming an unequalizing issue". And as urban authorities design their policies to compete for private real estate investment, revanchist urban policies are deployed which treat these neighbourhoods as spatial fixes to overaccumulation, and as frontiers where speculation with the extraction of potential future rents is exercised (Harvey 1981; Smith 1986).

However, in addition to the mapping, describing, calculating of correlations and discussing the harms of segregation for social cohesion, there has been little attention paid to explanation of urban inequality by critical urban scholars and political economists working in and on Finland. What has been missing from urban research on Finland, are sustained efforts by urban sociologists and political economists to explain urban inequality. Its very structural dynamics have been largely neglected. This book identifies this lack of attention to explanation as a serious gap in research concerning urban inequality in Finland. Instead of merely focusing on segregation, this book applies wider optics and also discusses housing dispossession, residential displacement, gentrification and withdrawal of key protective policies that all feed into the urban inequality that punishes the urban working-class. The focus of analysis in this book is on transformations in two key policies that have traditionally contributed to Finland's comparably even and equal socio-spatial, urban development – land and housing policies. In this book I explore institutional and legal transformations of the welfare state, entrepreneurial public land policies and a withdrawing state role over housing provision.

In my analysis of land policy transformations, I use case studies and analyse city strategies, policy documents and interviews with urban authorities to show how decentralisation, growing inter-city competition and the adopting of economic policies informed by an ideology of efficiency, growth and entrepreneurialism in governance, have prompted the state and cities in Finland to adopt market rationalities for the use of urban land. Land is increasingly used to maximise land rent revenue to public treasuries. The selling, privatising and leasing with market rent of public land, are seeing cities develop according to the corporate interests of speculative developers, jeopardising the interests of residents. I also explore drastic changes in housing policy, which has slowly abandoned targets it once had of the state supplying affordable social housing. Instead, housing policy in Finland is restricted to subsidising the supply and demand of housing in the private market. In my investigation of the role of housing policy for urban inequality, I couple the political economy approach with a critical, sociological analysis of mainstream scholarly narratives and dominant policy discourses regarding urban inequality and I unpack the symbolic use of housing tenure to categorize people. Essentially, I am interested here in the production of what

Loïc Wacquant (2008) calls territorial stigmatisation – the toxic reputation of working-class neighbourhoods, social housing and their residents.

The aim is to explain how recent transformations in the key policies of a Nordic welfare state that have traditionally worked to curb multifarious urban inequalities, now allow for them to become exacerbated. Regulation and planning in urban development, which aimed at securing the welfare of residents, are increasingly giving way to urban policies that prioritise competitiveness, growth and rent maximisation from public landed assets. We see not a withdrawal of the welfare state but its transformation into an institutional scaffolding of the capitalist economy. The arguments I defend in this book are that while land and housing policies continue to reflect idiosyncrasies of the Nordic welfare state, in Finland they have increasingly been transfigured to also answer to neoliberal rationalities of deregulation, privatisation, efficiency, urban growth and competitiveness. These policies are now part of a state apparatus that increasingly supports the use of land and houses as instruments of accumulation. And in responding to the diktats of capital, the policies are in fact themselves mechanisms contributing to and exacerbating urban inequalities. Through a combination of sociological and critical political economic analysis of these policy transformations, in the chapters that I briefly outline next, I contribute to an explanation of the structural dynamics of urban inequality in Finland.

Outline

This book is divided into three parts. Chapters 1, 2 and 3 constitute Part I. Chapters 1 and 2 provide, first, an overview of international and Finnish research into urban inequality. Chapter 3 explores transformations of the Finnish welfare state. Part II is made up of Chapters 4 and 5. From a political economy perspective, they investigate the traditional and contemporary land policies in Finland and illustrate their links to urban inequality. Finally, Chapters 6 and 7 make up Part III. They focus on housing policy and changes in the provision of social housing. The Coda discusses some main findings and proposes lines of further research. For an extended note on the research material, see the Appendix.

Chapter 1 is an overview of inequality as a research topic for international urban studies. I introduce general approaches to, and concepts used in the study of urban inequality as the discipline has developed over the last century. I do this by distinguishing key theoretical debates in this research field and introducing some of the key authors. Methodological and ontological approaches change and overlap between periods and the purpose of this historical account is to illustrate where ideas and concepts of contemporary research, including this book, derive from. Chapter 2 is a critical analysis of contemporary research on urban inequality in Finland. This research, populated by the use of geographic information systems (GIS) analysis and descriptive segregation mapping by geographers and a positivist sociology of neighbourhood effects research, has relied heavily on statistical data to describe the differentiation of urban populations. The focus of segregation research has been on the housing preferences and migratory patterns of residents, and particularly investigating the moving out of middle-class, Finnish-speaking households from working-class neighbourhoods where immigrants or ethnic minorities are also concentrated. I discuss how a heavy reliance on describing and mapping has left explanations only a marginal role in these studies. Drawing on the literature around the sociology of territorial stigmatisation (Wacquant 2008, 2009) I suggest that one of the major issues with segregation research literature is that its descriptive approach and use of colloquial language may in fact add to negative blemishes of social housing estates and their residents, ultimately exacerbating the phenomenon it simply intends to record and describe.

Hoping to transcend the received wisdoms on spatial differentiation in Finland, Chapter 3 studies transformations in the institutions and conditions under which the state and municipalities in Finland practice land and housing policies. The Finnish welfare state transformed drastically in the 1990s. The idea that a redistributive state should yield to a competitive state (Sipilä 2006) gained momentum, meaning that success in international economic competition became in many respects emphasised over national success of promoting welfare. In the 1990s the tenets of neoliberalism and new public management (NPM) were eagerly adopted in Finland. NPM brought lessons from the business world to the public sector. Consultants and politicians advocating deregulation and privatisation promoted a transformation similar to that studied by David Harvey (1989) in the US, namely a change from managerialism to entrepreneurialism in urban governance. NPM meant a move from central governance to market-led management of the public sector (Anttonen and Sipilä 2000; Kuusela and Ylönen 2013). The strong public sector was seen as heavy, expensive, overly bureaucratic and a hindrance to economic growth. NPM sought efficiency from within the public sector and without, by looking at ways to outsource responsibilities to non-governmental organisations and private companies. The streamlining rationale of the era had great ramifications for how public bodies manage public assets, meanwhile the universalism of public welfare provision and, for example, public housing was criticised.

Next, in Part II, I turn to closer analyses of state and municipal land and real estate policies under the rubric of the above transformations. First, in the introduction to Part II, I discuss the traditional public land policies of the Finnish welfare state that have worked to curb the domination of public good by private interest in land use. Around the turn of the millennium the legislation, administration and objectives of land policy in Finland changed. The law on land use and planning gave more room for public-private partnerships than before. Instead of the traditionally strong public control over urban development, private developers have since had more say over the way Finnish cities are developed. As the central state's role as the funding body of welfare services changed, and its supportive mechanisms to the municipalities have withdrawn, cities have been driven to compete with each other for fiscal resources and external investments. Many cities choose to sell and lease their land to maximise what Anne Haila (2016) has called fiscal rent, land rent used to boost municipal revenues. I illustrate how, ultimately, this fiscal rent policy has made the addressing of urban inequalities through land policy of secondary importance.

I analyse in Chapter 4 these policy changes and the new type of land policy that intensifies inter-city competition; is used to market cities to attract corporate investments; tries to maximise land rent; is practised through the use of public-private partnerships and contracts; and replaces the traditional, robust public planning and redistribution driven approach with growth goals. These novel urban policies drive cities to adopt practices that subject them to the risks of market competition. Cities and the state in Finland have established real estate corporations that manage public lands in an entrepreneurial fashion, prioritising the revenues to be made from land over social targets of land use. Traditional welfare objectives of land policy – preventing and alleviating urban inequality, ensuring open public spaces and housing affordability – are being tested. As the conditions for practising active and systematic policies have deteriorated, public protection has weakened and regulation has loosened, urban dwellers have been left vulnerable to interests of private actors.

Chapter 5 then looks in more detail at the outcomes of the local government of the Finnish capital city of Helsinki selling off public lands and maximising land rent. The chapter draws on a case study of the City of Helsinki deviating from its traditional land and real estate policy of allocating space by leasing. The city sold land in a prestigious city centre location for private developers who built exclusive, high-end housing. The chapter explores why the city favoured the building of exclusive, luxury housing instead of continuing its successful tenure mixing policies. I use the concept of entrepreneurial public real estate policy (introduced in Hyötyläinen and Haila 2018), to explore the switch to selling land and privatising city land. The justifications for entrepreneurial public real estate policy and for privatising land are explored by analysing policy documents and interviews with municipal authorities. I discuss how the new policy risks aggravating urban inequalities by enabling an uneven development of the built environment. Land policy is used to get money to the public treasuries and promote the needs of private companies. Cities in Finland today use their land and real estate in ways that are favourable to developers, bring revenue to the public treasuries and attract highly educated, foreign labour force and taxpaying companies. Yet, such land and real estate policies may lead to increasing displacement and dispossession of local residents from territories of their city, a topic explored in the next part.

In Part III, the final section of the book, I study housing policy and its role in urban inequality. First, a historical analysis of the role of social housing in the Finnish regime of housing provision explores transformations in Finland's housing policy. Chapter 6 shows how Finland has always lacked a robust housing policy that would have allowed the careful planning of future provision of affordable housing for all Finns. Instead, policy has been sporadic and frequently changing its emphasis on subsidising either housing supply or demand. Today, 60 per cent of Finns are homeowners, and owner occupation is the expected goal of any successful housing career. The role of social housing is seen as merely providing an ambulance service for those deemed market incapable, who cannot meet the market price of housing and buy into ownership. Furthermore, housing policy jargon tends to call people who rely on social housing special groups. The rhetoric and practice of housing policy symbolically and physically differentiate people based on tenure. As homeownership is the expected norm, social housing and its residents are seen as abnormal in housing policy language and practice. Housing policy language risks stigmatising the people and their homes who live in social housing, exacerbating the pressures towards urban inequalities, increasing territorial stigmatisation and spatial differentiation. The differentiation of residents in housing policy language enforces the symbolic distancing of owners, private renters and social tenants, possibly exacerbating spatial differentiation.

Chapter 7 further elucidates the follies of housing policy and presents a case study of housing displacement in the working-class neighbourhood of Sörnäinen in Helsinki, Finland. Finland's largest pension provider used to also operate as a non-profit housing company that developed affordable housing for workers with state subsidies. In 1999 the pension company built a rental apartment building in Sörnäinen with state subsidies, under the condition the rents were kept affordable for a minimum of 20 years. During the preceding two decades, the neighbourhood began to see heavy gentrification. In 2019 the company terminated all current rental agreements, justifying its actions with urgent renovations – renovations tenants had been requesting for years. Now as the renovations are over, the pension company is renting out the apartments with market rent. To investigate this event, the state housing policy that has allowed non-profit housing corporations to begin privatising affordable, state subsidised housing stock, is scrutinised. And, making use of interviews with members of four displaced households, the chapter explores the experiences of housing dispossession. They illustrate the painful event of locking out working-class use values from a gentrifying neighbourhood, as families are dispossessed of their homes, everyday routines, place-based identities and communities.

Finally, after Part III, a concluding chapter discusses the most recent changes in Helsinki's land and housing policies in light of the main results drawn from the studies presented in this book. I look to the future and ask how well contemporary land and housing policies are equipped to answer urban inequalities in the coming years.

Notes

1. In addition to an urban inequality, the pandemic lay bare wider, global inequalities. For instance, people in high-income countries were the first to receive the vaccine. And as wealthy nations stocked up on doses, vaccine distribution to low-income countries was severely delayed. Europeans had received several rounds of booster shots and were fully vaccinated against the virus when people on the entire African continent were still waiting for their first dose ("Covid vaccine figures lay bare global inequality as global target missed", The Guardian 21.6.2022).
2. "On average, top CEOs make over $12.3 million. Can that continue after the coronavirus?" (Fortune 27.5.2020).
3. "Covid-19: Pandemic restrictions magnified discrimination against most marginalized groups" (Amnesty International 31.5.2022).
4. For example, US left-wing Democrats Bernie Sanders and Alexandria Ocasio-Cortez have in recent years espoused the Nordic countries and their welfare state model in public debates:
   "Bernie Sanders and AOC support the 'Nordic model'" (Business Insider 3.2.2020).
   "Bernie Sanders is fan of the 'Nordic Model'. Finland's leader says it's the American Dream" (The Washington Post 3.2.2020).
5. World Happiness Report 2023.
6. "I'm a psychology expert in Finland, the No. 1 happiest country in the world—here are 3 things we never do" (CNBC 5.1.2023).
7. To borrow the term from Brett Christophers (2013), who raises this question with regards to the Swedish housing sector in particular.
8. Tuloerojen kehitys Suomessa – tuloerot kasvoivat vuonna 2021 (Statistics Finland 19.12.2022).
9. The number of people at risk of poverty or social exclusion was 894,000 in 2021 (Statistics Finland 24.3.2023).
10. My translation from Finnish original.

PART I

Urban Inequality and the Nordic Welfare State

At the time of writing this, from the window of a spare room in our apartment that during COVID-19 work-from-home restrictions has doubled as an office for my partner and I, I can see the European rowan tree bearing its clusters of small red fruit. The rowan in Finnish is called *pihlaja*. The neighbourhood of the Finnish capital city of Helsinki in which we live is called Pihlajamäki, which translates to Rowan Hill. But despite the copiousness of its namesake shrub, Pihlajamäki is much better known for something else altogether. It is the quintessential working-class apartment-block suburb built in the forests around central Helsinki from the 1960s onwards using new construction technologies and standardised designs, replacing the traditional brick and mortar with prefabricated concrete elements. Pihlajamäki, built as a trial run of its sort of neighbourhood, is also the first of its type of development project in Helsinki that followed the development principles of the era. These principles defined how millions of people across the Nordic region live today. For example, roughly one and a half million Finns live on housing estates (Ministry of the Environment 2022) and two thirds of them on estates built in the 1960s and 70s (Stjernberg 2019). As part of its Million Programme, Sweden built over one million units between 1965 and 1974 which now make up a major part of the country's housing stock. And a majority of this housing was in multi-family housing blocks, which came to form large residential areas in peripheral locations (Hall and Vidén 2006). And even in the least urbanised Norway's biggest city Oslo, about a third of the city's population of 500,000 live in suburban areas dominated by large post-war housing estates (Brattbakk and Hansen 2004).

American, English and Swedish influences saw to a major transformation in Finnish planning ideals in the late 1940s.[1] New residential space was no longer developed as a continuation of the existing urban fabric, but green spaces were left between the congested city centre and the new neighbourhoods where residents would enjoy open spaces and the great outdoors right in their backyard.

The faults of the industrial city – its mixed land uses that saw overcrowded and insanitary residential space next to polluting industry and traffic – were frowned upon and discouraged by separating commercial, industrial and residential space (Turpeinen, Herranen and Hoffman 1997). During the 1950s highly appreciated new neighbourhoods by well-known planners and architects were developed, following functionalism and embracing the garden city ideology. An important but neglected sign of things to come, was the adopting of new development terminology. Whereas in the past the main concern was that buildings were suitable in design concerning the architectural image of an area, the efficiency of urban development now came to the fore. With a newfound focus on calculating plot ratios and floor spaces, the price of development also gained in importance more than ever before (Ibid.).

In the late 1950s Finland began to urbanise rapidly. The traditional, burdensome public planning and development process could not meet the sudden growth in housing demand. (Or so the argument has been worded in hindsight by policymakers. As I shall discuss in more detail in Chapter 6, if there is one constant in Finnish housing policy it is that it does not answer the long durée housing question, but tries only to come up with piecemeal solutions at times of social and economic change.) It has been argued that cities in this period did not have enough developable land in their land banks ready to lease out, and that returns from land leases were not enough to finance public utilities in new areas fast enough (Turpeinen, Herranen and Hoffman 1997; Perhiö 2017). Finland's neighbour to the west was already manufacturing residential spaces as vast development areas, using prefabricated materials. The Swedish Million Programme was fast underway by the mid-60s, answering the same great urbanisation pressures of the time as Swedes flocked to cities in search of work. Finnish cities looked to Sweden for lessons on how to house their own urbanising masses quickly and efficiently.

The influence of new international planning ideologies and development technologies on the development of Finnish cities has been well rehearsed by Finnish planning scholars and architects. Much less discussed, however, is the growing importance of the economic driver of this change at the time – capital accumulation via the development of the built environment and the importance of public land use policy in assisting that accumulation. The land question has changed through history. Drawing on international, historical accounts of urban development, Haila (2016) suggests that the general tendency is that during urbanisation the land question revolves around housing the masses, and during suburbanisation it concerns speculation with fringe land. But I would argue that in Finland the substantial urbanisation of the 1960s was about its peculiar type of suburbanisation. The heaviest period of urbanisation during the 1960s was met not by building housing for the new urbanites in the city centres, but by developing it on marginal land acquired by developers. Apartment block suburbs were erected in the forests, disconnected from the existing urban fabric, by speculative private developers. By the 1960s the garden city lessons of innovative planners and functionalist dreams of architects were replaced by rather more mundane targets for efficiency, cheap construction materials, increasingly commodified housing and maximisation of land rent. Pihlajamäki represents the transition from one period to the other (Kervanto Nevanlinna 2012). To implement their projects, developers needed long term financing thus creating lending opportunities for banks and financial institutions and creating links between the construction industry and banks. Banks then became key agents in financing land purchases and the subsequent development of land in Helsinki (Hankonen 1994).

In 1959 the City of Helsinki initiated a competition for the development rights of an entire new neighbourhood planned eight kilometres north-east of the city centre, Pihlajamäki. Two large Finnish cooperative housing companies called Sato and Haka, made a proposition to the City of Helsinki regarding the sharing of the development between the two. The offer was for the companies to develop the residential area from scratch, beginning with public utilities and ending with the renting and selling of apartments, without input needed from the city – besides allocating the land for the developers and ratifying the plan, greatly alleviating the costs for the city. This became the model for developing new apartment block suburbs in Helsinki. In the 1960s developers were called non-profit companies. They had been established mostly by labour unions to answer the post-war housing needs by developing affordable and high quality housing (Turpeinen, Herranen and Hoffman 1997).

Later on, the developers were the ones initiating the projects. They had acquired inexpensive marginal land in the urban periphery and would persuade the city to sign land use contracts (Kervanto Nevanlinna 2012). The public officials found the proposals increasingly attractive – the city could simply roll over development responsibilities to the private companies and rest back. Important new actors in the development game came to the fore, and new policy instruments that allowed for speeding up housing development were introduced in the form of public-private partnerships. First, the contractee was supplanted by the developer. The developer was a new type of entrepreneur. It was someone who leased, but more preferably bought large tracts of marginal land; instead of a few houses had an entire neighbourhood designed by in-house architects; developed the buildings and made other improvements on the land; and finally, even marketed and sold or rented the homes. Profits to be made in potential land rents were increasingly attractive to private developers.

In her impressive comparative work on segregation in European cities, Arbaci (2019) suggests that Northern European post-war housing development was carried out on public land with strong public planning. The Finnish experience of development areas sheds a contrasting light on this suggestion. After Pihlajamäki, the East and North-East Helsinki neighbourhoods were all implementations of the development area.[2] Here, developers had managed to buy or lease inexpensive fringe land. Vast tracts of this peripheral land were allocated to just a few developers with land use and development contracts, who now came to have a much stronger say in planning and the development of the built environment. In Helsinki's development areas, in fact, the strong public planning system was for the first time purposefully neglected in order to increase building volumes (Hankonen 1994). By the 1970s the developer was a rent-seeking[3] player, who instead of simply following the orders of public officials, was eager to lobby the municipality in the very initial planning phase. Getting its voice heard in planning gave the developer the opportunity to negotiate for more development rights, rather than simply having them assigned by the city planners. Innovative take-over of the different phases of the development process opened all new vistas of capital accumulation for large developers of marginal land. Rapid development of fringe land was then the outcome of development contracts between the municipality and the developers who had bought land outside the city (Mäkinen 2000).

Development areas and contracts gave birth to large monopolies, favouring large landowning developers that were able to build entire neighbourhoods. In some instances, the city's role in public-private partnerships was little more than a rubber stamp as development areas were assigned to developers hastily. The rent seeking and lobbying of politicians by developers has been criticised. Developers have been suggested to have contributed to funding political parties, leading to a reluctance from politicians to regulate them too much in planning (Mölsä 2016). Furthermore, as the city rolled over payments for planning and utilities to developers, developers were moving these costs to housing prices and hence to individual residents (Kortteinen 1982). In the past, such costs would have been more evenly divided between all local taxpayers. Development areas on fringe land forged an increasingly scattered urban fabric and not enough attention was paid to coherent urban development, transportation infrastructure between areas, nor the location of public and private services. Development areas became physically differentiated from the existing urban fabric, reflecting not just planning ideals of yesteryear, but the speculative interest in fringe land of developers (Hankonen 1994). The city became highly differentiated between the city centre with its mixed land uses and the functionally uniform, concrete block suburbia. Yet, the welfare state now ensured that people of different means could find their home in new and at the time highly appreciated housing estates.

In fact, prior to the large-scale development of apartment block suburbs, Helsinki had been socially a divided city. The city centre had been clearly divided into the southern bourgeois neighbourhoods of Eira and Ullanlinna, and working-class neighbourhoods of Sörnäinen, Harju and Kallio to the north. In the 1960s the stark concentrations of wealth and poverty began to disperse, and due to socio-spatial policies aiming at regional equalities – discussed in more detail in Chapter 2 – by 1990, the deep urban divides of the early 20th century had dissipated, and people of different social and economic backgrounds lived throughout the city (Lankinen 1997). Although neighbourhoods like Pihlajamäki were geographically separated from the city centre, they provided good quality housing for different income groups.

The new construction technologies had had a great influence on the planning and development of residential areas. Concrete element construction methods were adopted mainly from the French construction business (the building of the French concrete tower-block estates was a key influence) but were soon found not to be completely suitable for the drastic weather conditions and sub-zero temperatures of the Nordics. And although brick and mortar materials could be as much as six times the price of new, prefabricated concrete elements, the introduction of new technologies did not bring housing prices down as was projected (Hankonen 1994). But now, buildings deteriorated in condition much more quickly. Public oversight for repairs was lacking (Mäkinen 2000). Marxist geographers have taught us that the uneven development of the built environment is how capitalism materialises as urban space. Capital circulates in the built environment, looking for lucrative investment opportunities. These opportunities arise unevenly as capital moves from one place to the next in search of potential land rents. But improvements on land would require continued investments to be maintained. Once investments leave, those who can afford to do so usually follow (Harvey 2006; Smith 1982, 1989). Since the 1990s many housing estates have seen piecemeal disinvestment. Over the years many of the areas did not see the needed repairs. These suburbs seldom saw upgrading investments; services were poor and declined even further when higher income groups moved out. Some of these demographically heterogeneous neighbourhoods became increasingly working-class, as middle-class residents left soon after the investments did. Socio-spatial unevenness was aggravated, as the municipalities of the HMA had different resources and policies to answer housing need. Helsinki has built social housing, small apartments and practised social mixing in neighbourhoods. Espoo has concentrated on semi-detached owner-occupied housing. Kauniainen maintains its villa settlement nature. The different responses to urbanisation by the municipalities slowly contributed to social differentiation (Haila and Le Galès 2004).

Despite the humane planning ideals, capital accumulation should be seen as a primary motor of introducing development areas. Housing companies like Sato and Haka that were established in the post-war era, have turned into listed companies, and have since turned from developers to rentier capitalists. Their main shareholders are domestic and international banks and investment funds. Municipalities are today the sole providers of a residualizing stock of social rental housing, which they direct increasingly at so-called special groups. This housing is today disproportionately found concentrated in peripheral housing estates. Since the turn of the millennium, socio-spatial differentiation has become a growing concern. A new type of differentiation along markers such as employment status, income and household education levels, but increasingly also ethnic background, is found in the HMA. This differentiation has since been one of the key concerns of urban geographers and sociologists in Finland.

By 2015 soi-disant segregation researchers who had been studying and mapping spatial differentiation for nearly two decades published a paper in which they called the preceding twenty-year period the "age of segregation" (Kortteinen and Vaattovaara 2015). They were now convinced that segregation had been growing and had become a key feature of life in the capital region. This was an important and unsettling finding, one of major public interest and policy implication. It pointed to increasing urban inequality and spatial division of the lived realities of social groups. Despite the importance of their findings, the explanations given for this phenomenon have been left wanting and research outputs have been predominantly descriptive. Alas, I suggest, descriptive segregation research has gone a long way in shaping the contemporary dominant discourse (Bourdieu 1998) around urban inequalities in Finland. But before unpacking the implications of that suggestion in Chapter 2, let us look at how urban inequality has been approached by international urban scholars over the past century. Chapter 1 will help in understanding the theories and concepts adopted by Finnish researchers.

Notes

1. In 1947 Finnish professor of urban planning O. I. Meurman published a seminal work *Asemakaavaoppi* which introduced overseas influences on Finnish planners' desks overnight.
2. The neighbourhoods of Kontula, Jakomäki, Myllypuro and Mellunmäki are well-known examples.
3. Rent seeking means lobbying public officials for extended and intensified rent extraction opportunities. For example, increased development rights. See Haila 2016.

CHAPTER 1

Inequality as a Research Topic in Urban Studies

Urban inequality is a major research topic for urban studies and researchers approach the topic in vastly different ways. One takes it as a natural situation simply to be observed, mapped, and measured, a second regards it a blemish on the image of the city and a hindrance to urban competitiveness, while a third might argue it reflects poorly on the quality of urban life and should be tackled with appropriately designed policies. Urban scholars draw their concepts and theories from disciplines such as anthropology, economics, geography, political economy, political science, and sociology. This multidisciplinarity partly explains the different approaches to and analyses of one of its central topics. The approaches to the study of urban inequality have developed in historical periods of interdisciplinary critiques and their responses. Methodologies overlap between periods. The approaches of one period might be heavily criticised and omitted in the second, only to find applications again in the third. This book also adopts an interdisciplinary approach as it draws on political economy and sociology. I draw the main theoretical approaches and analytical concepts from two pertinent critiques of mainstream urban research: critical urban political economy formulated and developed in the works of authors like David Harvey, Neil Smith, Brett Christophers and Anne Haila, and the sociology of territorial stigmatisation introduced by Loïc Wacquant and developed by Tom Slater and several others. In this chapter I introduce some key traditional and contemporary approaches and concepts used in the study of urban inequality within the field of urban studies. This is not an all-inclusive overview but focuses on European and American major research traditions in order to introduce the key influences behind contemporary research on urban inequality in Finland. Although this is a well-rehearsed history, it bears some repeating as it allows one to understand more fully the roots of the methodologies, concepts, research designs and their key critiques used and developed by contemporary urban scholars.

In this chapter I discuss first the segregation research of the Chicago School of Sociologists that arguably birthed urban studies. Second, I introduce the bid rent theory and concentric land use model of the urban economists. Third, I present the Marxist geography as a critique to both of the above, and the way it revolutionised the discipline. The fourth research tradition I discuss deals with the notion of the global, post-industrial city and the related concept of social polarisation. Related to the polarisation thesis, I then introduce the revival of the populist notions of the ghetto and the underclass, their ill-suited transfer to the European context and, finally, their powerful critique in the sociology of territorial stigmatisation. Lastly, I discuss contemporary European segregation research. Contributing to the field of critical urban studies, the ontological position I take is that ultimately, urban inequality reflects the inherent inequality of capitalism and its unjust class relations. To understand urban inequality is to understand how class inequality is translated into urban space through uneven capitalist development, and importantly, the role of the state in this. For a brief period, the social democratic Nordic welfare state kept inequalities relatively in check. This book investigates how some of the equalising mechanisms of the welfare state have now been recoiled, and the ramifications of this policy retrenchment for urban inequality.

Segregation as a natural and market process

Questions regarding spatial divisions and differentiation of people in cities have puzzled urban scholars for over a century. The birth of urban studies is commonly associated with a group of sociologists at the University of Chicago working from the 1920s onward. Robert Park, Ernest Burgess, Roderick McKenzie and Louis Wirth, among several others, made up a group of scholars widely referred to as the Chicago School of Sociology. "The first true school of urban sociology" as Hall calls it, the Chicago School was characterised by their work "towards a total understanding – based on theory, tested on observation – of the social structure of a great city" (Hall 1996, 366). For the Chicago School, the object of study was the American city, a city of immigrants. The most important social structure they observed was the segregation of ethnic groups and social classes. To analyse segregation Chicago sociologists adopted a terminology from the natural sciences. The competition for space and the concentration of people with similar preferences were depicted as natural phenomena, not unlike animals and plants competing for space in the natural world. Park (1926, 9) writes that "the Chinatowns, the Little Sicilies, and the other so-called 'ghettos' are special types of a more general species of natural area which the conditions and tendencies of city life inevitably produce". Segregation was defined as the outcome of competition for space and the voluntary self-segregation of distinct groups, who selected the neighbourhood based on their interests and tastes (Park 1926; Wirth 1964). The Chicago School produced two bodies of work, one associated with the ecological mapping of the so-called "natural areas" of Chicago, the other with a series of ethnographies of diverse social groups in the city (Savage and Warde 1993, 9).

First, the goal of mapping was to systematise a general model of segregation. Ernest Burgess (1925) famously depicted the expansion of the city with an ideal-type illustration consisting of a series of concentric rings designating successive zones of expansion and types of areas differentiated in this process. In the centre of a city a central business district (CBD) was to be found, surrounded by first an area of light manufacture. The second ring was a residential area of workers, the third a district of detached homes and high-end apartments. Finally on the last, outermost ring one could find suburbs and satellite towns. Burgess explained how urban expansion happened through the "tendency of each inner zone to extend its area by the invasion of the next outer zone. This aspect of expansion may be called succession, a process which has been studied in detail in plant ecology" (Burgess 1925, 50). On these concentric rings different groups would then find their place in the city. Burgess explains how "this differentiation into natural economic and cultural groupings gives form and character to the city [. . .]. These areas tend to accentuate certain traits, to attract and develop their kind of individuals, and so to become further differentiated" (Ibid., 56). This idea that distinct neighbourhoods attract, develop and accentuate distinct types of individuals was widely accepted. As I will discuss later, it resonates even today in the tradition of so-called neighbourhood effects research.

The second body of work consisted of ethnographies of distinct people in distinct neighbourhoods, essentially focusing on categories of people outside the white bourgeoisie. From anthropology, sociologists borrowed the method of participant observation. Where anthropologists worked abroad to understand foreign lands and people, sociologists worked in their home city hoping to understand "unfamiliar" neighbourhoods and their residents – immigrants, gangs, the poor, Black and Asian people – sociologists were predominantly white, middle-class men producing knowledge about their 'Other'. A recent critical reading of the Chicago School ethnographies by Montalva Barba (2022) provides an analysis of how the white bourgeois standpoint of Chicago sociologists was inscribed as the ordinary, native and organised position, indicating who would become the subject of research. And the ecological terminology characterised this knowledge production, as segregation was regarded as a natural phenomenon. As Robert Park wrote of poor neighbourhoods "Association with others of their own ilk provides . . . not merely a stimulus, but a moral support for the traits they have in common which they would not find in a less select society. In the great city the poor, the vicious, and the delinquent, crushed in an unhealthful and contagious intimacy, breed in and in, soul and body" (Park 1925, 45).

Cementing the white middle class as an organising agent of the city, research focused on racialised groups and ethnic 'Others', those viewed as culturally and socially distinct, those of lower socio-economic classes, the poor and the delinquent (Montalva Barba 2022). Further perpetuating the racist methodology and the idea that the University of Chicago was the primary source of American sociology, the Chicago sociologists systematically omitted mention of the works of the Black sociologist W. E. B. Du Bois. Du Bois had been writing a sophisticated sociology of race relations decades before the Chicago School, while criticising capitalism, protesting Jim Crow laws and discrimination, and championing full civil rights for Black people (Morris 2015). Du Bois' (1899) work in *The Philadelphia Negro* was in fact the first American sociology to combine registry data and surveys, hence providing the theoretical and empirical basis for the works of the Chicago School, a basis they never referred to or acknowledged. There is reason to argue for a rewriting of the canon of American sociology to have begun not in the white department of sociology at the University of Chicago in the 1920s, but in the predominantly Black Atlanta University in the 1890s (Morris 2015).

The approach of Chicago School urban sociology was empirical and positivistic. It used statistics and illustrated them with case studies, observations and ethnographies of individuals, households and their communities. From the 1920s to the 1950s the Chicago School of Sociology solidified the study of socio-spatial difference and social disorder within the city as a key objective of urban studies. The mapping of neighbourhoods, ethnographic studies and quantitative methods has been essential for urban sociologists ever since. The contribution of the Chicago School to urban studies is of undeniable importance, not least for defining an object of study for empirical urban research (Hall 1996, 370). The school's influence was profound and international in reach. In Finland, professor of social policy Heikki Waris, in his seminal doctoral dissertation of 1932, conducted a detailed, Chicago-School-style, empirical study of the social and material conditions of daily life in the working-class neighbourhoods on the north side of the city centre in Helsinki. These were communities spatially, socially and culturally differentiated from the bourgeois South Helsinki. In Finland the study is regarded as a classic in social sciences and a formative text for urban studies. It is an invaluable window into the urban class hierarchies and socio-spatial divisions of Helsinki at the end of the 19th century. In Chapter 2 I will discuss the enduring legacy of the Chicago School in contemporary segregation research in Finland.

The concentric zone theory was the foundational tool used by Burgess in his sociological study of the city. However, it is the location theorists and the urban economists who have made the most use of a concentric model of the city in their analyses regarding the competitive bidding for land. Mainstream urban economics is broadly the economic study of allocation of resources in urban areas and urban land use. It involves using the tools of neoclassical economics – namely the framework of marginal utility and equilibrium – to analyse urban spatial structures and things like the location of households and firms. The planner and economist William Alonso (1964), and economists Edwin Mills (1967) and Richard Muth (1969) are perhaps the most noted thinkers behind location theory and mainstream urban economics, the formation of land rent in urban areas, and spatial modelling of population distribution. First, Alonso translated the 19th century German landowner, farmer and economist Johann Heinrich von Thünen's agrarian land use model to one of urban land uses. For von Thünen land rents – the abstract concept denoting a payment made by the user of land to its owner – were a function of distance and transportation costs to a central marketplace. Therefore, land that is closer to the market has lower transportation costs and commands higher rent. Land users all compete for the most accessible land closest to the market. The amount they are willing to pay is called "bid rent". There are competing uses of the land in terms of what agricultural commodity the farmer produces, and some products need shorter transportation times to the market (e.g. dairy products) than others (e.g. grain). The result is a pattern of concentric rings of land use, commonly known as von Thünen rings (Richardson 1977).

Like von Thünen, Alonso assumed a central node, in the urban context the CBD, and rising transportation costs as one moves away from the CBD. Urban land use would then be determined through a process of competitive bidding for the use of land. Alonso (1964) expected poor people to have little money to spend on transportation costs and so their ability to bid for the use of land (housing) declines with the distance from the city. Meanwhile the rich may choose to live further out and pay more towards transport costs to own a larger plot of land. The approach was amended by Mills (1967) and Muth (1969) with more detailed deliberation on urban growth, housing and equilibrium of locational costs and benefits. Eventually it became known as the Alonso-Mills-Muth model, or the standard urban land use model, a mainstay of mainstream urban economics. As it pertains to urban inequality, segregation in this model is taken simply as an outcome of the different abilities of households to bid for residential space. Attesting the endurance of the model, in Finland contemporary urban economists such as Heikki Loikkanen and Seppo Laakso (2019) notably build their analyses and arguments on it. They have been advocating Helsinki's new land policy, which sets the leases on public land according to market rent and profits from the allocation of land in auctions based on highest bids. I discuss and problematise this in more detail throughout the book. But despite the endurance of the naturalising narrative around segregation of the Chicago sociologists and of the market determinism of mainstream urban economics, a powerful critique of both had developed already in the 1970s and 80s.

The urban revolution

In the 1970s criticism and alternatives to the approaches of urban ecology and urban land economics were emerging on both sides of the Atlantic. In 1970, the French philosopher and sociologist Henri Lefebvre's influential book *The Urban Revolution* was published. In the revolts against capitalism, imperialism, war, racism and patriarchy that shook cities worldwide in the 1960s, Lefebvre saw symptoms of another profound revolution: the changing of a world once agrarian, then industrial, to now an urban world. Lefebvre voiced an urgent task: the urban needed to be theorised, a task in which urban ecology had failed. Marxist urban scholars were ones to take this provocation for theorisation most seriously. First, in 1972 Manuel Castells's *The Urban Question: A Marxist Approach* saw the light of day. Castells took Lefebvre for "one of the greatest theoreticians of contemporary Marxism", but also heavily criticised the way Lefebvre's ambiguous urban ideology in the end overpowered any robust Marxist analysis (Castells 1977, 86–7). Hence, Castells wanted to develop a Marxist approach to the city based on theoretical work around the question of what the process of social production of the spatial form of a capitalist society is, including the actions of administrative state policy, productive market forces, and human action in the form of lifestyles and culture.

A year later, also drawing on Lefebvre's insights, but attacking more directly the question of urban inequality, the geographer David Harvey's (1973) *Social Justice and The City* was published. In this work, nothing short of revolutionary for the discipline of urban studies, Harvey understood that competitive bidding over space and segregation was not a universal and natural characteristic of cities, as the urban economists and Chicago Sociologists had claimed, but a characteristic of a very distinct kind of city, the capitalist city. Capitalism was the condition for the contemporary urban process, and Harvey developed the approach of Marxist political economy to understand the process. The approach focuses on the importance of analysing capital accumulation and circulation and investment flows as the drivers of the urban process. And to understand urban inequality it stressed the importance of the unequal social relations under capitalism, the class conflict between capital and labour.

Harvey worked in the context of the American metropolis where Black Americans were predominantly living in inner city ghettos. Ghettos were seen as a social problem, and social scientists and public commentators continued to be concerned about segregation. Using the segregated city of Baltimore as his case study, Harvey put forth a critique of the descriptive sociology of mainstream urban studies based on liberal formulations. Instead of empiricism and ethnographies of Black and poor people, Harvey called for a critical approach to urban theory, one that would not merely entail more empirical investigations of the social conditions in the ghettos. Harvey (1973, 144–5) writes:

> This kind of empiricism is irrelevant. There is already enough information in reports, newspapers, books, articles and so on to provide us with all the evidence we need. Our task does not lie here. Nor does it lie in what can only be termed 'moral masturbation' of the sort which accompanies the masochistic assemblage of some huge dossier on the daily injustices to the populace of the ghetto over which we beat our breasts and commiserate with each other before retiring to our fireside comforts . . . Nor is it a solution to indulge in that emotional tourism which attracts us to live and work with the poor 'for a while' in the hope that we can really help them improve their lot.

Yes, cities are segregated, Harvey concurred, but this segregation can hardly be understood by visiting the ghetto, by mere statistical reporting or by mapping population distributions. Nor could it be explained by individual choices and decisions. Harvey coupled his criticism of liberal sociological formulations with an unpacking of central notions of mainstream urban economics that are based on neoclassical models and marginalist land use theories. If the objective was to eliminate segregation, surely one should not merely shrug it off as the outcome of competitive bidding. The land use models of economists took for granted the question *why*, and simply described the reality – different groups forced to compete and bid for land in the city, the winners always ending up with the first pickings. For Harvey, it was this reality that needed to be understood, the reality that gives truth to the von Thünen theory (Harvey 1973). To understand ghetto formation the question we must ask is why are urban residents forced to compete and bid for land in the first place, and what is the cause of the vast difference in their ability to pay for space?

Harvey (1973, 177) writes how rent is accepted by urban land use theory:

> in an innocent state as if there were no serious problems attached to its interpretation. This fact may be accounted for by the pervasive and complete acceptance in micro-economic urban land-use theory of the neo-classical view that rent is the return to a scarce factor of production and that land is in essence no different from labour and capital.

Turning to the Marxist conceptualisation of rent meant understanding rent as a social relation; that it is the private property in land that allows real estate owners and developers to extract surplus value in the form of rent and force households to enter these bidding competitions for residential space that gives truth to the theories of mainstream urban economics. Later Harvey has also discussed the role of land as a pressure valve in capital circulation. The major destination for surplus value produced through labour exploitation is the primary circuit of capital, the productive sector. But when production wavers, excess capital investment is switched and directed in land and buildings, or the secondary circuit of capital (Harvey 2006; Beauregard 1994; Christophers 2009). Private property in land enables investors to keep accumulating even if production has halted while the secondary circuit dampens capital's crises.

Marxist urban political economy thus emerged as a critique of the urban economics paradigm, particularly the latter's explanation for the growth and structure of cities and regions. In emphasising the spatial competition for resources by individuals, groups and institutions, mainstream urban economics had neglected political hierarchies, power relations of domination and exploitation. By introducing class and power relations to the discussions on urbanisation, Marxists were able to move away from the descriptive concentric land use models and come to a fuller understanding of the central role of land in urban politics and class struggles. Marxist political economy has shown how the specific functions of land and rent under advanced capitalism underpin uneven spatial development, which is a major aspect in urban inequality (see Smith 2008). Capital invests in areas where higher returns are expected, but also disinvests from existing areas where the potential for profits is lower. The resultant unevenness spatialises class conflict. An example of uneven geographical development is residential and commercial investment in suburban development, which I discussed in the introduction to Part I, where land and development costs are much lower than in the urban core. When developers attract households to these areas and retailers and office users follow, capital establishes a new location of investment opportunities to replace a previous location (the inner city, now financially superseded). The result is an uneven landscape with areas of growth and decline.

Marxists called for a paradigm shift in urban studies. Instead of accepting the status quo, scholarship was to be critical, and instead of a narrow focus on communities and individuals, wider optics were adopted to investigate the political economy of the city and uneven development of the built environment under capitalism. The task for critical urban scholars was to theorise and explain urbanisation, not to describe segregation. The works of Marxist geographers helped to redefine the 'urban' in urban studies. They saw that urbanisation under the conditions of private property in land and maximisation of rent was bound to produce uneven development of the built environment and lead to urban inequalities such as the spatial differentiation of classes. As John Friedmann (1986, 69) writes:

> Henceforth, the city was no longer to be interpreted as a social ecology, subject to natural forces inherent in the dynamics of population and space; it came to be viewed instead as a product of specifically social forces set in motion by capitalist relations of production. Class conflict became central to the new view of how cities evolved.

One scholar engaged directly and in a profoundly important way with the topic of urban inequality through the concept of rent was Neil Smith (1982, 1986), who developed the rent-gap thesis to make sense of gentrification or the middle-class takeover of working-class neighbourhoods to the displacement of their original inhabitants. For Smith, it was uneven capital investments in the built environment, emerging of rent-gaps – or the difference between actual and potential land rent – and speculation by land and real estate owners for potential rents, which caused gentrification, not simply the whimsical changes in the housing and lifestyle preferences of the middle class. I return to the topic of gentrification and the rent gap thesis in the final chapter. In Finland, Anne Haila (1988, 1990, 2016), though not a Marxist scholar nor specifically writing on questions of urban inequality, can be largely credited for introducing critical urban studies and urban political economy through her writings and lectures. Her corpus of work on urban land rent theory has been of great importance internationally. For Haila, it is the speculative behaviour of developers and private landowners that cause housing unaffordability and urban inequality, as land use is coordinated by the landowners' endeavours to maximise land rent. As an urban scholar Haila (2015, 2016) advocated for practical urban policies such as large public landownership, strong housing officials and robust housing policies, and the eradication of land speculation. I return to the works of Haila when discussing transformations in Finland's land policies in Part II.

Polarisation in the post-industrial city

By the late 1970s, in advanced capitalist countries the manufacturing sector was in decline and as the significance of the service sector increased, occupations shifted from manual work to managerial, professional, secretarial and service work (Mollenkopf and Castells 1991). Class divisions in the so-called post-industrial society (Bell 1973) were diversifying. The big industrial middle and working classes were descending, while a class of low-skilled service workers and a highly skilled, highly paid professional class were emerging. More than before, alongside these arguably novel class divisions, intersecting racial, ethnic and gender divisions and inequalities were also being recognised. Scholars debated the question of how to best depict "new" social divisions and urban inequalities in the post-industrial city. A key concept that was introduced in this period was "social polarisation". The idea was that the new division of labour in the post-industrial society – the formation of social classes of a highly-skilled, well-paid professional elite on the one hand and a low-skilled, poorly-paid service class on the other, with an ever-widening gap between the two – was seeing to the disappearance of the robust, homogeneous classes of the industrial era.

The new division of labour and its spatial organisation as polarisation was seen as a characteristic feature of the world city, or global city (Friedmann and Wolff 1982; Sassen 1991). For Friedmann and Wolff "the primary social fact about world city formation is the polarisation of its social class divisions" (1982, 322). A new cleavage had emerged between the dominant class of transnational elites and a class of service-labour tending to the needs of elites. And urban scholars were interested in the spatial manifestation of this polarisation and suggested that world cities were characterised by a spatial organisation that reflected this division. On the one hand, there is a citadel of the ruling class, answering the lifestyle demands of the elite. On the other hand, there exists a city that serves the servant class, physically separated from the citadel: the ghetto of the poor (Ibid.). Saskia Sassen (1991) argued that the number of highly paid professionals and those in the low paid service class were increasing, whereas the middle-income groups were declining. The appreciation of urban living by the cosmopolitan elite led to the gentrification of centrally-located working class neighbourhoods in global cities. In this way, social polarisation resulted in spatial polarisation and deepening segregation.

Like Friedmann, who wrote about two cities, Mollenkopf and Castells (1991) wrote about dual cities. The concept of the dual city refers to the division of the city between the haves and the have-nots, the rich and the poor. Mollenkopf and Castells (1991, 16) write that "the dual city metaphor has the virtue of directing our attention to the new inequalities that define the post-industrial city, just as depictions of 'How the Other Half Lives' defined the emerging industrial city a century ago".[1] Dickensian tales of divided cities have been common in western literature, journalism and scholarship. However, even if done with the best of intentions to depict and study urban inequality, a danger lurks in the metaphor of the dual city. Instead of raising awareness of urban inequalities, the metaphor risks reinforcing them. Peter Marcuse (1989) for one has criticised the metaphor of the "dual city" for being "muddy". If we hold the city divided into two cities, a city doing well and a city doing poorly or "a city of light" and "a city of darkness", Marcuse suggests, we most likely make our interpretations from the point of view of the city of light. Like the Chicago sociologies, the social-polarisation-works risked reserving the city of darkness for the 'Other', the poor, the immigrant, the destitute, but analysing them from the perspective of affluence. For Marcuse, the dual city metaphor places too strong an emphasis on exploring differences between the two halves. The muddy metaphor is then put forth at the cost of investigating the structural dynamics of a capitalist economy built on unequal and exploitative class relations, and the type of urbanisation processes that result in the spatial reflection of said inequality as geographic differentiation. The metaphor of the dual city may be muddy, but there are other metaphors perhaps even more detrimental to the process they attempt to describe.

The ghetto and the underclass

In the 1980s, urban scholars were again readjusting their view on inequalities. In the United States, deepening racial segregation continued to occupy urban sociologists. Sophisticated methods to measure and analyse segregation were employed. Studies such as Douglas Massey and Nancy Denton's (1987) *Trends in the Residential Segregation of Blacks, Hispanics, and Asians: 1970-1980* and William Julius Wilson's (1987) book of the same year *The Truly Disadvantaged – The Inner City, The Underclass and Public Policy* showed the poor Black population was being increasingly pushed into an ever-deteriorating ghetto. In their book *American Apartheid: Segregation and the Making of the Underclass*, Massey and Denton (1993) introduced the idea of "hyper-segregation" to depict the multidimensionality and intensity of the segregation of Black and white Americans. Escaping sophisticated analysis of the multidimensionality of segregation, however, was the hijacking of the concept of the "underclass" that regained momentum in its popular use in this period.[2] The term had already been used by scholars in the 1970s, but by the 1990s "urban underclass" had become a widely used folk concept in the United States. It was used particularly to depict the populations locked in the ghetto.

The word underclass was adopted from aforementioned scholarly works by American journalists who turned it into a behaviourist term. In its new meaning, the underclass was used to refer to "mostly poor black people, who behaved in criminal, deviant or just non-middle-class ways" (Gans 1999, 142). The term "urban underclass" became a pejorative and stigmatising moniker used at times in research literature, but mainly in the American media, to blame those locked in the ghetto, who were accused of being "disengaged from the regular labour market and engaged in unacceptable behaviour ranging from producing children through consuming drugs to committing murders" (Fainstein 1996, 154). The underclass is comparable to Oscar Lewis's (1959) infamous "culture of poverty" thesis, which has been used to depict poverty and destitution as outcomes of the behaviour and values of the poor themselves. The term underclass had the effect of obviating a search for an explanation for urban poverty and marginality. It was a way to blame the single mothers, the unemployed, the drug addicts and basically all Black, ghettoised populations for being part of a dangerous group of deviants. With its populist and racist connotations, the term urban underclass became a moral accusation. It avoided any understanding of the realities of Black American victims of systematic racism, of their detachment from the labour market and from mainstream white America, how they had been cast into disinvested and dilapidating neighbourhoods. Instead, it blamed the victim for their predicament.

In Europe, the post-war welfare-state policies, universal education, health care, unemployment benefits, pensions and income redistribution had the effect of keeping in check growing poverty and urban inequality. Policies also tackled the process of segregation. Public land ownership ensured municipal control over planning and the development of the built environment, and the provision of public housing. European cities were less segregated than cities in the United States (LeGales 2002; Haila 2004). As van der Wusten and Musterd (1998, 239) noted, "welfare states formed major barriers to segregation and exclusion when they were, for one brief generation after the Second World War, the hegemonial project of state formation in the western world". I return to the topic of welfare state formation as barrier to segregation in more detail in Chapter 3. However, by the 1980s and 1990s, concerns over social differentiation and urban inequality were growing in European cities. Of special concern was the concentration of marginalised populations in peripheral housing estates. Scholars compared the growing urban inequality in Europe to segregated US cities and this led to anxiety over the birth of a dangerous "underclass" also in Europe. The idea of an underclass or a "class outside the class structure" was of course nothing new in

European literature. Marx and Engels had already written about the *lumpenpro-
letariat* or "a dangerous class, the social scum, that passively rotting mass thrown
off by the lowest layers of the old society" (1848, 20). What was a new feature in
the analysis of the European underclass of the late 20th century was that it took
on an "ethnic" component.

Because of an "increase in the settlement of immigrant populations formerly
thought of as guest-workers or colonial subjects" (Wacquant 1996, 234), there
was a growing number of disenfranchised, racialised minorities located in the
same post-war housing estates as the working-class victims of economic restructuring. The concern over the birth of an underclass of the unemployed and the
poor in Europe was combined with the concern over its territorial concentration
in "ethnic enclaves", comparable to the Black ghetto of the American city. In
their attempt to understand the processes of growing urban inequality, some
European scholars borrowed the concepts and methods from American sociologists. According to Loïc Wacquant (2008, 164),

> European analysts and commentators have turned to the United States for ana-
> lytic assistance in their effort to puzzle out the current deterioration of urban con-
> ditions and relations in their respective countries . . . European poverty was being
> 'Americanized' – that is, falling in line with a pattern of segregation, destitution
> and violence (mis)identified with the Black ghetto.

This criticism by Wacquant gave shape to one of the most fascinating, critical
contemporary sociologies of urban inequality.

Territorial stigmatisation

A major contribution to contemporary sociological research regarding urban
inequality and poverty is Loïc Wacquant's work on urban marginalisation (2008,
2009). A source of inspiration and contestation for many contemporary, critical
urban sociologists and geographers (see e.g. Kirkness and Tijé-Dra 2017; Makki
and van Vuuren 2017; Slater 2017; Tyler and Slater 2018; Sisson 2020) we find
Wacquant's corpus of work informed by the following central arguments. First,
social marginality maintained under advanced capitalism throughout the world's
cities involves a new type of relegation of the populations on society's lowest
rungs to decaying neighbourhoods where the continued social fall of working-
class households and settling in of immigrant populations meet and intensify.
And second, a powerful, toxic narrative regarding distinct areas of relegation
then attaches itself to marginalised populations of those areas – people who
already carry the social blemishes of poverty, ethnicity and race – locking them
further in place. As this process of territorial stigmatisation unravels, local daily
lives and social realities are veiled by the reputation of the neighbourhood which
works its way from public discussions to local understandings, turning slowly into

a self-fulfilling prophecy; as a territory becomes known for some perceived social evil, its residents will develop coping mechanisms. They will find symbolic and material ways to distance themselves from their neighbours who are suddenly viewed as the sole causes of those very same evils. Social atomism, disorganisation of the community and cultural anomie are then exacerbated by the very territorial stigma that described them (Wacquant 2008).

The spatial dynamic of urban marginality refers to both a concentration of poverty in distinct neighbourhoods and micro-locales within neighbourhoods, and the symbolic denigration of those territories. To understand and explain the symbolic disparagement of neighbourhoods of working-class, racialised and marginalised populations through comparative empirical studies on French housing estates and the Black American ghetto, Wacquant built his notion of territorial stigmatisation of urban territories of marginality from two theoretical traditions. On the one hand is Erving Goffman's (1963) classic sociological study and conceptualisation of stigma, on the other is Pierre Bourdieu's theory of symbolic power. First, Goffman explored three distinct, socially discrediting and disqualifying elements: "abominations of the body" (e.g. disability), "blemishes of individual character" (imprisonment, addiction, unemployment etc.), and "tribal stigma of race, nation and religion". These bodily, moral and tribal stigmas had serious social consequences for the individual as they constituted for Goffman nothing less than "a social impediment, a major axis along which all other characteristics are measured and evaluated" (Cohen 2013, 114). And second, Bourdieu drew our attention to symbolic power and the symbolic struggles between different classes. His work focused on the different ways in which agents, authorities and institutions insist and exert their specific characterisation and meaning of the social world, so as to shape that world according to their own interests. Here symbols become "instruments of knowledge and communication in the production of consensus on the meaning of the social world" (Slater 2015, 4).

Pairing these classic sociological approaches, Wacquant then suggested that space was also to be seen as a distinct anchor of social disrepute. Just as bodily, moral and tribal stigmas carried serious social penalties for the individual, so did territory. Wacquant was concerned with how noxious representations of urban space are produced and disseminated by those wielding symbolic power such as state and commercial agencies, as well as in everyday power struggles to define social identities and urban hierarchies (Wacquant, Slater and Pereira 2014). And so, from the ethnically heterogeneous working class housing estates of Europe where residents struggle in the face of austerity and withdrawing of welfare services, to the Black American ghetto where residents struggle with systemic racism and are forced to develop parallel institutions for survival in the face of a complete lack of welfare services, Wacquant was convinced that in every metropolis of the world we tend to find territories of dereliction, where space increasingly is a source of social stigma and an instrument of symbolic power. In Finland a noteworthy work on territorial stigmatisation is Lotta Junnilainen's (2019) ethnography of experiences of life on stigmatised social housing estates.

By now territorial stigmatisation is well-rehearsed by urban sociologists and judging by the sheer volume of international empirical research on the topic, it is safe to agree with Wacquant's assessment that in most advanced capitalist cities there are neighbourhoods known and shunned for their concentrated poverty and deprived populations. Symposiums and special issues on the topic have been published in many journals, including *City* (2007), *International Journal of Urban and Regional Research* (2009), *Urban Geography* (2010) and *Environment and Planning A* (2014). Instead of another extensive literature review on the topic here, I will refer to the very similar conclusions drawn from two overviews of this field of research that are especially appropriate for the purposes of this chapter. Relatively recently Slater (2015) and Larsen and Delica (2019) have pointed out that there is an abundance of research on the consequences of territorial stigmatisation, but that new avenues of inquiry should be opened by looking at its causes. Slater (2015, 6) notes that "very few studies have taken up the challenge of tracing the production of territorial stigmatization". And Larsen and Delica (2019, 540), after a detailed review of the literature, conclude "most studies have focused more on confirming and expounding the impact of territorial stigmatization than its production". Despite the impressive comparative setting in Wacquant's analysis, further analyses are called for to understand the nuances of how territorial stigmas are produced under, for instance, different regimes of welfare, housing provision and local governance (Slater 2015). In an earlier work, Hastings (2004, 234) emphasised the same gap in research and noted that we still lack "research and analysis capable of fully investigating the causes of stigma. Clearly, without in-depth research, evidence on the causes of stigma will be slight, even impressionistic and, crucially, will be insufficient to support effective policy and practice".

To heed the call of these scholars, in the next chapter I explore how policies, research outputs and public discussions in Finland play into a powerful narrative about social housing estates and their problematic residents. Later, in Chapter 6, I explore how the recoiling role and targeted purposes of Finnish social housing provision have a major role in the production of stigma for social rental housing. But before that, let us look finally at the recent European research on urban inequality that has been most influential for Finnish segregation research.

The return of segregation research

In the 2000s and 2010s segregation research influenced by the urban ecology of the Chicago School gained popularity in European urban studies. Research focused on housing preferences and migratory patterns. Of particular interest is the tendency for white European populations to move out from the neighbourhoods where immigrants or ethnic and language minority groups are concentrating. European segregation researchers share what Andersson and Bråmå (2004) call a "process-oriented understanding of segregation". This means accepting that the decisions of individuals and households are important forces in the formation and transformation of urban social space. As Andersson and Bråmå (2004, 520) write:

> central to this analytical framework is the concept of selective migration, which refers to a situation in which the composition of out-migrants differs from the composition of in-migrants (and those staying in the area). [. . .] This way of addressing segregation goes far back into urban research history; the Chicago school sociologists, for instance, talked about succession and invasion and filtering processes.

With the "process-oriented understanding" of segregation as a starting point, various forces contributing to the process have been investigated. For example, Aldén, Hammarstedt and Neuman (2015) investigate what they call "tipping behaviour of native Swedes". They are not interested in gratuities paid by Swedes, but in what is known as the tipping point, i.e., how many immigrants are needed in a neighbourhood in order for so-called "native Swedes" to move out. Bråmå (2006) suggests that "immigrant concentrations" have formed because of a "Swedish avoidance", i.e., native Swedes avoiding areas where many immigrants live. In addition to studying a variety of processes like tipping and avoiding, European segregation researchers have dedicated themselves to exploring what are widely known as "neighbourhood effects". According to Friedrichs, Galster and Musterd (2003, 797), studies on neighbourhood effects assume that "spatial concentrations of poor households and/or ethnic minority households will have negative effects upon the opportunities to improve the social conditions of those who are living in these concentrations". Worry about segregation is coupled with concern about the influence of poor and minority populations on other groups of people. As Morris (1996, 161) writes, "[a] vocabulary of contagion is common to much of this work; the idea that certain sections of the population can contaminate society's more respectable members". European researchers have been interested in how neighbourhood background may affect residents' school success, employment and health. The rush to analyse how neighbourhood affects life chances has been so overwhelming that it deserves the name that Tom Slater – in his piercing critique of the neighbourhood effects school of thought (2013) – has introduced: a "cottage industry of neighbourhood effects research", characterised by a "complete disregard of what happens outside the neighbourhood" and of the complex structural dynamics of "policies, capital, housing commodification and structural unemployment".

One influential proponent of the process-oriented approach to segregation is Hans Skifter Andersen (2002, 2003, 2019) who argues that segregation is a self-perpetuating process. Skifter Andersen suggests a cyclical model of segregation based on the idea that segregated areas themselves, in fact, create segregation. Skifter Andersen (2002, 154) suggests:

> deprived neighbourhoods are not merely a simple result of social inequality and segregational forces; they are also by themselves creating new segregation and inequality. The areas can be seen as magnetic poles that attract poverty and social problems, and repel people and economic resources in a way that influences other parts of the urban space.

The way segregation works, according to Skifter Andersen (2002, 157) is that these "magnetic poles" attracting poverty and problems and repelling people, become inhabited by, as he writes, "marginalized ethnic and social groups, who have little in common. Some of these people have a culture or behaviour that deviates from general norms or have less regard for the comfort of their neighbours, making noise and carrying out other annoying activities." In a more recent study (2019), Skifter Andersen argues that the desire to live close to others with a shared ethnic background – instead of concentrations of ethnic minorities with "little in common" – is a major dynamic of those very locational preferences, feeding into ethnic segregation.

Subsequently, the "annoying activities" and "deviant culture and behaviour", argues Skifter Andersen (2002, 167),

> tends to make 'ordinary' people flee to other parts of the cities making room for an increasing concentration of low-income and socially excluded groups and thus increasing the spatial division of social groups. This effect is even more serious when looking at the segregation of ethnic minorities where the forces at work are much stronger.

Finally, Skifter Andersen claims that segregated areas come to have a devastating influence on urban space beyond the segregated areas, as "these neighbourhoods display visible physical and social problems that can disfigure the perhaps otherwise attractive urban landscape. They could in severe cases even be termed sores on the face of the city" (Skifter Andersen 2003, 1).

Skifter Andersen sees segregation as a cycle, as a self-perpetuating process that he calls "succession and decay". Essential to it are several detrimental changes such as the concentration of marginalised people, the decay of buildings and the fall in middle-class demand. The starting point of the cycle is the migration of poor, low-income people and immigrants to an area. With their "annoying activities, deviant behaviour and culture, and little regard for the comfort of their neighbours" these new residents drive out the "ordinary people". In these studies, the legacy of the Chicago School's urban ecology and 'Othering' from the perspective of the white academic is alive. Skifter Andersen (2002, 2003, 2019) argues that the self-perpetuating process of segregation initiated by the poor, the immigrants and the destitute creates "magnetic poles", drawing in – to borrow Robert Park from nearly a century ago – "others of their own ilk". Skifter Andersen describes how the invading hordes of the poor drive out the "ordinary people" and that segregation comes to contaminate the city around these polluted neighbourhoods. Skifter Andersen (2019) specifies four "types of moving behaviour" which he calls "white flight", "white avoidance", "ethnic attraction" and "ethnic retention". The key question for him (ibid., 111) is "which kind of moving behaviour has the dominant importance for the creation and maintenance of ethnic segregation and multi-ethnic neighbourhoods?" White avoidance, or Danes – whom the author equates with white people – who avoid moving into multi-ethnic neighbourhoods, is found to be of most relevance for ethnic segregation. Calling segregated, ethnic minority and working-class neighbourhoods "urban sores" on the face of the affluent, white European city provokes immediate nausea towards the politics of Skifter Andersen. Such rhetoric, and the notion of segregation as a self-perpetuating cycle of contamination, runs a very high risk of exacerbating the territorial stigmatisation of the neighbourhoods of marginalised populations. Wacquant (2007, 2008) for one has voiced the urgent call on social scientists to be aware of the rhetoric and words they use to avoid aggravating urban inequality.

*

This chapter provided a brief overview of some of the main research approaches to urban inequality during the past century, including the urban ecology of the Chicago School and the bid rent theory of mainstream urban economics, followed by their Marxist critiques; the post-industrial era and the polarisation thesis; the revival of a moral panic regarding the ghetto in America and its transatlantic transfer to Europe; and the latter's critique in the territorial stigmatisation thesis. Finally, I discussed how contemporary European segregation research has resuscitated the fear and loathing of a deviant underclass. I discussed how a circular reasoning of succession and invasion does not make it necessary to find an explanation for segregation but simply suffices to describe it. It too readily emphasises the behaviour of the poor, suggesting that the most important things to investigate about urban inequality are the outcomes of the living together of poor, unemployed people and the 'Other' to white Europeans, instead of asking why they are poor, unemployed or marginalised and why they end up living in disinvested neighbourhoods. Finnish segregation researchers, whose work I turn to next, have unfortunately applied the very same circular reasoning, taking for granted many of the tenets of urban ecology and mainstream urban economics and omitting their important political economic and sociological criticisms.

Notes

1. How the Other Half Lives was a photojournalistic investigation of life in New York's working-class tenements in the 1880s by Jacob Riis.
2. The origin of the concept of the underclass can be traced to the work of Swedish economist Gunnar Myrdal (1963). In its original form, the concept of the underclass was used in Sweden in the 1800s to denote the poor in general. *Underklass* was a derogatory folk term used especially by the wealthy to depict "something uncouth, bad-mannered, lacking in breeding and status" (Stewart 2002, 137). Myrdal however revived the term because he wanted to depict the economic victims of American economic progress. He described how not all were sharing in the affluence of the American economy, but instead the very economic organisation was creating "an unprivileged class of unemployed, unemployables and underemployed who are more and more hopelessly set apart from the nation at large and do not share in its life, its ambitions and its achievements" (Myrdal 1963, 10).

CHAPTER 2

The Age of Segregation Research in Finland

A spectre haunts Finnish cities – the spectre of segregation – and an alliance has been formed to exorcise this spectre. A successful exorcist is of course one who gets rid of the apparition once and for all. But a lucrative exorcist is one who manages to ensure the continued need for their services by repeatedly summoning the ghoul back for another round of spells and condemnation. The spectre of segregation is summoned back through the reciting of a powerful narrative concerning working-class and marginalised residential spaces. This narrative endorses the view that the reason we should be concerned with urban inequality is that neglect, delinquency, poor educational achievement and poor health and lifestyle choices are endemic to the spaces of the working-class and unemployed households. Coupled with the presence of people of immigrant background and non-Finnish speaking households, the narrative states, these spaces allow for an unwanted, deviant culture of neglect to be implanted. And it is the concentration of households on the lower rungs of the society and their neglectful culture that is also driving out the middle-class and, in this way, working to self-perpetuate the further segregation of neighbourhoods, reflecting poorly on the overall attractiveness of the city. In Finland the spectre of segregation is strategically drummed up by three members of the alliance of exorcists who appear to share a liberal consensus on the matter; liberal in the sense that Harvey (1973) defined years ago – they recognise inequity but address it without wanting to disturb or question existing sets of social mechanisms. Instead of transformative solutions to urban inequalities, they affirm the status quo (Fraser 1995).

The first members are made up of urban scholars, particularly in the disciplines of urban sociology and geography. Within the field of urban studies most research into urban inequality for the better part of the preceding two decades has concentrated on a specific type of knowledge production regarding segregation. The Helsinki Metropolitan Area (HMA) has been its primary geographical point of focus and it has been undergirded by a two-pronged methodology of spatial description and multivariate analysis. First, urban geographers and sociologists have systematically produced maps that depict what they suggest to be segregation: concentrations approximately the size of two apartment blocks of low income, unemployed and ethnic and language minority households scattered around the HMA. Second, they have conducted an assortment of multivariate analyses of how segregation affects learning outcomes and school choices

(Bernelius 2013; Bernelius and Vaattovaara 2016), experiences of safety and disorder (Kemppainen et al. 2014; Kemppainen 2018), house prices (Harjunen et al. 2014), selective migration (Vilkama et al. 2014), wellbeing (Koskela 2008), alcohol consumption and other health behaviour (Kunnas 2013).

The second member of the alliance is the mainstream media. Leading the pack has been *Helsingin Sanomat* (HS), the biggest daily newspaper by subscriber numbers not just in Finland but across the Nordics. It has actively disseminated the findings of segregation research to the public by reprinting the research results verbatim during the past two decades. This repetition has helped instil and normalise a very particular, descriptive way of discussing urban inequality, focusing on the differences between neighbourhoods and their residents from the perspective of the white middle-class. It has also risked stirring moral outrage about working-class and immigrant neighbourhoods. As Jahiu and Cinnamon (2022, 4548) explain "When places are labelled in the media with descriptions or imagery suggestive of poverty, ill health, disorder, or crime, negative portrayals over time come to represent the totality of the place and the people associated with them. Media discourse is thus complicit in advancing the "blemish of place" (Wacquant et al. 2014), an outcome that serves as an important pathway by which individuals and social groups are vilified (Wacquant 2007).

The third party in the alliance of exorcists are politicians for whom segregation and the public outrage regarding it offer convenient diversions. Through the incantation of segregation and its dangers in speeches and policy-papers, decision makers seem to release themselves of the arduous task of addressing the actual structural dynamics of urban inequalities and social marginality, such as housing unaffordability and uneven development. Segregation has become a useful buzzword that allows politicians to beat their chests over so-called problem neighbourhoods and problem people. The liberal policy approach suggests that the very causes of unemployment, marginalisation, poor health behaviour and low education levels are found in the homes and the neighbourhoods of working class and the marginalised. This is then used to justify place-based policies often amounting to little more than state-led gentrification masquerading as "social mixing" to target the lived spaces of working-class and minority households (Slater and Hannigan 2017; Sakizlioglu and Uitermark 2014).

The critical focus of this chapter is on the methodological descriptivism and lack of theoretical explanation within research, which I argue has been instrumental in developing a circular and unanalytic approach to segregation in Finland. In the first part of the chapter, I discuss two points related to the poverty of theory and methodology of segregation research. First, there is a degree of what we might call spatial fetishism in these works. They tend to assign causal powers to space in favour of discussing the development of urban space as a social process. And second, the century-old urban ecology idea that within certain spaces a deviant cultural brew is boiling and spilling over from one household to the next,

is favoured over discussion on class-struggle and the importance of social communities in working-class neighbourhoods. The main focus and object of analysis in
the chapter are the outputs of the first member of the alliance: the works of urban
scholars. However, in the final parts of the chapter I briefly illustrate how segregation is discussed in the media and by politicians. This is important to reflect on
how through a kind of "symbolic drip-feed" (Bourdieu 1998) between research
products, media and politics, segregation research has been influential in producing many of our received wisdoms regarding urban inequality in Finland.

One struggles to establish causality in such matters, but in what follows I argue
that segregation research outputs in Finland have added to the symbolic denigration of working-class and immigrant neighbourhoods, the process described by
Wacquant (2008) as territorial stigmatisation. Regarding this, my attempt here
is to answer the invitation of Larsen and Delica (2019, 44) who point out in
their thorough review of recent literature on territorial stigmatisation, that "the
issue of how academics take part in the production of territorial stigmatisation
through their research, the production of knowledge, the legitimation of policies
etc. barely receives any attention at all". I concur with their call that there is not
only a scholarly, but a social and a political urgency to provide better understandings of said issue. The purpose of this chapter is to answer that call.

The poverty of theory in segregation research

Segregation or "the degree to which two or more groups live separately from one
another, in different parts of the urban environment" (Massey and Denton 1988,
282) has been a topic of intense focus for urban studies in Finland since the turn
of the millennium (see for example Kortteinen, Lankinen and Vaattovaara 1999;
Kortteinen and Vaattovaara 2000; Kortteinen, Tuominen and Vaattovaara 2005;
Virtanen 2007; Vaattovaara and Kortteinen 2007; Kauppinen, Kortteinen and
Vaattovaara 2009; Vilkama 2011; Vaattovaara and Kortteinen 2012; Vilkama,
Vaattovaara and Dhalmann 2013; Kortteinen and Vaattovaara 2015; Kemppainen 2017; Saikkonen et al. 2018; Stjernberg 2019). One of the most widely
publicised arguments of segregation researchers is that the formation of a new type
of spatial differentiation can be identified as having been taking shape since the late
1990s in the HMA, which includes the four municipalities of Helsinki, its north-
east neighbour Vantaa, Espoo to the west of Helsinki, and the small bourgeois
municipality of Kauniainen, sitting wholly inside of Espoo.

Using surveys and Geographic Information Systems (GIS) data, geographers
have drawn detailed maps which portray the locations of households based on
educational, employment, income and ethnic background. A main source of survey data for segregation research is census data supplied by Statistics Finland.[1]
This data is then presented on grid cell maps, where a grid made up of cells 250
metres by 250 metres in size is placed on top of a map of the HMA. Comparing

the maps of different years, segregation researchers have observed a worrying trend – the grids show growing differences between these cells. When the first grid-cell comparisons were conducted at the turn of the millennium the differentiation between cells was showing moderate concentrations of low-income families, the unemployed and ethnic minorities, and larger enclaves of wealthier, Finnish speaking households (e.g. Kortteinen, Lankinen and Vaattovaara 1999; Kortteinen and Vaattovaara 2000; Vaattovaara and Kortteinen 2003; Kortteinen, Vaattovaara and Alasuutari 2005).

In the late 1990s and early 2000s the key conclusion drawn from this cell differentiation was that there were small pockets of low-income, low-education and unemployed households scattered evenly across the cities of the metropolitan area. Several reasons were then offered for the cell differentiation depicted on segregation maps. The first is found in studies of the late 1990s, which suggest that the differentiation takes place along residents' educational background and housing preferences (Kortteinen, Lankinen and Vaattovaara 1999). It was suggested that analyses of segregation should account for experiences of social disorder and its effects on selective migration of the highly educated (Kortteinen and Vaattovaara 1999). Here, the researchers drew on Gerald D. Suttles's (1968) classic study called *The Social Order of the Slum*, which was seen as helpful for interpreting segregation in Helsinki (Kortteinen and Vaattovaara 1999). Translated from Finnish,[2] their overview (ibid., 347) of Suttles's argument is as follows:

> If the social networks of the proper folk cannot control and govern their environment and the troubled folk begin to behave in disturbing ways, then micro-areas the size of a stairwell, house or apartment block will be formed. The proper folk will want to move away from these micro-areas. Socio-economic segregation takes place through this type of incremental everyday selection.

What was disclosed in the abovementioned piece was the researchers' understanding of who differentiates – those they called "proper folk" on the one hand and "troubled folk" on the other. One could of course excuse the crude depiction of the agents of segregation in this work from over two decades ago. However, this way of obscuring class hierarchy and inequality and the favouring of colloquial categories in analyses has been characteristic of much later segregation research and it has framed public understanding of what the problem with segregation is – troubled individuals and households and the ungovernable spaces they inhabit. Second, as will be illustrated later, the idea that neighbourhoods require management by strong social networks of "proper folk" has influenced policies to this day. Finally, the notion that segregation takes place primarily through everyday selection has persisted as a central argument of segregation research in Finland. The legacy of urban ecology endures and the dominant discourse on why the lives and spaces of residents of the metropolitan region are differentiating is that people are simply choosing to segregate.

In 2000, segregation researchers had drawn new grid-cell-maps and in their interpretation a vocabulary of social problems was adopted. The ideas of the Danish scholar Hans Skifter Andersen were found particularly helpful. Skifter Andersen for one did not shy away from defining people and areas as problematic – recall his naming of low income and ethnic minority neighbourhoods "urban sores" and "magnetic poles that attract poverty and problems". He also suggested their residents have annoying activities, little regard for the comfort of their neighbours, "cultures and behaviour that deviate from general norms", and, in his final analysis, accused segregated neighbourhoods themselves of creating segregation and inequality. Of him, the Finnish segregation literature wrote approvingly: "Hans Skifter Andersen has made an empirical study of the cycle of deprivation in Danish rental houses. His research skilfully summarises previous Nordic experiences of such processes" (Kortteinen and Vaattovaara 2000, 116). This cycle of deprivation, which Skifter Andersen (1995, 1998) called a "process of succession and decay" was explained by him (1998, 112–13) as follows:

> The immigration of people with lower incomes to a neighbourhood leads to lower demand and limitations on rent, which results in less investments in maintenance, which causes physical deterioration, and which in turn accelerates the migration of people with higher incomes out of the areas followed by immigration of low-income groups – a process called succession.

The argument clearly locates the beginning of the process in the moving into a neighbourhood of low-income people who are claimed to then lower demand, limit rent and investments, and drive out the middle class. This oversight of the structural dynamics of urban inequality – uneven investments in the built environment, land rent maximising actions of landlords and class conflict – leads to accusing low-income people of segregation. But there is obviously another way to begin the argument than blaming the poor.

Urban political economists have discussed at length how capital derives profit from a process known as uneven spatial development (e.g. Smith 1982; Slater 2013; Lees, Shin and López-Morales 2015). Preventing neighbourhoods from dilapidation requires repeated investments of labour and capital, yet often more is invested in those neighbourhoods with higher potential for land rent and less in other places. Hence, some environments become neglected as better opportunities for investments with more potential for future rents arise. Capital then disinvests from existing areas in search of areas where new investment is expected to yield higher returns. This leads to the successive development, underdevelopment, and redevelopment of given areas as capital jumps from one place to another (Smith 1982). Due to the circulation of interest-bearing capital in the built environment, in the case of residential neighbourhoods with less potential, the wealthy and middle classes leave along with or soon after investments leave. They are replaced by poorer residents who "can only afford to move in after a neighbourhood has been devalorised – after capital disinvestment and the departure of the wealthy and middle classes" (Slater, 2013, 377). Uneven capitalist urbanisation explains how disinvestment takes place before the low-income populations settle in, not after. This helps us untangle the theoretically poor notion of cycle of effects and move towards a robust analysis of the uneven development of the built environment as a fundamental causal mechanism of segregation.

However, in applying the succession and decay theory, researchers in Finland found it unfathomable that a physical decay of buildings would be taking place in the East Helsinki housing estates (Kortteinen and Vaattovaara 2000). This nega-tion of the disinvestment of housing estates is curious as some of these areas are well-known for their planned obsolescence – they were deliberately built to last no longer than 30 to 40 years (Mölsä 2016). Even the City of Helsinki had awoken to the poor condition and disinvestment of its housing estates as early as the mid-1990s and began a programme focusing on their redevelopment (Wallin 2017). Yet on many estates, buildings have stood in poor condition for years and only those with few other options in the harsh housing market reside therein. But segregation researchers concluded by suggesting that the cycle in Helsinki is simply one of "suc-cession" – the concentration of poor and ethnic minority households on its own is enough to make the area unwanted and push out the middle class (Kortteinen and Vaattovaara 2000). This approach is again reminiscent of the original Chicago School sociologists and urban ecologists, who argued that the urban environment develops towards equilibrium like an organism and individuals and groups find and sort into their "natural" areas. As Park (1925, 8–11) wrote:

> one of the incidents of the growth of the community is the social selection and segregation of the population, and the creation, on the one hand, of natural social groups, and on the other, of natural social areas. [. . .] Such segregations of popu-lation take place upon the basis of language and of culture and upon the basis of race. [. . .] Natural areas are the habitats of natural groups.

The theory of succession quite readily blamed the low-income and minority households for their own spatial exclusion. Researchers then pointed out where Helsinki's neighbourhoods that have fallen into such a negative social process exist: "East Helsinki has fallen into a vicious circle of underdevelopment where socio-economic deterioration of the population structure and declining desirabil-ity as a residential area seem to be feeding one another" (Kortteinen and Vaat-tovaara 2000, 124). Without isolating meaningful dynamics of urban inequality, such works suggest that the working-class households – who during this period were living under the violence of post-recession austerity and welfare cutbacks and novel forms of insidious employment precarity and competition of advanced capitalism – were pushed into disinvested and dilapidating housing estates as the increasingly tight housing market left them few options. They were also some-how deemed the culprits of not only all their own predicaments, but guilty of making residential spaces increasingly undesirable too.

Reminiscent of Skifter Andersen's accusation over "urban sores", one Finnish segregation researcher then went on to call these areas of east Helsinki "black holes of urban development". Coupled with the omission of robust analysis of inequality, such descriptors can be harmful to the very neighbourhoods and their residents the research is concerned with describing. These types of claims risk becoming entries in the lexicon of the dominant discourse on urban inequality. Such arbitrary abstractions (Sayer 1998) not only fail to distinguish what is relevant, but can be misleading and enforce territorial stigmatisation of people and neighbourhoods. Territorial stigmas work to turn our attention away from the structural reasons for poverty, marginality and social and ethnic segregation. Derogatory and unanalytical abstractions coined by scientists, spread by journalists and erroneously taken on board in public policies may soon become common knowledge and affect how we see the world. As Wacquant argues (2008, 239):

> whether or not these areas are in fact dilapidated and dangerous, and their population composed essentially of poor people, minorities and foreigners, matters little in the end: when it becomes widely shared and diffused, the prejudicial belief that they are is suffices to set off socially noxious consequences.

Throughout the 2000s concentrations of unemployed and non-Finnish speaking households the size of an apartment block were found in the east and northeast of the HMA (e.g., Kortteinen and Vaattovaara 2007). High income, well-educated and Finnish-speaking households were shown to live in great numbers in the west of the HMA (Kortteinen, Vaattovaara and Alasuutari 2005). The question why unemployment was increasing in segregated neighbourhoods was explored. The rapid development of the information and technology sector at the end of the 1990s was correctly pointed out to have created new occupational opportunities for a highly educated professional class (Vaattovaara and Kortteinen 2003). Meanwhile, the industrial labour of yesteryear, struggling under the long shadow of the 1990s recession was falling into long-term unemployment (Kauppinen, Kortteinen and Vaattovaara 2009). I have suggested elsewhere that the Marxist political economy approach can have much to say about the techno-economic development of the time (Hyötyläinen 2022). Marx argued that capital seeks to forge a reserve army of surplus labour to keep wages down and provide checks on the power of organised workers. Importantly, with the introduction of new technologies workers also undergo a process of deskilling or a change from skilled to abstract labour. Marx (1993, 104–5) explains abstract labour in *Grundrisse*:

> indifference towards specific labours correspond[ing] to a form of society in which individuals can with ease transfer from one labour to another, and where the specific kind is a matter of chance for them, hence of indifference [. . .] labour in reality has here become the means of generating wealth in general, and has ceased to be organically linked with particular individuals in any specific form.

David Harvey (2006, 118) has expanded on the notion of deskilling as appearing "through the technical division of labour, mechanisation, automation and scientific management". In short, it is in the interest of capital that an organised labour transforms into a disorganised, flexible and substitutable precariat of surplus and abstract labour with homogeneous machine tending abilities. A cadre of highly educated innovators and designers of new technologies sees itself well remunerated. The hardware of those technologies is increasingly compiled by an exploited cadre of the working-class in "countries of cheaper labour force" on the one hand. On the other, labour at home is first displaced by the software – applications and programs – and then works in precarious platform economy and machine-tending-occupations. A Marxist interpretation views potentially emancipatory technology under capitalism reduced to an instrument for reorganising skilled workers into an exploitable, precarious surplus faction of abstract labour (Hyötyläinen 2022).

Frustratingly, however, segregation research brushed aside the option of any critical analysis of this new class division in Finland taking place between a professional elite and an increasingly precarious surplus population. It was argued that

> it is not the Marxist class theory that seems to be most relevant in the interpretation of this new change. With new growth at the upper end of the social scale, new social and spatial divisions emerge, and specific segments of the new elite gather into special neighbourhoods, each on the basis of their peculiar preferences. (Vaattovaara and Kortteinen 2002)

Researchers then accused Finland's tax and transfer payments and social services of leading the cadres of unemployed into "benefit dependency" (Vaattovaara and Kortteinen 2003). Because of the low employment rates, Finnish segregation researchers later argued that the neighbourhoods have witnessed signs of social deprivation and themselves now negatively affect residents' employment (Vaattovaara and Kortteinen 2012, 63–4).

As the "unemployed benefit-dependents" now concentrate in distinct neighbourhoods, a concern over the spreading of a culture of poverty and welfare-dependency was voiced. In 2012 (64), referring to their own, co-written article from three years prior, Kauppinen, Kortteinen and Vaattovaara wrote:

> studies show that the neighbourhood will prevent residents' employment if the unemployment rate in that neighbourhood rises to 13 per cent. The negative effect of the neighbourhood's unemployment rate on an individual's employment opportunities appears to function in the way that heavy drinking, smoking and other bad health behaviour are more common in the neighbourhoods with a high unemployment rate. (Translated from Finnish original)

This sweeping generalisation was a rehearsal in the demonisation of the working-class, playing out as an "ideological battering ram" (Slater 2021) in two parts: first, announcing, with no justification provided, that a class analysis was not relevant, and second, building a stigmatising narrative about the working class as a lazy band of benefit dependents who concentrate spatially and make neighbourhoods unattractive sites where poor lifestyle choices of smoking and drinking spread from one individual to the next.

After announcing that unemployed people and the spaces they inhabit were the cause of unemployment, the presence of ethnic minorities and people of immigrant backgrounds in certain neighbourhoods was another theme causing concern among segregation researchers. Grid-cell maps were now showing that non-Finnish speaking households were concentrating increasingly in the same neighbourhoods as working-class and unemployed households. The concern of researchers, however, was not in explaining why this was happening. The concern that drove studies was that the increasing presence of ethnic minorities in a neighbourhood may drive out and discourage so called "native Finns" from moving into these neighbourhoods, a phenomenon resembling what was known from American literature as "white flight" but which researchers dubbed "native flight" in the Finnish context (Vilkama, Vaattovaara and Dhalmann 2013). Researchers used the term "immigrant concentration" and defined it as a neighbourhood in which at the end of the year 2007 the share of people born outside the Nordic countries from the total population of the neighbourhood was 11 to 24 per cent (ibid., 488). They explained that such neighbourhoods were now experiencing native flight as Finnish-speaking middle-class households were fleeing these neighbourhoods due to the presence of immigrants. These conceptualisations are highly ambiguous and problematic.

First, even in statistical terms, immigrant concentration was a problematic definition. Having been born outside the Nordic countries does not automatically mean that one is of an immigrant background. For instance, some of those people born abroad have been born to Finnish families, meaning the people are Finnish speakers and citizens of Finland. The more serious problem is that a concept such as "immigrant concentration" is what Andrew Sayer (1992, 138) calls a "bad and chaotic abstraction"; it lumps together features of the Finnish demographically heterogeneous, multi-ethnic and mixed neighbourhoods without isolating what is significant about these neighbourhoods. And as Sayer (1992, 139) continues, "abstractions, whether good or bad, can form part of the object of study in social science and have real effects".

Second, the authors noted that their theory of "native flight" was insufficient and that a wish to escape from social problems, uncleanliness, bad reputation, bad architecture and feeling of insecurity also affects the selective migration – what they called "social flight" – of middle-class households (Vilkama et al. 2013, 495). But even after such reservations, they collected all these other aspects under the derogatory concept of an "immigrant concentration", which suggests that all the other issues mentioned are both of less relevance and endemic to the places where large numbers of people born outside the Nordic countries live. The result of such vocabulary is that the status of immigrant neighbourhoods becomes synonymous with social problems, uncleanliness, bad architecture, insecurity and social disorder. The concept of immigrant concentration was not only statistically unsubstantiated, but it was also an arbitrary abstraction that ran a high risk of stigmatising neighbourhoods and aggravating the predicament of their residents. Social scientists should avoid chaotic abstractions and distinguish journalistic folk concepts from analytical concepts that help to explain and understand social phenomena.

Finally, in 2015, an article was published which argued that segregation had been a consistent event during the period beginning in the late 1990s which the authors had been following in their series of publications. The article and the period in question received the title "The Age of Segregation" (Kortteinen and Vaattovaara 2015). It introduced the latest results of grid-cell mapping of groups of different income, ethnic and educational background while summing up and comparing these to the corpus of Finnish segregation research. And yet, after the better part of two decades of research, the authors concluded "on the basis of this data and analysis, it is not possible to sufficiently state what explains [segregation]" (Kortteinen and Vaattovaara 2015, 569). The neglect of a methodological design that would allow for explanation had left the field wide open for interpretations. A poverty of theory in research has left it descriptive rather than explanatory, characterised by a refusal to isolate what is relevant about socio-spatial differentiation. Research had been driven less by a hope to understand urban inequality and why the life-worlds of social classes and other groups differentiate, and more by building a descriptive sociology and cartography of undesirable territories of disadvantage in the HMA (Aalbers 2011; Rolnik 2013). It had served to summon the spectre of segregation by symbolically denigrating the same areas researchers wanted to describe, fuelling a stigmatisation of these areas as unwanted.

Repeatedly defining distinct groups and territories as troubled and problematic can serve purposes beyond mere description. It can be a strategic research move. A sociologist, for instance, who can establish convincingly that problem populations exist in problem areas and that those areas need to be closely watched in the future, and who then re-announces year after year that the problem groups still exist and perhaps in even greater numbers, well, that is a sociologist who has found a way to stay "policy-relevant". Sociologists are servants of power, notes Sharon Zukin (2011, 13) who writes:

> sociologists depend on the state for research funds, social recognition, and 'policy relevance'. Often, therefore, sociologists adopt public officials' view that urban populations should be 'integrated' into a more or less harmonious, well defined urban society. 'Problem' populations are sociologists' bread and butter whether they are deviants and delinquents, ethnic minorities or immigrants, or the working class and poor. The presence of these populations opens the gates to government

intervention in 'problem areas' and funds for research. But to qualify for funding sociologists must define these groups at least implicitly as problematic.

In Finnish segregation research the definition of working-class and immigrant neighbourhoods and their residents as problematic has been more or less implicit. There is a growing international trend of what Slater (2021) calls the "heteronomy of urban research", that is research motivated not simply by the questions scholars want to ask, but increasingly motivated by the concerns of policymakers and those aired in the media. In Finland strong feedback exists between segregation research, journalism, and policymakers, which fuels both the heteronomy of segregation research and researchers' strategies to stay policy relevant.

The symbolic drip-feed

Territorial stigmatisation is a complex process. One key element in the process is how external representation of residential territories are produced and reproduced. Recently interest has grown in the relationship between the media and the production of territorial stigmas (e.g., Butler 2020; Schwarze 2022; Watt 2020), and specifically in "how place representation through images, maps, and textual descriptions come to matter greatly in how the public understands places" (Jahiu and Cinnamon 2022, 4548). An interesting feature of the Finnish age of segregation research is how the arguments and concepts used in the studies discussed in this chapter have been consistently repeated by journalists. In fact, there has been a rather strong feedback loop between mainstream segregation research and the media during this period that has allowed the wide dissemination of research findings. Illustrating this feedback loop is a curious link between one academic journal and the liberal newspaper media. The foremost academic outlet for segregation research has been the respected *Finnish Journal of Public Policy*, which has published the series of research articles on segregation since the late 1990s. This journal has a so-called 'embargo agreement' with the largest subscription newspaper not just in Finland, but in the Nordic countries, *Helsingin Sanomat* (HS), which enjoys the attention of roughly 700,000 subscribers and 1.2 million daily readers. The embargo agreement means that research articles gauged to be of particular interest to the public are selected and shared with the newspaper by the journal's chief editor, often before the journal issue comes out. In September 1999, just a few days before the very first article that kicked off the series of segregation studies discussed here (Kortteinen and Vaattovaara 1999), HS ran a piece[3] in which it referred to and summarised the findings of the – at the time forthcoming – research article. Back then, the concern was still with spatial class division.

Since then, instead of questioning research findings, HS has often printed the main conclusions and cited the authors of segregation research verbatim. Bourdieu writes of this systematic repetition of research findings as a "kind of symbolic drip-feed to which the press and television news contribute very strongly – to a large extent unconsciously, because most of the people who repeat these claims do so in good faith – [and how it] produces very profound effects" (Bourdieu 1998, 30). The drip-feed is a nice analogy of the process, depicting how certain research results find their way from the pages of niche journals to public awareness. I would argue, however, that HS has been very conscious about its role in shaping the public perception regarding segregation, and the descriptive methodology of segregation research has suited the liberal media's style of reporting on the matter well. The studies regarding concentration of people of immigrant background in the HMA have been a particularly publicised event in HS. I use a series of HS articles over the years to briefly illustrate the drip-feeding to the public of a noxious narrative regarding the segregation of immigrant households.

The first initial research findings on the segregation of immigrant households (Vilkama 2006) were published in HS under the title "Immigrants are concentrating in the same municipal rental houses".[4] The paper reported how households in which languages other than Finnish were spoken as a first language were concentrating in east and north Helsinki. The article paid no attention to why households belonging to language-minorities or those of immigrant background might be spatially concentrating. Instead, citing segregation researchers, the news article explained that a worrying development would get underway in rental housing when the share of households of immigrant background in an apartment building exceeded 20 per cent, as the 'native' population would then begin to shun the building. Instead of exploring whether non-Finnish-speaking households and communities might benefit from proximity to one another, the article insinuated that there is something intrinsically sinister and unwanted about non-Finnish-speaking households and people of immigrant background living together. However, it was five years later that this concern saw major attention. The title of a piece in HS from 2011 disclosed the source of this concern, "The Finnish language is withering away on housing estates – Immigrant concentrations are forming in the capital city region".[5] Citing the author of a study that sparked this particular headline, the article reminded readers how in central Europe the situation is "much worse" and "even in Sweden" there were housing estates where the native population is but a small minority.

The article warned that around the HMA there were tens of clusters of "immigrant concentrations" and it let the readers understand that it was now high time to address these unwanted socio-spatial formations. Referring to interviews with researchers, the article then spelled out two contradictory formulations of why said concentrations are unwanted. First, it accused the immigrant households of self-segregation and explained that "when immigrants isolate from the native population this causes various problems. Their assimilation into Finnish society gets more difficult if contact with the native population is lacking."[6] And second, it explained that immigrant households will move to municipal rental apartment buildings, which are already inhabited by long-term unemployed native Finns.

The high-income families will then feel insecure in these areas and be susceptible to moving out. Clearly the issue taken up in this formulation of the problem was not that people of immigrant background live separate from Finns, but that they live separate from and fail to assimilate to the expectations of certain kinds of Finns, namely the so-called native middle class.

Later the same year, HS interviewed the social democrat housing minister on the question of how to tackle this unwanted concentration of immigrants. Her solution was twofold: to build more owner-occupied houses for the middle class in the vicinity of "problem estates" and to regenerate and renovate the old apartments in order to increase the overall attractiveness of housing estates.[7] The minister pondered that social deprivation should not be allowed to concentrate in distinct areas. The article emphasised that "the inequality between areas of the capital region carries the risk that the native population will move away from housing estates where many immigrants are locating".[8] What is illustrated in these formulations of the issue of segregation is the paternalism of the dominant discourse of liberal researchers, media and politicians. Instead of a discussion on structural inequities, why policies and urban development focus social rental housing into peripheral estates and why socio-spatial inequalities persist, HS and the housing minister lamented the disappearance of middle-class households from housing estates. The primary concerns from the liberal perspective are that the concentration of marginalised immigrants and precarious working-class households make uncomfortably visible the deeper urban inequalities of the HMA and the paternalist worry over formation of "ungovernable" neighbourhoods that lack the supervision of robust, middle-class, native social networks.

Two years later a string of news articles in HS reported on the latest segregation research. First urban economist Seppo Laakso was interviewed about his analysis of differentiation. Laakso explained how the key solution was to find employment for young people on the estates. This was but a superficial remark, and Laakso then turned to his analysis of segregation, in which he explained: "the differentiation of housing estates happens so that alcoholics cause disturbances and normal families move out of social rental apartments. These families are then replaced by immigrants." His solution to the differentiation among other things was "housing estates spiralling out [of control] must be improved for example by building more owner-occupied housing in the areas".[9] Again, both the analysis of the situation and its following policy suggestion reflect the researcher's underlying cognitive division of households into the folk categories of unwanted alcoholics and immigrants whose presence reflects negatively on housing estates and causes them to "spiral out", and the wanted "normal families" whose homeownership in the areas should be promoted to strengthen the status of the areas.

Later that same year an article on the "native flight" of Finnish speaking households was published in *The Journal of Public Policy* (Vilkama, Vaattovaara and Dhalmann 2013). Soon after HS published at least three exposés on the article's findings titled, "The great number of immigrants is already a reason to move out of housing estates" (27.10.2013), "'White flight' is real and we need to be able to talk about it" (30.10.2013) and "Differentiation accelerates in urban housing estates" (27.11.2013).[10] Journalists and commentators stated that a native flight was true in Helsinki; immigrants were concentrating and "the large number of immigrants is reason enough for natives to move out of these neighbourhoods" (HS 27.10.2013). While researchers cannot be held responsible if the media misinterprets, popularises and makes unwarranted generalisations, researchers do bear a responsibility for making correct abstractions and being careful in their concepts. As was discussed earlier, this particular journal article had explained that other factors were much more relevant in middle-class residents' choices to move out than the presence of immigrants. But because the authors had framed the clustering of immigrants as the main issue and titled the article to insinuate a "white flight", this was the narrative that the media was also attracted to. All the other, more relevant issues pertaining to the neighbourhoods' systematic disinvestment were dominated by the moral panic over the presence of immigrants. The gamble that researchers take with using such rhetorical exaggerations is fuelling the flames of powerful xenophobic discourses in public debates.

In 2015 *The Journal of Public Policy* published the "Age of Segregation" article and thanks to the embargo agreement, HS was again running headlines even before the journal issue was out: "Disadvantage becomes visible when we look at individual blocks of housing"[11] and "Insecurity a reason to move out of some neighbourhoods – Check where people want to move to and from in Helsinki".[12] Providing a useful soundbite for journalists profiting from the muddy metaphor of the divided city, sociologist Matti Kortteinen gave his thundering warning concerning segregation in an interview and exclaimed: "The nation is on the verge of rupture!" HS ran this as a title of an article: "Differences between neighbourhoods are still growing in Helsinki – 'The nation is on the verge of rupture'".[13] A common line of fearmongering in liberal and conservative media builds on tales of two cities and suggests that parallel worlds to the mainstream society are being created. These tales, focusing on the differences between the two halves, as Marcuse (1989) noted, are told from the perspective of the white middle class. The tacit concern behind such tales is that in the parallel worlds of the Other, people might become collectively aware of class exploitation and share their frustrations with racism and marginalisation. With this awareness the threat of social unrest familiar from international cities could also grow. These neighbourhoods and their residents are then labelled problematic while the liberal academic and journalistic focus that has been directed at problem groups in problem neighbourhoods is reflected in policy. To address worries over socio-spatial "ruptures" the chief policy instruments have been the "positive activation" and "participation" of problematic residents, and the outright gentrification of problematic housing estates masked under the notion of social mixing.

The follies of anti-segregation policy

By refusing to interrogate the structural dynamics of inequality, such as those related to the housing market or state policies and institutions, mainstream segregation research better works in service of those institutions, representatives of which might find such interrogations uncomfortable (Tyler and Slater 2018). The spectre of segregation is summoned by policymakers in favour of addressing vexing issues of systemic inequalities. The Association of Finnish Local Authorities (2021, 6) – a local governments' advocacy group – recently published a report on urban social sustainability, outlining its view of the key issues regarding segregation:

> The spatial concentration of marginalization and disadvantage causes radicalization and other types of security risks. Exclusion and disadvantage create a fertile ground for crime. Crime is realised not only as acts but also as a feeling of insecurity. The fear of becoming a victim of crime grows. This in turn feeds a cycle which further increases the isolation of disreputable areas from the rest of society.

And even when local and national government strategies on urban policies and development are more nuanced than such scaremongering over radicalisation and crime, they tend to portray segregation as the main social issue to be tackled via area-based policy design that targets the residents more than their predicaments.[14]

Two types of key policies that reflect a paternalist approach to working-class housing estates and their residents in recent years can be discerned. First, projects claiming to "empower" the residents of estates, build "social cohesion" and "activate" the residents through participation in neighbourhood and community matters are noted in the research of Junnilainen (2019). In her in-depth sociology of experiences of living on stigmatised housing estates Junnilainen found participation and cohesion to be policy notions applied from outside the neighbourhood. Residents found such projects patronising and unhelpful and felt that the real and existing importance of their communities, participation and social lives were seldom acknowledged. Residents in Junnilainen's (2019) study felt that in the implementation of participatory policies they were being asked to respond to and fix territorial stigmas that are in fact produced outside of their neighbourhoods. And while the importance of their existing, complex communities went unrecognised, they were being asked to build a community life that better answered to middle class expectations of homogeneity (Ibid.).

And second, in addition to this middle-class conceptualisation and expectation of participation and social cohesion, goes the outright class-antagonistic project of gentrification as a novel attempt to invite the middle class to working-class estates is devised to mix the population (Kukkonen 2022). In recent years the policy goal of social mixing has found an answer in infill (re)development of peripheral housing estates, with an emphasis on building owner-occupied dwellings for the middle class. As Lees (2008) points out, policy language never uses the word gentrification to deflect criticism and resistance. Usually, redevelopment is justified with some ambiguous notion of spatial equality and renewal. Recently the ambiguity was shed by one popular commentator, when widely respected, long time city councillor and urban environment board member in Helsinki, Osmo Soininvaara (2020) of the Green Party suggested how best to tackle the problems of East Helsinki housing estates: "What the neighbourhoods of east Helsinki crucially need is a little gentrification." There is an international trend of designing gentrifying policies that aim to disperse concentrations of groups distinct from the white middle class on the neighbourhood scale (Lees 2008). Lilius and Hirvonen (2021, 122) for example note how

> Many housing estate neighbourhoods in the Helsinki Metropolitan Area are also the target for regeneration processes, often with the aim of enhancing a social mix, in particular, by diversifying the housing supply with more owner-occupation housing. For example, in 2006–2008, the city planning department of Helsinki created a general plan of 'the renaissance of the suburbia' with the aim to densify the suburbs.

And yet there is a "poor evidence base for the widespread policy assumption that gentrification will help increase the social mix, foster social mixing and thereby increase the social capital and social cohesion of inner city communities" (Lees 2008, 2450).

Infill development and social mixing are thought to bring in the middle class to working-class neighbourhoods. Concepts used in policy, like renewal, rejuvenation and revitalisation, are familiar from international policy designs and rhetoric. The budget plan of the City of Helsinki (2022, 118) for example notes that "in tackling segregation, practices directed at urban renewal and strategic urban rejuvenation areas require commitment from across government sectors". To promote "vibrant areas and preventing segregation" the plan suggests that "planning and housing policy can be used to influence the population structure and maintain the attractiveness of residential areas". Again, the concern is with middle-class preferences concealed under terms like attractiveness and vibrancy. Instead of housing policy that would promote and ensure housing affordability, it stresses that no more than 50 per cent of housing should be social rental housing and where this is not the case, the city should build more owner-occupied houses. What appears to escape the understanding of policymakers rooting for gentrification to tackle segregation is that *both are symptoms of urban inequality*. One is not a policy solution to the other, but merely a way to open working-class neighbourhoods for capital accumulation and deepen the crises of housing affordability. Gentrification is the tool of liberal consensus, an instrument of a neoliberalising state to answer to middle-class concerns over concentrated poverty by distilling and spatially dispersing the Other of the white middle-class (Slater 2021). Only recently has the problematic aspect of enforcing social mix via redevelopment been investigated in Finland by Kukkonen (2022) who correctly calls it a practice in state-led gentrification. Building owner occupied houses for the well-off is based on the age-old notion of "proper folk" controlling their neighbourhood.

Instead of improving the socio-economic standing of locals and investing in their well-being, revitalisation projects without proper regulation of rents and protection of tenants' right to stay put, will in the worst case displace original residents (Kukkonen 2022). Rather than exploring the difficult questions of systemic inequalities and the very sources of socio-spatial marginalisation of ethnic minorities, the institutional and state transformations that punish and concentrate the unemployed and low-income households, the liberal consensus on the harms of segregation points the finger at problem populations and problem areas. This spatial fetishism and class antagonism also conveniently justifies socially pacifying displacement that remove barriers to capital circulation, and open working-class neighbourhoods for gentrification and new rounds of capital accumulation.

*

The purpose of this chapter has been to critically analyse some of the main research outputs of Finnish segregation research between 1999 and 2015. This chapter unpacked some of the methodological and theoretical shortcomings of mainstream segregation research during a period I have called the age of segregation research. During this period, both an analytical neglect of state institutions, policies and urban governance, and an oversight of the inherent inequalities of capitalism, class struggle, accumulation imperative and uneven development of the built environment have characterised research. Urban sociologists and geographers have conducted descriptive research of segregation which has nursed colloquial notions of difference and differentiation. Urban research of this period has been foundational to the way urban inequality is understood and studied. Today a new generation of segregation researchers[15] continue to describe segregation as an outcome of the housing preferences of individuals, ruminate over the negative experiences of social disorder in housing estates, search for the neighbourhoods' negative effect on employment and education, and study the clustering of ethnic minorities and its implications for the moving patterns of 'native Finns'. The survey and grid-cell mapping methods are still widely used in contemporary segregation research in Finland.

The problem is not merely methodological, however. An orthodoxy of a descriptive style of knowledge production about segregation has influenced public narratives about urban inequality. Few urban studies topics have received as much attention in the public eye and are of similar policy concern in Finland as segregation. The research output of this period has been instrumental in producing much of our received wisdom on it, a body of work that has described socio-spatial differentiation and reproduced the spectre of segregation but failed to explain urban inequality. Until now, as Larsen and Delica (2019, 544) point out, the issue of how academics take part in the production of territorial stigmatisation has barely been discussed. In this chapter I have attempted to address this very issue. Due to a lack of explanation, segregation research in Finland has risked taking part in the production of the symbolic denigration of working class and immigrant neighbourhoods. One cannot understand urban inequality by simply describing the neighbourhoods and lives of those who are suffering from urban inequality, or by mapping the moving patterns of those who leave disinvested neighbourhoods. No matter how persistently one summons this spectre by beating their breasts and repeating the chant that neighbourhoods are becoming different, they will get no closer to explaining the underlying dynamics of urban inequality.

A guiding concern of segregation research over the past 20 years has been that housing estates on the urban peripheries are showing signs of novel socio-spatial concentration of problematic groups. On the one hand, scholars have refused to say anything too conclusive about the phenomenon, justifying the need for further research. On the other, the repeated external classification of certain areas and their residents as problematic has shaped colloquial, journalistic and policy under-standing regarding them. From the perspective of territorial stigmatisation, par-ticularly damaging is that the dominance of this powerful, descriptive discourse and its folk-rhetoric has seeped out of academic texts and affected the public per-ceptions about urban inequality and chosen policy instruments to address it. As Junnilainen writes "there are no problem estates in Finland, but there is a housing estate problem, which primarily reflects external notions of what kinds of people live in particular areas" (2019, 289). I would add that it also reflects the structural dynamics of uneven development. The estate problem is the problem of estates not seeing lasting investments and lacking attention in terms of the well-being of their residents, the quality of their residential spaces and necessary services.

Even under the Nordic welfare state, which traditionally has worked to curb some of the inevitable inequalities produced by the capitalist economy, the uneven development of the built environment, abetted by the state, is directly connected to the ebb and flow of capital accumulation. In 2002 the geographer Mari Vaattovaara argued that "there is no political turn that could account for the growing segregation pressures in the HMA". Perhaps the turn was too close at the time to see, or maybe it did not fit with the story of segregation scholars. Nevertheless, there is a very discernible political turn, which began as far back as the 1980s, became more prominent in the 1990s and continued during the preceding decades that must today be brought to our analyses of urban inequal-ity – the transformation of the welfare state and the turn to neoliberalism. This class-based, political project has had significant impact on those policies which the old welfare state relied on to develop urban areas in a just and equitable manner. It is this political turn that I inspect next. The next chapter discusses the historical project of welfare state transformation. The rest of the book then, while also paying attention to the experiences of residents where they illustrate the urban inequalities, turns the focus away from housing estates and segregation maps and then readjusts the focus on the transformations of two policies that play a key role in how urban inequalities have traditionally been managed: land and housing policies.

Notes

1. Statistics Finland is an independently acting government agency under the Ministry of Finance. It collects statistics from different register data such as the Population Register and the Incomes Register, but also directly from citizens and organisations.
2. "Jos ns. kunnon väen verkostot eivät pysty hillitsemään ja hallitsemaan ympäristöään ja moniongelmainen väki alkaa käyttäytyä avoimen häiritsevästi, syntyy rappukäytävän, talon tai korttelin kokoisia pienalueita, joista tämä ns. kunnon väki tahtoo pois. Sosioekonominen segregaation tapahtuu tällaisen arkisen valikoitumisen kautta vähittäin, liukuvasti."
3. Luokkayhteiskunnan mukainen aluejako palaa pääkaupunkiseudulle (HS 6.9.1999).
4. Maahanmuuttajat ovat keskittymässä samoihin kaupungin vuokrataloihin (HS 29.9.2006).
5. Suomen kieli hiipuu lähiöissä – Maahanmuuttajien keskittymiä syntyy pääkaupunkiseudulle (HS 29.4.2011).
6. "Maahanmuuttajien eristäytyminen kantaväestöstä aiheuttaa kuitenkin monenlaisia ongelmia. Heidän sopeutumisensa suomalaiseen yhteiskuntaan vaikeutuu, jos kontakti kantaväestöön puuttuu."
7. Kiuru: Asuinalueiden eriytyminen luultua pahempi ongelma (HS 29.11.2011).
8. "Pääkaupunkiseudulla alueiden eriarvoistumiseen liittyy riski, että kantaväestö muuttaa pois lähiöistä, joihin sijoittuu paljon maahanmuuttajia."
9. Tutkija: Lähiöiden eriytymiskierre pysäytetään työtä luomalla – Monet ongelmalähiöt ovat omia eristyneitä ja sulkeutuneita saarekkeita. (HS 25.10.2013).
10. Maahanmuuttajien suuri määrä on jo syy muuttaa pois lähiöstä (HS 27.10.2013). "Valkoinen pako" on totta, ja asiasta pitää pystyä puhumaan (HS 30.10.2013). Eriytyminen kiihtyy kaupunkien lähiöissä (HS 27.11.2013).
11. Huono-osaisuus näkyy, kun tarkastelee yksittäisiä kortteleita (HS 10.12.2015).
12. Joiltain asuinalueilta muutetaan turvattomuuden takia – Katso, mistä ja minne helsinkiläiset haluavat muuttaa (HS 12.12.2015).
13. Asuinalueiden väliset erot vahvistuvat yhä Helsingissä – "kansakunta on vaarassa haljeta" (HS 10.12.2015).
14. For example Lähiöohjelma 2020–22, the government programme on development of housing estates; City of Helsinki programme for housing and land use 2020.
15. More relevant than beginning to name these young authors and studies, I would argue, is to understand which ontological traditions and methodologies steer their work. The point of this chapter has been to unpack and criticise the works of the first generation of segregation scholars, well established and respected researchers in their fields, whose outputs have been central in forming academic and public views on the matter in Finland.

CHAPTER 3

The Nordic Welfare State in Transformation

In both the Western left and liberal political imaginations Denmark, Finland, Iceland, Norway and Sweden represent an egalitarian economic and political model that maintains a high quality of life for their populations. A widely accepted narrative flaunts these Nordic welfare states as exceptionally successful in tackling inequalities (Fritzell et al. 2012; Kangas and Kvist 2019; Kvist and Greve 2011; Righard et al. 2015). Behind their success, it is suggested, are the combined societal arrangements of collective agreement between capital and labour, and a universal welfare state based on high levels of redistribution. In political imaginaries and popular interpretations, these countries still reflect a post-war "Nordic model", built around strong central state and bureaucracy, decommodification, vast public ownership of assets, collective consumption and public provision of key services, and a general willingness for progressive income redistribution and provision of universal social protection made possible by relatively high taxation (e.g., Kettunen 2012; Olsson 2018).

The idea of a Nordic model of welfare state is intact and it tends to find strong popular support from its traditional, social-democratic wardens. But the welfare state today has various other spokespersons. In Finland, the pleas of business elites for enhanced competitiveness and less state regulation are justified by the preservation of the welfare state (Finnish Business and Policy Forum 2011). When the Ministry of Finance argues in favour of penalising workfare policies, it is to defend the welfare state (Ministry of Finance 2021). And when the far-right Finns Party make calls to "bring back the welfare state" (The Finns Party 2021) what they advocate is a welfare chauvinism that provides services exclusively for the "native population". This is not only a Finnish feature. In Sweden a quarrel over the conceptual ownership of "the Nordic model" broke out between the Swedish political parties. "After the Swedish centre-right government made an ownership claim toward the concept, social democrats swiftly reacted and applied for a patent for it (Edling, Petersen, and Petersen 2014, 28–29)" (Kuisma 2017, 433). While different sides claim to save and maintain their version of the welfare state, research suggests that welfare states across the Nordics have in recent decades been increasingly subjected to significant reforms and transformations of some of their traditional features (Moisio and Leppänen 2007; Righard et al 2015; Olsson 2018).

Processes of privatisation of public services and assets, move from universalism to selective, means tested, and residualised policies, rescaling of statehood and a growing entrepreneurialism in local governance, which have been studied extensively in European core areas and Anglo-American contexts, have been observed and analysed in the Nordic countries (Moisio and Leppänen 2007). Peeling back the imagery and rhetoric of the enduring success of the Nordic welfare state, currents of structural readjustment, administrative decentralisation and social fragmentation are revealed. Some suggest, however, that international scholars tend to be "relatively unaware of this situation and continue to think of the Nordic countries as leading examples of successful social-democratic societies with progressive socio-spatial politics (and policies)" (Baeten et al. 2015, 210). The legacy of Esping-Andersen's classic (1990) analysis of the Scandinavian variety of social-democratic welfare capitalism, characterised by vast decommodification and universalist programmes, is still carried to contemporary analyses. It is worthwhile discussing how the Nordic model has been diluted under pressures of neoliberal restructuring, before exploring its policy implications in the following chapters.

This chapter looks at the Nordic welfare state in transformation with a particular focus on state spatiality in Finland. The book deals with urban inequality in light of two policies that have direct and indirect socio-spatial consequences: land and housing policies. This brief historical overview-chapter serves the purpose of setting the scene of a changing institutional framework under which these policies are practised today. This chapter begins with a discussion on the notion of policy universalism and social equality in the Nordic welfare state. Next, it introduces the concept of spatial Keynesianism (Brenner 2004) to talk about the traditional, spatial policies aiming at regional social and economic equality. The third section turns to explore recent neoliberal reforms of the so-called Nordic model. It distinguishes a change from universal welfare policies to increasingly selective social services and it discusses the widely influential public administration reform of the 1990s called New Public Management (NPM), which was much more eagerly adopted in Finland compared to the rest of Europe, including its Nordic neighbours (Temmes 1998; Haveri 2002). NPM was instrumental in the decentralisation of decision making and bringing an entrepreneurial logic to the management of public assets in municipalities. Finally, the chapter discusses the spatial restructuring that resulted from these reforms. Specifically, there has been a transfer of emphasis from regional equality to highly localised urban policies that boost the competitiveness of key urban areas.

Universalism and social equality

Fascinated by Sweden's rapid recovery from the Great Depression in the 1930s, the American journalist Marquis Childs (1936) famously declared that Swedes had succeeded by taking "the middle way". Flanked by state communism to the east and liberal capitalism to the west, Sweden had struck a practical compromise between the two. While fascism reared its ugly head in Europe, Sweden held onto its parliamentary democracy, catering for both industrial working-class and land-owning agrarian interests. Although Childs used the journalistic notion to describe specifically the Swedish experience, the middle way has been largely understood as a shared Nordic characteristic and it has greatly shaped the international narrative of the Nordic model (Dahlqvist 2020; Hilson 2011).[1] Starting in the 1930s Nordic countries did indeed venture down a similar developmental path of modernisation and tension-reducing institutional solutions, largely based on political consensus and state-regulated capitalism. Characteristic of social democratic welfare states in general has been to "seek to curb excessive exploitation of labour power and place themselves behind the class interests of labour without abolishing capital" (Harvey 2003, 92).

Kettunen (2012) describes the three features of the Nordic modernisation process as equality, efficiency and solidarity, based respectively on the idealised heritage of the free peasant, the spirit of capitalism and the utopia of socialism. The cooperation between the state, capital and labour, and the Keynesian principles of economic theory were already adhered to across the Nordics before the Second World War (Veggeland 2016). A culture of negotiation and agreement in the labour market was more widely established in the Nordics during the 1930s and 40s. Norway and Sweden signed basic agreements between trade unions and employer associations in 1935 and 1938 respectively. In Finland the corresponding agreements were signed in January 1940 in what is known as the Betrothal of January. The Civil War of 1918 had pinned the proletarian against the bourgeois, ending in the violent repression of the former. This outcome gave Finnish employers in manufacturing industries enduring power to refuse collective agreements with trade unions (Kettunen 2012). In the era of rebuilding after World War II, however, compromise was emphasised partly as the working-class efforts in the war had to be recognised. After the war all Nordic countries began to follow a similar social, economic and administrative model. Its features included the favouring of extensive state intervention to achieve full employment and social redistribution combined with an extensive welfare state, broad political consensus, developed on a platform of a state-regulated capitalism. The Nordic model saw economic growth, democratisation and social policy development go hand in hand (Kildal and Kuhnle 2007).

Political legitimacy for the Nordic model was gained with economic justifications for the significance of state intervention, public expenditure and anti-laissez-faire policies. Employment and economic growth were promoted by high public and private spending. Strong public planning was a common feature on different scales of administration. Moving on, the welfare policies launched in the 1960s and 1970s were growth-oriented, and they continued to represent a widely agreed upon need for a redistributive state. The state development in

Finland during this time was built on the principle that domestic competition was undesirable – be it between classes, institutions, companies or regions. The promotion of social equality was seen as important for liberating human productive capacities and promoting economic effectiveness. And economic prosperity, in turn, was seen as a fundamental precondition for achieving social equality (Kettunen 2012). The welfare state worked to curb inequalities created by the market, although "social security systems and public services followed and supported labour-market rationalities" (Kettunen 2012, 32). By the 1980s Finland had the lowest income inequality in the OECD countries (Atkinson et al., 1995).

Social policies in the Nordic welfare state were established on the notion of universalism. The right to a good standard of living was a much-favoured political goal in the rebuilding of post-war Europe, deeply traumatised by the violence of war and economic turmoil. The Nordic countries sought to develop welfare states that included the entire national population (Erikson et al. 1987). Universalism was rooted in the idea of social rights. If civil rights – such as the right to private property and freedom before the law – were a product of the 18th century in Europe, and political rights – the rights to association and political representation – of the 19th century, then social rights are a product of the mid-20th century post-war era (Marshall 1987). The civil and political rights were about basic rights of liberal citizenship, but social rights refer to the right to a certain quality of life and social equality. The objective of the welfare state project was equality and social justice by way of ensuring a high standard of living for all. Welfare was, then, a universal question and this was highlighted in the development of the Nordic welfare state in particular. The Nordic hallmarks were that services such as education, health care and social security were de-commodified. All children were to receive a child allowance and all retired people were entitled to basic old-age pensions. Universal coverage was ensured through progressive taxation, hence public provisions did not simply provide a safety net for the poor, but were an equaliser, intended for all segments of the society as a right (Anttonen and Sipilä 2000).

For their wide acceptance, policies that targeted the promotion of social rights needed justification. What helped in the acceptance and justification of universalism in social entitlements and public provisions was a homogeneous population with a low degree of division between people based on things such as ethnicity, religion or territory (Anttonen and Sipilä 2000). High taxation was politically easier to justify, when individuals felt they were paying for the benefits and services for themselves and people like themselves. The Finnish welfare state is restricted to Finland and Finnish nationality. Finnish nationality entitles people to similar services and benefits. The development of the welfare state was also about nation building. For individuals it meant receiving the same, free education as their contemporaries. A shared curriculum had a nationally homogenising, unifying tendency. Free health care for individuals also ensured a healthy and productive nation. Belonging to a society is historically and nationally contingent and despite calls for universalism, the citizenship-based welfare state worked on its own exclusionary logic and nationalist sentiment (Barker 2013). Importantly, to increase its own power and legitimacy, a strong central state also worked towards regional homogeneity and spatial equality within its national borders.

Spatial Keynesianism

A degree of localism has been a feature of the Nordic model. In Finland municipalities begun collecting taxes already in the 1880s and the municipal tax was made income based in the 1920s.[2] The central government finances statutory local services by transfer payments to local governments. The state transfers for municipalities were for a long time earmarked for each sector, such as schools, hospitals and social services (Anttonen and Sipilä 2000). The purpose of the transfer system was to even out inequalities between local administrations and ensure equality in access to services throughout the country. Despite local self-governance, municipalities are restricted by legislation regarding where they may allocate these revenues. After the Second World War, municipalities' responsibilities grew, and they were seen as an essential part of national, socio-economic development. The municipality was perceived as part of the national state apparatus and its tasks concerned the production and distribution of state-assigned commodities (Yliaska 2017). This instigated the development of what Ahlqvist and Moisio (2014, 28) call the "cartel polity" – a particular regime of distribution, following the principles of social and spatial universalism and "predicated on the dominance of national-scale regulation, with local governments acting as intermediaries for centrally determined policies".

During the 1950s and 60s several new institutes of higher education were established in Finland. New needs for education, a move from elite universities to the education of the masses and the ensuing explosive growth in the number of people in higher education was a European trend (Kohvakka 2021). But apart from answering educational needs, establishing universities and vocational schools across the country was also considered of great importance. This was part of the project of promoting spatial evenness and regional equality on the national scale in economic and infrastructure development, or what Peck (2002, 331) calls a "nation-centric scalar fix". Key elements of the Nordic model were a strong, central bureaucracy and state infrastructure monopolies. This included not only soft infrastructure such as welfare and social-security services, education and labour-market services. It also adhered to hard infrastructure (such as telecommunications and road construction), public land monopolies and real-estate ownership. These monopolies enabled distribution and redistribution not just socially but regionally. The transferring of institutions of education and jobs from rich regions to the periphery was not simply a question of justice, but a question of promoting higher degrees of effective demand (Veggeland 2016). The distribution of universities in Finland is an example of the distinct landscape of what is known as "spatial Keynesian" capitalist development (Lobao et al. 2009).

Spatial Keynesianism was a project concerning the evenness in the placement of education and jobs – particularly, at that time, in branch plants of key industries – state offices and public services with the aim of building regional equality in living standards and employment opportunities. Over the period lasting from the late 1950s to the mid-1980s most western European states established comparatively uniform, national, standardised administrative arrangements and designed policies to ease spatial inequalities by extending industrial and infrastructure development also to peripheral areas (Brenner 2004). As Moisio and Leppänen (2007, 68) point out the "primary scale of a European government's political and economic operations during Fordism-Keynesianism was the national scale. Despite various degrees of local autonomy within a particular state, 'state space' was treated as 'single entity'." Spatial Keynesianism also developed "the distinctive urban built environments, land-use patterns, regional agglomeration economies, and nationwide infrastructural networks associated with Fordist urbanization" (Brenner 2004, 161). For Brenner it represented "the historical high-point of twentieth-century state strategies to alleviate uneven geographical development and territorial inequality within national borders" (Ibid.).

In Finland, the "scalar fix" of spatial Keynesianism was a project based on developing standardised frameworks for capitalist production and collective consumption on a national scale. Behind this project was, first, the political agenda of easing and preventing patterns of uneven spatial development by spreading state investments as evenly as possible across the surface of the national territory. And second, spatial Keynesianism was an attempt to increase state power throughout the nation with the help of substantial transfer payments and regional development. The central priority of the government was to "produce economic growth with the help of nationally scaled political structures and social welfare" (Ahlqvist and Moisio 2014, 27). Socio-spatial equality of distribution and development was a matter of national importance which both central and local state governments were thought to work towards.

The welfare state and the city

In the Nordic countries, particularly the relatively late-to-urbanise Finland, the development of the welfare state and urbanisation are intricately linked, but social policies were not categorised as urban policies. As Lehto (2000, 118) writes:

> On the contrary, a firmly stated goal of the [Nordic] welfare state has been to create equal opportunities for using welfare state benefits and services in terms of socio-economic groups, central and peripheral regions, urban and rural population. To label social policy as urban would have been against this universality principle.

However, the welfare state did also pull people from the countryside to the towns and cities where many of the increasing number of public sector occupations were located. Meanwhile, suburban, working- and middle-class households were being reorganised as women entered wage labour. Dual incomes were needed to pay for the cars and appliances that the modern household now required. The dual-earner households allowed for the growth in demand that the economic arrangement of the Fordist-Keynesian pact of the time was based on. This in turn required more from the welfare state: day care for the children and care homes for the elderly, social security networks in case of sickness and unemployment. The welfare state enabled two breadwinner families and the middle-class way of life to develop in the cities, and vice versa.

State institutions essentially mediate the geographies of capitalist urbanisation within their territories (Brenner 2004). And capitalist urbanisation had its idiosyncrasies in the Nordic welfare state, where welfare policies assisted in opening new urban terrains of accumulation. As it pertains to urban development, spatial Keynesianism was a project of encouraging urban growth throughout the national territory. The main function of municipalities was to deliver state funded public services, while their plans and budgets had to be ratified by a state official. The central state created the conditions for land use policy practised by the local state. The state gave land for municipalities' social housing needs and municipalities allocated land free of charge for schools, health care centres and libraries (Haila 2016). State transfer payments were earmarked to municipalities according to need and they aimed at equality between municipalities. In the development of urban residential space this target of equality demanded active land policy. Public bodies worked collaboratively and the state subsidised housing development, while cities would buy raw land or use compulsory purchase to build their land bank and prepare for urban development. Using their planning monopolies, the cities drew their city plans; these were however overseen by a state official, who was responsible for ensuring that plans did not create unwanted unevenness within and between cities. Again, the equalising and redistributive Keynesian state aimed at spatial equality as much as social.

Diluting the Nordic model?

In Chapter 1, I introduced the Chicago School of Sociology. The University of Chicago is also known for another famous school, the Chicago School of Economics. The Chicago School of Economics, originating in the 1920s, is a highly influential economic school of thought and American hub of neoliberalism, represented over the past century by the likes of Frank Knight, Ronald Coase, Friedrich Hayek and George Stigler. Perhaps of most wide influence are the ideas of Nobel laureate and advisor to Augusto Pinochet, Milton Friedman, whose monetarist approach proposed an alternative to Keynesian economics. The main attributes of the Chicago economists can be summed up as follows: free markets are the best and most efficient way to allocate resources in an economy, government intervention is unwanted from the perspective of economic prosperity, and economics and price theory are applied to "every nook and cranny of life" (Cate 2013; Miller 1962). The Chicago economists espoused free market libertarianism and promoted the idea that individuals are best left to their own devices, free to choose how to conduct their own affairs. For an account of the history and thought of the Chicago School of Economics, particularly how it relates to the neoliberal political project, see Van Horn and Mirowski (2009). Suffice it to state here that neoliberalism is, rather than a project to completely withdraw the state, a class-based project to reengineer the state as an institutional framework to favour capital. The Chicago School economists' criticism of state regulation and the support for rolling back of government responsibilities in favour of market mechanisms are the ideological underpinning for the drastic, neoliberal changes in the Finnish welfare state.

The global onslaught of the neoliberal, class-based political project of state reengineering then came to challenge and profoundly transform many of the principles of the Nordic model. Among key normative principles that became questioned were the social, economic and spatial equalities and universalism that had so far informed the operations of the state. As different countries deployed their neoliberal reforms, a substantial international transfer of ideas and examples was under way (on the notion of policy transfer see Peck and Theodore 2001). International examples and debates have affected the development of Finnish governance models on many often not so apparent levels. There has been a push to transform the social value system incrementally from values that uphold the welfare state with its strong institutions and bureaucracies, towards a very different view of the state and its role and tasks.

In the 1980s, following the example of other Nordic countries, Finland underwent major financial deregulation and credit expansion, which was reflected especially on the housing market. New private investments were made in residential real estate development. Prices and rents set on the market were favoured over state regulated rents and subsidised development, and household debt was an increasingly favoured way of boosting demand for housing and commodities. The Bank of Finland relaxed its restrictions, allowing commercial banks to lend lavishly to firms and households. Suddenly available credit saw house prices escalate, driving households that had entered the housing market even deeper into debt and eventually overheating the real estate market. From 25 per cent of GDP in 1980, household debt rose to 45 per cent in 1992. Starting in 1989 corporate debt rose from 70 per cent of GDP to nearly 90 per cent of GDP in just a couple of years. Housing prices doubled between 1986 and 1989, while the Finnish stock market tripled in value between 1985 and 1988 (Nygaard 2021). In 1990 this boom turned to a bust. Combined with the collapse of the Soviet Union and the withering of this important export market to the east – the Soviet

Union had accounted for approximately 15 per cent of Finnish exports – the result was a serious economic depression. From an all-time low of four per cent in 1989, by 1993 unemployment had climbed to 22 per cent (Statistics Finland 2012), and thousands fell behind on their mortgage payments and other household loans, causing banks and companies to drift into bankruptcy. With little political support to be found for increasing state debt for public investments, national unemployment turned long-term and saw the state's tax income shrink even further. Cutbacks and privatisation were increasingly attractive to municipalities struggling with the depression of the early 1990s (Haveri 2002).

The ground had now been prepared for increasing outside pressure for transformation, which was exerted on the Finnish state by a familiar crew of transnational actors including the EU, the WTO, the OECD, the IMF, the G8 and also the World Bank, and the World Economic Forum, and various transnational business elites (Moisio 2008). The neoliberalisation advocated by these players concerned a production of polity that fosters and favours increasing competition. Also, policy reforms and changes in state arrangements that follow the doctrine of neoliberalism are often displayed as economically sensible and pragmatic, presented as "systemic, rationalistic, and naturalized" (Peck 2002, 334) and as such, apolitical. Such referrals to ideas of rationality and economic reason, however, are utterly political endeavours and neoliberalism is a very material, class-based project (Cahill 2014). Neoliberalisation is often depicted as a vast state retrenchment and roll-back. Neoliberalism does not, however, mean replacing the political with the economic, or the state with the market. A more insightful analysis posits it as a reorganisation of the state's functions, including a market penetration of its institutions and policies.

Neoliberalism entailed a critique and a following reorientation of the historically and geographically specific form of the Keynesian welfare state (Jessop 1999; Peck 2002). Ahlqvist and Moisio (2014, 22) write how neoliberalisation "displays a will to generate the state increasingly as an enterprise association which promotes the commodification of its own activities and structures, resulting in a sort of consolidated corporate polity". Under this neoliberal state transformation, the tradition of collective agreement becomes questioned. The moving of industries and production to countries of cheap and unorganised labour where workers are often practically enslaved has given the employer heavy bargaining power in the labour market. We have seen an increase in precarious employment and "the growing fluidity of the boundary between wage work and entrepreneurship", and while growth in finance capital saw companies growing and becoming global players, "the idea of the worker as the weaker part of the worker-employer relationship tended to be pushed to the margin through the ethos of entrepreneurship" (Kettunen 2012, 32–3).

Redistribution and spatial Keynesianism were also re-evaluated. Neoliberalisation means that state intervention in wealth redistribution makes room for intervention that assists in creating markets, supporting commodification and protecting property rights. "This polity operates on a lexicon that resonates with corporate concepts and which is premised on concerns about competitiveness" (Ahlqvist and Moisio 2014, 22). The depression in Finland gave political ammunition for austerity politics and a new, entrepreneurial approach to the management of public assets. If the previous arrangement between state and market was for the state to curb laissez-fair ideology, the new arrangement is for the state to allow the private sector growing operational room and responsibility over service provision. Policy design is less about public provision and administration, but geared more towards alternative ways of making money for the public treasuries to pay for these services.

Coupled with the creative, entrepreneurial and highly individualistic approach to work under neoliberalism, are the deterioration of the basic conditions of employment, remuneration and social insurance for wage-earners. For contemporary European "deproletarianized" populations the wage-labour relation itself has become "a source of fragmentation and precariousness" (Wacquant 2008, 265–7). Instead of a community of people with shared experiences, the working-class in advanced capitalist countries, including the Nordic states, is an increasingly atomised precariat of abstract labour navigating part-time contracts, temporary and short time work, challenges to union protection and growing privatisation of social goods and digitalisation of social services. Furthermore, neoliberal discourse then depicts coping with unemployment as both an individual responsibility and a cause of social dependence, further eroding a sense of solidarity (Pemberton et al., 2016). During the past 20 years access to social support has been reduced, growth of social budgets minimised, and penalising welfare-to-workfare practices implemented in Finland. Austerity politics have increased inequality and hit hardest the workers and deskilled individuals already suffering from insecurity in the labour market. The equalising and poverty-reducing effects of redistribution have been weakened due to tax reforms since the 1990s. Taxing of capital income and wealth as well as wealth transfers have been reduced. Tax reliefs have been justified as necessary to keep up with the tightening international competition. As a result of tax reforms, the benefits of neoliberal restructuring have indeed gone to those groups whose taxation has been lightened (Karvonen et al. 2022; Rajavuori 2022). The weak development of basic security in relation to wages has seen to the failure of income transfers in equalising income differences (Saikkonen et al. 2018). The reorganisation of the responsibilities of welfare state has led to increasing inequality.

In the previous chapter I noted how Finnish segregation scholars allude to a culture of "benefit dependency" in low-income neighbourhoods. Yesterday's moral justification for universalism, based on equal social rights, has turned to today's moral panic over benefit dependent households. The result is that both liberal scholars and mainstream commentators appear to have bought into diktats of the "workfare offensive" (Peck 2002). The fear is that generous social benefits lead to indolence and work avoidance at the expense of the righteous and hard-working taxpayer. Universal benefits and services are questioned and criticised because they are expensive (Anttonen and Sipilä 2000). Furthermore, the growth in global migration has seen to the diversification of the Finnish population. Social life is characterised by a new heterogeneity. Ethnic and language differences are abused by populists to weaken a sense of solidarity. Nationalist political parties grow in popularity, largely on the ticket of welfare chauvinism and by criticising the provision of social benefits to people of immigrant background. The social rights of the previous welfare era, including the universal right to a standard of living via redistribution, are easier to reproach and austerity politics are easier to justify when all are not seen as equal. While the principles of universalism are giving in, welfare provision is increasingly based on eligibility criteria. Helping to slim down the welfare sector in the 1990s was a new approach to public administration that argued against state bureaucracy, looked to the private sector for more efficient administrative practices and, importantly, advocated shedding public assets that it saw as a surplus.

New Public Management

Reforms that aimed at savings in public administration and efficiency through privatisation of public services were introduced first in the UK and USA in the 1970s and 1980s, followed by New Zealand and Australia. Their experiences motivated other OECD countries to put similar changes on their agendas. Academics identified the common characteristics of a set of public administration reforms and began discussing them under the umbrella concept New Public Management (NPM) (Gruening 2001). NPM is an approach to governance that combines neoclassical economic theory and private management studies (Hughes 2003). It is rooted in the approach of New Institutional Economics (NIE) and although NIE introduced certain criticisms of neoclassical economics, it builds heavily on its paradigm and draws from the work of Chicago School economists. Generally, NPM holds that in order to promote the efficiency of the public sector, attention must be redirected from input and processes to performance and output. Advocates of NPM hope to transform institutions of public management so as to allow for market practices and business world lessons to penetrate the public sector. They increasingly view the citizen as a customer exercising consumer sovereignty in the market for services. NPM practices are characterised by an alleged separation of politics and administration on the one hand, and the separation of service provision and production on the other. Among these practices are budget cuts, privatisation, user charges and vouchers (see Borins 1995; Hood 1991; Hughes 2003; Osborne and Gaebler 1992).

NPM played a major part in the transformation of the Nordic model, much more so in fact than in the local government reforms of central Europe. And in the Nordics, Swedish and Finnish municipalities were the most enthusiastic about implementing NPM practices (Haveri 2015). In Sweden, NPM has underpinned several national and local reform processes aiming at the use of market mechanisms in public welfare service provision outsourcing service provision to commercial and third sector organisations, voucher systems that allow 'consumers' of welfare services to shop and choose things such as senior care and education in the market instead of the municipality providing the services itself. Market liberalisation policies advocated by the European Commission have seen Swedish municipalities increasingly selling their assets to private investors (Wollmann 2004).

But it was Finland that was the most persistent and consistent of the Nordic countries in applying the doctrine of NPM to its fullest (Temmes 1998). The lightening of bureaucracy, the empowerment of market mechanisms, the reduction of regulation and the shift from input budgeting to a stronger focus on results were the main means adopted during the Finnish reforms of the post-recession 1990s (Haveri 2002). NPM was introduced to local governments under the name of the Free Municipality Experiment,[3] the point of which was a thorough "disaggregation" – a decentralisation of governance and the establishing of the municipality as the baseline unit of governance (Dunleavy et al. 2006). The main objectives of the experiment were the strengthening of municipal autonomy, resident participation in local decision making, efficiency in local governance and service provision. Municipalities were granted more flexibility to deviate from state regulations and transfer tasks belonging to state officials onto local decision makers, freedom to organise local governance more particularly, and experiment with inter-municipal collaboration. The act removed many of the obligations of municipalities to have the state ratify their plans and decisions. The local decision-making bodies were now granted more freedom to reorganise their tasks and responsibilities between different municipal boards. The Free Municipality Experiment was essential in dismantling the supervision and steering of local administration by the central state. The transformation had begun from a welfare state to what governance researchers have called the welfare municipality (Kröger 2011) and the local welfare state (Rose and Ståhlberg 2005).

A major reform, which further marked the beginning of a more market-based welfare system in Finland, was made in 1993 with regard to state transfer payments to municipalities. The state transfer reform removed much of local governments' budgetary planning responsibilities and removed state oversight of how municipalities organised their welfare services. The previous system had incentivised municipalities to expand, improve and develop their services as state transfers were cost-based. But now municipalities would receive the same amount of state transfers per capita despite the extent and expenses of their social and health services (Yliaska 2017). The state allowed for differences to grow between municipalities. Local governments began to adopt increasingly entrepreneurial governance practices, a trajectory in the US in the 1980s discussed by Harvey (1989).

The municipalities and municipal enterprises were free to use their state funding as they wished. State funding was also cut, and municipalities were encouraged to look for other ways to fund their services. This trend has persisted. The ministry of finance calls this new model "performance management". Since the introduction of NPM, the municipalities have looked for the best ways to organise their services in an economically "well-preforming" way – i.e., a way that saves money and brings more money into the public treasury. Two related changes this has brought are the diminishing role of municipalities as service providers and the growth in buying services from the private sector. An example is the privatisation of municipal care homes for the disabled and the elderly.

Most importantly for our considerations, the approach to public ownership and management of land and buildings was changing under NPM. One aspect that the roots in NIE reflect is the strong favouring of private property rights, suggesting that negative externalities can be negotiated when property rights are well defined. NIE emphasises that public institutions should work not only to protect property rights, but transfer public properties to the private sector for the sake of efficiency. Public monopolies are seen as too burdensome, inefficient and market distorting, and state and municipal real estate are questioned (Haveri 2002). As efficient managers, NPM proponents argue that officials should concentrate on outputs and revenue and getting rid of surpluses. The state essentially becomes the purchaser of private services as opposed to acting as a direct public service provider, and this is especially true for providing space and premises for public offices and services. Instead of being an owner of public real estate, these property assets are sold off. The next part of the book explores this transformation in Finland in detail.

The Nordic universalism of public welfare provision became a focus of critique, and the state's arrangement with the markets since the implementation of NPM has been that the private sector has growing responsibility over service provision. NPM meant a move from central governance to market-led, decentralised management of the public sector (Anttonen and Sipilä 2000; Kuusela and Ylönen 2013). NPM also introduced managerial and leadership practices from the private sector to the public sector. Civil servants were replaced by technocratic, rational managers. The latest in this "cadre of technocrats" in Finland is the mayoral model recently adopted in Helsinki. The role of the mayor as compared to the previous city director is one of a manager compared to a civil servant. To quote at length the astute analyst of European urban governance, Patrick LeGales (2002, 243), who wrote of Finland, and Helsinki in particular, already twenty years ago:

> The dogma of universalism has begun to crack. Well aware of what is at stake in the European integration project, Finnish elites have rapidly seized the initiative. Gradually, the anonymous politicians who ran the city council of Helsinki and its related organizations have turned towards Europe, and they now stress the city's position in Europe, renovation of the docklands, and competition with

Stockholm. Politically, Helsinki has become a much more sensitive stake: even though the term had no meaning in Finland, Mrs Eva-Riitta Siitonen [Helsinki City Director 1996–2005] soon began to present herself at European conferences as the "mayor" of Helsinki. For the first time, the political role of mayor of Helsinki has gained consistency in terms of leadership and of building links with a project inside Europe. It is now a truly political role, which goes beyond internal party logics to issues of power, and which aims to articulate a plan, a special interest for Helsinki.

The mayoral model is the latest in the rolling out of novel managerial practices in this Northern pocket of Europe. European mayors convene in conferences to learn best urban development practices, speeding up and streamlining neoliberal urban policy transfer. They also have new types of interests to collaborate with the development industry. The previous mayor of Helsinki was recruited by the Nordic real estate investment company NREP before even the end of his term. But the newfound role of cities as key nodes in the national growth apparatus and the growing responsibilities and opportunities of urban managers had already been envisioned in the 1990s.

From regional equality to urban policy

Legal reform concerning the responsibilities of local governments was passed in Finland in 1995. One of the key purposes of the reform was to strengthen the role of the municipality in directing local, regional development. In addition, it intended to reorganise the system of local political decision making, to increase resident participation for the sake of local democracy. The same year the prime minister Paavo Lipponen established a working group to begin developing the idea of a specific urban policy. This was in anticipation of the growing centrality of cities and city regions in the global dynamics of advanced capitalism. And, as Salo and Mäntysalo (2017, 129) write, the main Finnish urban regions have since "become the focus of special urban policy programmes, administrative reforms and strategic planning". But according to Haila (1999, 177), the term urban policy was intended to substitute that of urban planning:

> This change of the vocabulary is indicative. The new word suggests that the previous mode of planning – coordinating from above, adjusting different land uses into each other, emphasizing targets and values like equality and social welfare – has been replaced with projects that are carried out by public-private partnerships and that are not only more economic and market oriented than the previous public projects, but also more controversial.

I would hesitate to say that targets of equality and social welfare have simply been replaced. Those targets still do exist, but planning, land use and land policy now have other targets that seriously hinder and contradict the reaching of traditional welfare targets. The aim of urban policy is often to open urban land and the built environment for new rounds of investment and capital accumulation. To explain how this aim is reached is in great part, as Haila pointed out, to explore urban politics, strategies and decision making regarding public land use. This is the task of Part II of the book.

The prominence of urban regions as growth machines and sites of increasing competitiveness and entrepreneurialism has been a global phenomenon since the 1980s (Harvey 1989; Logan and Molotch 1987). The new urban policy coupled with state transfer reforms came to encourage spatial restructuring and local autonomy, a process familiar from international literature on rescaling of governance. The city and the local government have become the scale at which "market-compatible coping systems are to be constructed not as a shield against globalization but as a way of maximizing its local potential" (Peck 2002, 334). National, regional and local state strategies were being developed "to position major urban economies optimally within global and supranational circuits of capital" (Brenner 2004, 3). And municipalities, while engaging in cutbacks, were now increasingly the loci of decision making and management. Across most contexts in which such processes of rescaling have been mobilised, they have accelerated marketisation and commodification and intensified uneven development across places and territories (Brenner, Peck and Theodore 2010).

In Finland, this was reflected in a situation in which cities – whose catchment areas as regards job markets, housing and retail reach beyond municipal borders – now increasingly compete with each other for investments, jobs and professionals or so-called "good taxpayers" (Salo and Mäntysalo 2017). In the next part of the book a case study of Helsinki, using its land and housing policies in novel, entrepreneurial ways with this objective of attracting high taxpaying households and companies, is introduced. The new urban policy of the mid-90s was inherently associated with the emergence of both the entrepreneurial city and the entrepreneurial self (Moisio and Paasi 2013). In this process, local policymakers' focus switched from prioritising service delivery in the best possible way to local populations, to redeveloping the urban form in a way that favours images and city branding, building an attractive business environment, recalibrating the attitude of labour towards flexibility and of encouraging the unemployed to accept the violence of workfare (Peck 2002). I discussed in the opening to Part I how peripheral housing estates of Finnish cities began to see disinvestment during the 1990s. The focus of urban policy had switched back to the core areas where capital investments were now being attracted.

Meanwhile, unwanted, large bureaucratic structures were being dismantled but also divided into smaller, more focused and particular offices, public enterprises and private companies. One important bureaucratic division concerned the corporatisation of public real estate management. Many cities chose to use their land to maximise what Anne Haila (2015) has called fiscal rent and have established separate municipal companies to do this. Local governments now want to maximise the revenue to be made from their real estate assets and compete with one another for investments and mobile capital; as will be discussed in the chapters that follow, this has serious ramifications for urban equality. Such projects of decentralisation and autonomy are as Moisio (2012, 49) suggests:

> [A] concerted political choice of privileging transnational capital and its interests. It is also fairly obvious that a development that is quintessentially based on territorial polarisation is not going to be equally beneficial to everyone. Quite the contrary, it is likely that the future Finland will see deeper divisions and a concomitant separation of societal spaces between those who initiate the whirlpool of transformations and reap the profits, those who lose their footholds and drop out of this vortex, and those who were excluded from this swirl in the first place.

This intensifying institutional whirlpool which reorganises the state from a break lever and countercyclical force to the market, into its auxiliary and supportive mechanism, has been under way in Finland for decades now. Yet intriguingly it has rarely been bridged with explaining growing urban inequalities by scholars working on Finland.

As expressed in the beginning, the welfare state enjoys wide public support across the political spectrum, and to call its transformations neoliberal does not sit well with this support. To repeat the insight from Christophers (2013, 886), the Nordic model also continues to play a "cathartic role [. . .] in international leftist narratives of political-economic alternatives to neoliberal capitalism". But the developments discussed here shed a contrasting light on the matter. In Finland, neoliberalism "as a new regime of accumulation has significantly shaken the 'equalising' structures of spatial Keynesianism" (Moiso 2008, 4). As noted earlier, the Nordic universalism of public welfare provision became a focus of critique, and the state's arrangement with the markets since the implementation of NPM has been that the private sector has growing responsibility over service provision. NPM meant a move from central governance to market-led, decentralised management of the public sector (Anttonen and Sipilä 2000; Kuusela and Ylönen 2013). Against this historical backdrop, the following chapters explore the shake-down of public land policy, real estate management and housing policies under the institutional reorganisation of the roles of both public actors and public resources in the face of a novel regime of accumulation. My particular focus will be on the role that transformations in the means and goals of these policies play in urban inequality.

Notes

1. The notion of the middle way is, of course, highly problematic. In Sweden the Saltsjöbaden Agreement of 1938 between the Swedish Employers' Confederation (SAF) and the Swedish Trade Union Confederation (LO) was signed at the glamorous Saltsjöbaden Hotel, a notorious bourgeois hangout, reflecting on whose home

turf the "compromise" was being drawn. The agreement can also be seen as a union-led pacification of the working-class as it quelled labour uprisings in a country which for decades up to that point had seen the highest rate of strikes in the industrialised world (Dahlqvist 2020).

2. Municipalities set their own income tax rate independently and today it ranges between 17 and 24 per cent of individual taxable income. Another tax collected by municipalities is the real estate tax, based on the value of both the land and its improvements. Together local income tax, real estate tax and a share of corporate tax account for almost half of municipal revenue. Municipalities in Finland spend EUR 44 billion on services and welfare annually.

3. Fin. vapaakuntakokeilu

PART II

Entrepreneurialism in Public Land Policy

This part of the book deals with land, its ownership, use, allocation and management, and how these relate to urban development and socio-spatial inequality in Finnish cities. Land policy has traditionally been a central means by which public authorities deter uneven development of the built environment and its related inequalities. Over the following chapters I will argue that in recent decades the goals of land policy have changed to such an extent that not only has the target of preventing urban inequality become jeopardised, but new policy goals themselves may also be exacerbating inequalities. Although I will illustrate this with examples, my interest is not in providing extensive data on segregation or mapping the location of classes and ethnic groups. We know from Chapter 2 that there is plenty of this kind of information in studies and reports. Instead, in the chapters that make up this part of the book, I do the following. Chapter 4 explores changes in the means and goals of municipal land policy in three Finnish cities and discusses the ramifications of an increasingly neoliberalised municipal land policy for urban equality. Chapter 5 presents a case study of selling public land in Helsinki that ensued in the development of an exclusive enclave for the wealthy, exacerbating inequality in the city.

When such matters are topics of social scientific research, it is useful to begin by recognising some of the special characteristics of land in general. First and foremost, land is literally matter of existence – it is indispensable for all human activity. Land is scarce. Apart from land reclamations like the Dutch Zuiderzee Works or the Palm Jumeirah in Dubai, no more habitable land will ever be available than there already is. Land is also spatially fixed and unique. The use of land creates externalities, meaning that what happens on one plot of land has environmental, public-health and other consequences outside that immediate plot. Land, and urban land in particular, is embedded in complex social relations (Hyötyläinen and Beauregard 2023). Issues of social reproduction, community well-being and socio-spatial equality often hinge on land tenure – whether we treat land, for example, as private or public property, manage it collectively or use it as a commons. Any owner of land will enjoy a position of monopoly. The treatment of land as a commodity to be exchanged for a price, made a profit on and allocated to its uses in the land market is also highly problematic. For instance, land is not a product of human labour, it does not have production costs and it does not wear out through use. Land is a fictitious commodity, as Karl Polanyi pointed out. Land cannot be substituted with another commodity, in the way wheat can substitute for rice, or nuclear power for fossil fuels. The land market will always be imperfectly elastic, meaning that the land market cannot dynamically respond to the fluctuations in demand for land by adjusting supply in the same way as the market for smartphones or skateboards might. Then again, land scarcity is often a social construct to keep land values high. How much weight is given to these different special features of land, its curious place in the economy, and their implications for both political economic theory and land use practices has shifted through history.

Even when land is commodified and treated as a financial asset, exchanged in the land market according to the rent it yields, the state performs important and necessary functions. Christophers (2016) summarises these neatly. First, the state plays the role of facilitator. It produces and polices the property rights that circulate in land markets as well as the actual, physical lands to which the property rights attach. Second, the state intervenes. It regulates land use and users, it expropriates land for its needs, it plans land use, and it invests in land. The objective of such intervention often is to limit the extent to which land is treated as a financial asset and make it less vulnerable to speculation. Third, the state itself also tends to treat land as a financial asset, according to the rent it yields, allocating it to its uses according to bid rent. Political economists have in recent years grown increasingly interested in the third of these functions. The state in different contexts has been found to take an active role in supporting accumulation through public land disposals, public-private partnerships in urban development programmes, and entrepreneurial urban policies that promote the competitive use of public land and its treatment as a financial asset.

Reforms of the Canadian, Swedish, French and UK states, and changing conceptions of public property have been studied in recent years and they provide evidence of the changing yet enduring role of the state in the use and organisation of land. The means and goals of public land use and policy have changed as the neoliberal era progresses. The previous chapter discussed how first in Anglo-American countries and later elsewhere, neoliberal lessons have influenced local decision-making and how cities are governed. Neoliberal ideology has been important in legitimating the new "entrepreneurial city" (Peck and Tickell 2002, 393–4). According to Neil Brenner and Nik Theodore (2002), despite political tradition, local level decisions on land use are often adapted to suit the increasing competition between cities and city marketing to attract investment and jobs. Neoliberal urban policies such as city branding, business parks and innovation hubs, as well as urban development corporations and public-private partnerships are also becoming much more common in the European and Nordic urban experience. By competing with one another and marketing themselves, entrepreneurial cities are encouraging businesses and workforces to move, while subjecting themselves to the risks of competition. What all this points to is not so much a withdrawal of the state, but state recalibration to accommodate businesses and seek for funds through privatising assets, commodifying land and attracting investment capital. There is "a lemming-like rush towards urban entrepreneurialism, which itself would only serve to facilitate, encourage, and even publicly subsidise the accelerated mobility of circulating capital and resources" (Peck and Tickell 2002, 385).

Drawing on case studies in France, Adisson (2018) has investigated public land management and privatisation by public administrations. The disposal and conversion of public properties are an outcome of very particular and deliberate state policies, strategies and projects that open public lands for new rounds of capital investment. Adisson suggests that beneath all this is an ongoing state restructuring in France which we must understand in order to unpack the rationales behind public land disposals. The new public management doctrine has introduced market-inspired policies and practices in the public administration of state land and real estate. And a state rescaling is underway, resulting in increased power and pressures on local governments in urban affairs, which consequently motivate the redevelopment of their landed properties too. Also focusing on France, Artioli (2016) explores how reforms in state administration have aimed at strengthening market coordination in both the management and sale of public real estate. In a context of national deficit reduction and budget cuts, public real estate has become the target of reduced state ownership. Meanwhile streamlining the management of remaining land resources was one aim of the French cross-cutting administrative reforms of the mid-2000s. Efficiency in land management was sought by setting clear sales targets, introducing market-oriented instruments for real estate disposal, and restructuring the central government along a task-specialised model.

One of the most notorious land privatisation programmes in Europe is applied in the UK. This programme is part of a broader, ongoing regime of privatisation initially kicked off by the first Thatcher administration. Since the 1980s reducing the size of the public estate by selling it to private-sector actors has been consistent. Instead of the state itself leasing, developing, trading, actively speculating with or otherwise directly exploiting its land as a financial asset, the state has rather enabled such a treatment to be generalised by strategically selling its land to private actors that do treat land in such a way (Christophers 2018). And in Canada, starting in the mid-1990s, Canadian public land and buildings have been subject to regular bureaucratic inspection with the aim of elimination of properties viewed as a surplus. Surplus land is transferred to Canada Lands Company, a state-owned enterprise charged with privatising public land in the name of efficiency (Whiteside 2019).

Finally, coming to the Nordic context, Olsson (2018) and Zetterlund (2022) have studied changes and continuities in the Swedish municipal land policy. The active facilitation and control of urban development via public landowner-ship, also known as the municipal land instrument, was an essential tool for local governments in the post-war era to tackle escalating rents, produce universal working-class housing and plan for the even development of urban areas. Ols-son shows how the land instrument still very much exists and the state actively uses it. However, it is now used more than anything to fit the requirements of commercial property development. The programmes of state restructuring (as opposed to retrenchment), administrative and legal reform, shedding off surplus lands, implementation of competitive urban strategies and their justification with increased efficiency find their implementation in the context of Finnish land policy. In the following chapters I explore transformations in land policy in Fin-land during recent decades, analysing and discussing their implication for urban inequality. But first, an overview of Finnish land policy is in order.

On land policy in Finland

Land policy is a key instrument in managing land use for Finnish municipalities.[1] It allows a city to answer for planning, housing development, economic development, corporate needs for land and the availability of services. The responsibilities of pub-lic authorities pertaining to land policy are stipulated in the Land Use and Building Act.[2] Land use scholars define land policy as the means of a public authority to deal with the acquiring, allocating and pricing of areas and the development of property rights and tenures (e.g., Virtanen 2000). Traditionally Finnish cities have allocated land administratively, free of charge, for public services. Some cities have carried out long-term land policy and bought land when the prices are low, building up their land banks. The principal method of conveying land for development has been leasing. Leasing has brought predictable, long term rent revenues for cities, allowing them to purchase raw land for the land bank and prepare for future requirements. Leasing land has also ensured city authorities have control over land use and urban development. It has kept the planning power in the hands of town planners and helped Finnish cities develop relatively evenly, without glaring spatial inequalities, concentrations of poverty or enclaves of wealth, and without private, speculative interests overriding the public good. Public landownership has also been a prereq-uisite for public planning of the development of the built environment elsewhere in the world, for example in Sweden (Olsson 2018) and the Netherlands (Buitelaar 2010), but also in Singapore (Haila 2016).

In Finland roughly 60 per cent of the nation's land area is private property. Three-quarters of the country is covered by forests, the majority of which are owned by private individuals and households. This reflects decisions made as far back as the 16th century when the Swedish crown allocated land to private farmers.

The state owns 30 per cent of all land, and municipalities, religious congregations and corporations own ten per cent between them. Finnish cities are owners of a significant amount of urban land, as is often the case in European cities (Häussermann and Haila 2005). Indeed, cities own the biggest share of municipal land. The history of city land banks also reaches back to times of Swedish rule, as the crown allocated land for urban development. In the case of Helsinki, for instance, the city received land as a donation upon its establishment in 1550. Land banks have given local governments great power over land use decisions, and the ability of municipalities to intervene in community development free from private influence has historically been given great importance.

In Finland, but again also for instance in Sweden, land policy has traditionally been called 'active' when the municipality collects rent revenue to the public treasury on a long-term basis via land leases, and then uses that money to buy raw land from private owners or the state into the municipal land bank. Leasing ensures that the land is maintained in public ownership even when it is in private use. When leasing land, an annual rent of between four and six per cent of the estimated market price of the plot has been common. The idea here has been to capture windfall gains in land value due to public investment back to the public treasury (Lawson and Ruonavaara 2019). Traditionally, land has been leased through a plot application round organised annually by the city. Residential land is then leased on a first-come-first-served basis to developers. We will see that this has changed in an important way as municipalities now allocate land through auctions in order to capture the highest bid rent. The land leases have traditionally been 60 years but for instance in Helsinki a land policy update will see new leases set at 80 years. When selling land, the pricing of municipal land may vary. For example, when selling land for an individual family who uses the land to build their detached house, municipalities tend to sell the land at some 70 per cent to 90 per cent of the market price. When the city sells land for social housing, the price is between 50 per cent and 80 per cent of the market price.

The most common way for a city to acquire land for future needs is by voluntary purchase of raw land. The second method for a city to obtain land is pre-emption. Pre-emption stands for the right of the municipality to acquire land with a price and terms already agreed upon by a landowner and a prospective buyer. Here, the municipality has the legal right to replace the original buyer, and purchases the land with the price and terms set in the deed of sale. A city may use pre-emption to acquire land that it needs for utilities and recreational and conservation areas. The third method is expropriation. Expropriation means the legal obligation of a property owner to sell the land or property they own to the city, if the city needs it. Private land may be expropriated by the city for public use such as for the use of a public road. The city also has the legal right to expropriate land that is designated in the city plan for the use of a public building, say, a municipal care home for the elderly. When expropriating land, the landowner is duly compensated and paid the market price. Furthermore, if the property owner loses their home or livelihood in the process, the city must compensate for the costs of acquiring a new property. Nevertheless, expropriation is generally seen as a last resort, as it often leads to long legal conflicts with landowners (Virtanen 2000). Finally, the fourth way to obtain land is with the use of a so-called land use contract. Land-use contracts are used when the land has not been purchased prior to planning, but the city plans on private land. It is an agreement between a city and a private landowner about the rights and responsibilities of each party over the planning and the implementation of the plan. The building of streets, parks, water supply and power lines are usually the responsibility of the city. However, with a land use contract it is possible to have the private landowner accept responsibility for the building of utilities. How much the landowner contributes to the building of utilities is usually based on what they gain in land value increase from the plan.

One of the central objectives of land policy has traditionally been to ensure the conditions for planning and the execution of plans. In Finland and in Sweden (Clark and Runesson 1996) the municipality has a legal right to decide the content, timing and restrictions included in plans. Planning monopoly means that municipalities have the sole right to assign development rights. The Constitution of Finland (121 §) states that local governance should be based on the autonomy of residents. This is the basic justification for a public planning monopoly – no private interest should be allowed to overrule public interest in the development of the built environment in Finnish cities. With a planning monopoly, a municipality can also discourage speculation and have a say in the development of land prices. A central question for planning is whether the municipality draws plans on only public or also private lands. Many other municipal duties such as planning recreational areas and tending to water areas also require land policy expertise (Virtanen 2000). The Land Use and Building Act (51 §) gives municipalities great power to decide when and where they wish to draw and implement plans. In the post-war era, municipal land policy in the Nordic welfare state enabled the housing production systems, which facilitated the rapid processes of post-war urbanisation and industrialisation such as the Million Programme in Sweden and the development of housing estates in Finnish cities. Public holdings of developable land enabled the restraining of land rent extraction and aimed at distributing affordable, quality housing throughout the city.

Today, very different targets for municipal land policy are being emphasised. The liberal conservative leaders of Helsinki for instance persistently drive for land policy that maximises rent revenue, counts the rent from alternative uses of public land as a cost, engages in public private partnerships, rolls back on the regulation of developers, and opens calls for corporate actors to express their ideas for new development projects instead of deciding projects from above, guided by public interest (Hautajärvi et al. 2021). In balancing public and private interests, the scales of land policy have in places tipped in favour of the latter. What has been paid little attention to by urban scholars, is how this is due in large part to the fact that public entities – the state and municipal governments – have started to treat their landed property as if it was a financial asset, much like private land-owners do, according to the rent it yields (Harvey 2006). As Zetterlund (2022) points out, public landownership on its own does not ensure the traditional wel-fare targets of land policy. In Finland the state and municipalities are large land-owners today just as in the past. The issues we must concern ourselves with are what these public actors do with their land today, what the means and goals of land policy are, and what their ramifications for urban equality are. These are the questions I turn to next.

Notes

1. Unless otherwise stated, details regarding land policy in Finland are sourced from The Land Policy Guidebook (Fin. Maapolitiikan opas), an online resource main-tained and updated by the Association of Finnish Municipalities.
2. Fin. Maankäyttö- ja rakennuslaki

CHAPTER 4

The Corporatisation of Public Property

Several significant institutional changes regarding state and municipal land and real estate policies were implemented around the turn of the millennium in Finland. First, an unincorporated state-owned enterprise known as Senate Properties was established to manage state real estate and allocate premises for different branches of state administration. Senate Properties operates under the Ministry of Finance and is tasked with reorganising state premises and disposing of any real estate that through this reorganisation becomes distinguished as a surplus. Second, the management of municipal land and real estate was moved from public offices to revenue-seeking public utility companies. Whereas the offices would traditionally have allocated land for schools, libraries and health care centres for free, under public utility companies public services were made rent paying tenants (Haila 2016). Like the central state, these utility companies of local states were increasingly concerned with two matters: efficiency in land use and getting rid of surplus land. And third, in 2001 the Land Use and Building Act replaced the old Building Act of 1958. The new act introduced important changes to the land use legislation. The act legalised land use contracts, giving more room for partnerships between municipalities, landowners and developers. And it removed the obligation to have city plans ratified by a state official, substituting it with participatory planning that purports to give residents a stronger voice in planning and land use. In this chapter I discuss these three changes regarding state land management, municipal land policy and land use legislation in turn. I suggest, that due to these reforms there are now new conflicts between the state and municipalities that have come to weaken the well-being of residents, new entrepreneurial aims for land use that prioritise exchange values over use values of residential space and more room for private interests to influence land allocation and use. I suggest, that due to these reforms and their outcomes, the traditional welfare goals of Finnish land policy have not only been jeopardised, but in places urban inequalities have even been exacerbated.

State land management

The very first central office established under Finnish autonomy was the Office of the Intendant, which began operating in 1811. The purpose of the office was to supervise the plans and construction budgets for new public buildings. More than a century later, in 1936, the office was renamed the National Board of Public Building. By now Finland was an independent republic and the office had grown into a government agency tasked with the management of state property. Its responsibilities included allocating land and developing premises for various state requirements and assigning land for municipal needs, particularly for housing development (Hanski 2011). The final task became more prominent in 1978 when an act was passed requiring that if city plans were drawn on state land, the municipality had a pre-emption right. The state was understood to have fulfilled its role as a landowner when it allocated land to municipalities at the price of raw land, and supervised evenness in the development of the built environment by ratifying city plans (Kokkinen 2008). The state, however, would soon assume a drastically different role.

The consequences of the severe, early-1990s depression in Finland, discussed briefly above in Chapter 3, were aggravated by the deregulation of the finance industry and great credit expansion in the preceding decade. Local savings banks had been liberated to supply mortgages to households, and more private finance had suddenly been available for the booming real estate industry. Meanwhile the Finnish, but also Norwegian and Swedish tax systems, had at the time started to encourage households to pile on debt by generous deductibility of the interest expenses on mortgages. The 1990s saw the aftermath of speculative attacks on and devaluation of the Finnish currency, rising interest rates that put a stop to borrowing, and the collapse of the trade partner to the east, with unemployment rates beginning to soar (Nygaard 2021). Households fell behind on their mortgage payments and developers could no longer sell their product. Insolvent households and developers saw loans turn into bad debt. Banks attempted to realise the collateral, but found real estate valued nowhere close to what had been estimated in the 1980s. Over the period of a few years, from 1989 to 1992, the Finnish real estate markets crashed – real estate values plummeted in places by half. Devalued real estate and bad debts drove savings banks into a deep crisis, while thousands lost their homes (Lehtiö 2004).

The state stepped in to rescue banks from the Finnish banking crisis, and arguably also to help bankrupt companies and households weather the depression. It began reorganising the devalued properties and managing bonds and real estate previously owned by savings banks. In 1991 the state established two asset management companies called Arsenal and Sponda, the first one to liquidate the problematic residential real estate and the second to make money by selling valuable state properties (Nygaard 2021). A substantial volume of private real estate was transferred in-kind from savings banks to these state companies. The depression was a convenient motivation for the state, informed by the tenets of NPM in the latter half of the 1990s, to adopt a new rationality: to save and use public resources as efficiently as possible (Haila 2008). In 1996 Sponda's activities were transferred under the Ministry of Finance, which demanded that the highest possible revenue be sought in the use of state properties. In 1998 Sponda was listed on the Helsinki

Stock Exchange. With a portfolio consisting of precious properties in Helsinki city centre, it was the largest listed investment company.

The National Board of Public Building was dissolved in 1995. The majority of the state property assets were transferred into the new State Real Property Agency, and two other state real estate companies, called Engel and Kapiteeli. Engel was established to develop government buildings and manage related real-estate services (Haila 2015). In 1999 government real estate worth €1.5 (today €2.2) billion was transferred from various government companies and agencies, including the State Real Property Agency to Kapiteeli.[1] The transfer consisted of buildings deemed redundant from the government perspective. This included former schools, empty government buildings, railway stations fallen into disuse, post offices, state hotels and other buildings that were considered unnecessary for the government to own. The need for the state to own land and buildings was being scrutinised more than ever before. A new approach to state-owned, public real estate assets was being adopted and a great deal of public land and real estate was increasingly viewed as a surplus. In the years that followed, the state real estate companies were privatised one by one. Engel was privatised in 2004 when the Danish ISS bought its entire stock. Part of Kapiteeli's property was developed and sold on the market between 1999 and 2006, until Kapiteeli was privatised in September of 2006. The buyer was Sponda, which itself was now a private real estate business. It bought 100 per cent of the shares. And in 2017 Sponda was sold on to the international investment company Blackstone, the world's largest asset management company.[2]

Out of this reorganisation emerged a central state with a new entrepreneurial logic of public land policy and real estate management; one that viewed land as a commodity and prioritises the market mechanism for public land allocation. In 2001, the State Real Property Agency was renamed Senate Properties. Senate Properties, the remaining state branch of real estate management, is now an unincorporated state-owned enterprise, which manages a major part of the real estate assets owned by the state of Finland. The assets managed by Senate are worth €4.2 billion and are made up of approximately 9,000 buildings. The facilities used by the state amount to six million square metres. The defence administration occupies the largest number of facilities, with the Finnish Defence Forces taking up almost half the total square footage. One fifth of this area consists of offices, the rest are premises such as courtrooms, museums, police departments, laboratories and storage facilities.[3]

Discussing the operational logic of the enterprise, a real estate development boss I interviewed in 2018 at Senate Properties explained the transformations in state real estate management:

> For the last 200 years the state has developed a huge amount of real estate all over Finland. Now, during the last ten years, the doors have been swinging in the other direction. We currently have over 500 locations for sale, and we make

about 100 real estate deals annually. And we receive about 100 million euros per year from these sales, to be returned to the taxpayers. The revenue goes to the Ministry of Finance.

Similar programmes to sell off state-owned land have been reported in the UK and Canada and analysed closely in the works of Christophers (2018) and Christophers and Whiteside (2021). A central question in their research is why, after all the time and effort that went into amassing public land and developing the state's real estate in those countries, did the state effect a radical U-turn and begin selling off public land? The exact same question should be asked of the state in Finland. After two centuries of developing and managing state land and real estate under different public boards and offices, why do the doors now swing in the opposite direction?

The real estate boss's reply above reveals part of the answer. Today, Senate Properties answers to the Ministry of Finance. That the government's real estate strategy is handled by the Ministry of Finance is indicative a new kind of thinking on public land and real estate policy closely related to state finances, as opposed to merely a question of management and allocation of uses. The Ministry of Finance[4] explains core elements of its real estate strategy:

> Significant economic benefits have been achieved by centralising ownership and, thus, increasing the efficiency of the central government's corporate steering. Capital tied up in real estate assets has been freed for use in the core functions of central government by matching central government real estate holdings to the needs of the central government's activities and its need for premises and by selling assets that the central government does not need [. . .]. Such sales will enable the more appropriate use of the properties and support their maintenance and preservation.

Senate Properties is expected to have its customers – different branches of state administration – to move to shared work environments to save up on government office space expenses. This is a very particular and deliberate state strategy to open public land for new rounds of capital investment, similar to those from Adisson's (2018) case studies in France. And according to the real estate boss, Senate Properties is very efficient at releasing public lands for new investments: "The main task of Senate is to reorganise premises for state employees. And we are so good at that job, that we have been able to reduce the need for space. As state premises become vacant, there is no reason to hold on to these spaces. Instead, we look for new users and we sell the real estate." But by what rationale is state land really being designated as a surplus?

Again, the work of Christophers (2018) and Christophers and Whiteside (2021) is instructive in how to answer this: they point to the tripartite, neoliberal reasoning put forth in favour of state land privatisations in the UK and Canada. Firstly, it is argued that the public sector by its very nature is a wasteful manager of land. It both owns great swaths of unused "surplus" land, failing to put it to innovative uses, and it even hoards it and refuses to allocate it to the private sector. The argument is that "[w]hatever steps are taken to improve efficiencies the public [sector] will continue to contain land-in-use that is not actually needed precisely because it is the public [sector]" (Christophers 2018, 126–7). Second, promoting efficiency in public land use means using less land for the same result. So, more efficiency will eventually create more surplus land, as the state can now do with less. And third, concluding from the above, there are two types of surplus land: pre-existing and produced (Ibid.). And whichever kind it is, the received neoliberal wisdom goes increasingly in Finland, as it does in the UK and Canada, that it should be sold off and allocated to the much more efficient private sector. By selling it off, public land is commodified and provided to market actors who are seen as more innovative and efficient landowners who better know what the land is needed for. Senate Properties is a nimble special-purpose actor with new capabilities of releasing "wasteful surplus" land by reorganising the state's premises, identifying surpluses and increasing operational efficiency, helping the state reach the desired results with less land and allowing for private sector improvements for the highest and best possible uses of land to be unlocked.

Some recent examples illustrate how Senate Properties is addressing the logic of surplus disposal. First is the initiative to privatise national railway stations and their adjacent developable areas throughout the country.[5] The state wants to develop, in partnerships with municipalities and private corporations, and then sell large tracts of land in valuable hubs of public transportation. Altogether 21 station areas across Finland, many in urban centres, will be sold off. As Senate Properties (2023) explains:

> Railway stations and their surroundings will play a significant role in the way housing, services and transportation are planned and organised in town and city centres in the future. Our new company is an efficient and competent partner for towns and municipalities in renewing their railway station areas and ensuring sustainable urban development. Our company primarily uses town planning as a means to develop station areas and to facilitate the diverse use of these areas for housing, business and transportation purposes. Our aim is to sell the developed properties.

What this means is that Senate seeks to add value to its real estate through the planning system (see Christophers 2020, 359) before it sells off public real estate via land auctions at a profit. This could be called a programme of "strategic surplus disposal" (Whiteside 2017); strategic in the sense that the selling of valuable transportation hubs across the country is likely to bring in impressive revenues. But is it a good urban policy or fiscal strategy in the long term? Recall Harvey's (2006) insight: what is bought and sold in the land market is not simply the land, but the title to the rent of that land. The buyer of land acquires a claim upon anticipated future rent revenues, and the price of land is determined by that anticipated future rent. The state strategy of surplus disposal is based on a neoliberal fiction that the government will never in the future need those lands again (Christophers and Whiteside 2021). It is also likely to mean that in the future those key urban areas around train stations will be owned by private entities who will pocket further land value increases. And as they are sure to maximise the land rent in these urban centres, the risk is that these areas develop into high-income residential and commercial spaces, excluding the opportunity for working-class residents to live close to transportation hubs and aggravating urban inequality.

Regarding housing, prior to the reorganising of state real estate management, a key task of state authorities in charge of public land management was to allocate state land for municipal housing production needs. The state gave land for cities' social housing programmes. Today, Senate Properties operates with a very different purpose. For example, in Helsinki between the years 2012 and 2016, 34 per cent of all housing production took place on either private or state land. Of this figure, 97 per cent was comprised of private rentals and owner-occupied housing (Helsingin kaupunginkanslia 2017). The numbers reflect the fact that the state no longer allocates land for social housing production. Haila (2008) suggested that the state's real-estate company is just one among other real-estate entrepreneurs. And what does a private real estate entrepreneur really want? For one, it wants to maximise development rights. Senate Properties is a rent seeking company, and it actively negotiates with municipalities for more development rights. It lobbies local governments and again, attempts to add value to its real estate through the planning mechanism (see Christophers 2020). Interviewed land use officials from the city of Tampere described how Senate Properties behaved in land use and planning negotiations: "It's a long fight, and no private developer is as hungry for development rights as Senate Properties."

Instead of a benevolent Leviathan watching over the public good and urban equality, ratifying city plans and allocating land to municipalities according to their need, the state now participates in planning as if it were a private real estate entrepreneur. A decade after Haila's (2008) analysis, the real estate boss at Senate Properties confirmed that this is still very much the case as he explained to me the lack of interest in providing land under the market rent for municipalities' affordable housing needs: "It is not our purpose to be a disturbance in the land market." Harvey (2006) explains the purpose of the land market under the capitalist mode of production as allocating land to its uses. Allocating land below the market rent is seen by Senate as unwanted interference that hinders the full and efficient working of the land market to set expected equilibrium prices and seek highest and best rent-yielding uses for the land. The state is rolling over its duties of land allocation to the market based on exchange values rather than itself allocating land based on use values for urban residents.

All this is of course reflected in what type of housing is produced and for whom. Senate Properties only sells land for high-end housing projects. In Helsinki, for instance, state land in new residential development areas is always sold for private housing projects instead of allocated for social housing or even mixed tenure projects. Recent examples from Helsinki illustrate this. First, Senate sold land for the development of owner-occupied apartments on the brownfield redevelopment project of Konepaja in the Pasila district. It tapped into an increase in land values in the area due to the gentrification and skyrocketing real estate prices in adjacent old, centrally located working-class neighbourhoods (Ilmavirta 2008). Second, a new high-end apartment building is planned on state land where a military premises[6] used to stand in the central, bourgeois neighbourhood of Töölö. In Töölö only 2 per cent of all housing is social rental housing and opportunities for new housing development in this dense, central urban area are scarce. If the public authorities were concerned over segregation in the Finnish capital city, they would use such opportunities to allocate land for affordable housing for working-class families. Instead, the American architect Steve Hull was hired to design a luxury apartment building for the wealthy – the building has its own yoga studio, wine cellars and other conspicuous amenities. From the perspective of the Ministry of Finance, unlocking the exchange value in the land in Töölö is simply good business. From the perspective of working-class Helsinkians, the city centre is increasingly developed in the image of the elites.

How does the state justify to the public the selling of public land and the fact that the state does not subsidise house prices through its land allocation? The new policy is being promoted with the slogan that it will see money return to the taxpayer. The real estate boss at Senate, for one, was unwavering in his faith in the market and justified that disposing of land with full market rent is in fact for the good of the taxpayer: "Supply and demand determine housing prices. That's just how it is. The fact that we get the full market price for land from the developers means that we can return more money to the taxpayers." But this idea of returning money to the taxpayer is a fiction. First, it relies on the fiction that the only true value of land is its exchange value (Christophers and Whiteside 2021). And second, nothing is in reality being returned – the notion is simply based on calculating rent from alternative uses as a taxpayer cost. As was highlighted in the previous chapter, the value of urban land for the residents of cities is its use value. As opposed to viewing exchange value as the only true value of land and maximising land rents to boost public revenues, public authorities could alternatively adopt a stronger role of ensuring that use values are maximised and distributed evenly, and for example that people of different means are provided housing in central locations. For a brief moment in the post-war era, this was the adopted approach in Nordic welfare states.

For the cities and the residents of cities in Finland the new state real estate management is problematic. The state's contemporary, business savvy real estate policy drives up land prices in cities. The relationship between the state and the municipalities has become conflictual. According to Kokkinen (2008) "we have forgotten that both exist to serve the wellbeing of citizens. The primary task of both entities is to serve the common good" (p.14). Hence both state and municipalities should weigh the total outcomes of their actions, not just the benefit to their organisation. The state should support the sustainable growth of municipalities and not hinder their possibilities to practise land policy (Kokkinen 2008). But as the central and local states have become competitive landowners, absurd events arise. For example, in 2007 the small city of Järvenpää expropriated state land it needed for urban development, as the state was refusing its traditional role of allocating land to the municipality (Haila 2008). At the beginning of the 2000s the state had made an agreement with the cities in the Helsinki Metropolitan Area to convey state land for housing production. However, a controversy flared up concerning the price of state land. The state real estate company demanded the price of developed land, whereas the City of Helsinki defended its right to buy the state land at the price of raw land. Helsinki's impression was, that any value increase due to planning and development should belong to the city. The city refused to yield to the state's demand and protected its right to the value increase (Haila 2008). Again, the state acted as a real estate enterprise attempting to convert municipal property into corporate private property. And so, it is no wonder, that interviewed civil servants in Helsinki considered the actions of Senate Properties at large to be "socially irresponsible" and "interfering in the City's practice of sustainable housing policy".

In yet another example, a 2003 government programme had promised to ensure that state land be made available for affordable housing production. To follow up, in 2010 the National Audit Office of Finland published a report (208/2010) on the social duties of the state land policy. The report found that the central task of state real estate policy since the 1990s has in fact been to use real estate business to refund the money that was used to buy out the bankrupt savings banks in the aftermath of the depression. Similarly, in the UK, land sales have been used to balance the books of a debt-ridden country after the 2007–08 financial crisis (Christophers 2018), and in France land sales are used to pay for government debt reduction (Artioli 2016). Expectedly, the Audit Office report found that state real estate policy is not in line with the wider social objectives of the public sector, such as ensuring housing affordability in growing cities. The report highlighted that the state could just as well allocate land under market rent for municipalities for affordable housing purposes. But it has in fact done the exact opposite, attempting to maximise development rights and land rent. State real estate policy has not, the report found, been integrated with the objectives of social and public policy, and the target of allocating land for affordable housing has not been reached under state real estate corporations. Instead, the state's real estate management has been in conflict with the goals of municipalities (Audit Office 208/2010).

Such policy contradiction should be taken seriously as a key dynamic in the growing urban inequality of Finnish cities, leaving urban dwellers increasingly vulnerable to the interests of private actors and the loosening of public protection and regulation. Under the state's new corporatised real estate management strategies, the prospects of developing just, inclusive cities and deterring urban inequalities become jeopardised. As the state develops high-end residential and commercial space in city centres, how such projects affect and possibly narrow down the "decision environment" (Harvey and Chatterjee 1974) in which working-class people can operate regarding their residential needs, must be kept under close analytic scrutiny in Finland. It seems the state real estate practices are making it ever more difficult for working-class residents to find affordable housing in central locations and they will have to look for housing in peripheral areas. But what about the role of local authorities? Are municipal land use policies better equipped to face urban inequalities like socio-economic segregation and uneven urban development?

Corporatisation of municipal land use

The differences between the land policies practised by Finnish municipalities are often explained with two things: the political tradition of the city and the amount of donated land received from the crown during their establishment. Cities with left-leaning local governments are thought of as more inclined to practise active land policy than conservative ones. And only cities that received large land donations during their establishment phase are seen as capable of land policy free from speculation and pressure from private landowners. The late Finnish land use scholar Pekka V. Virtanen (2000) questioned both explanations. For example, the traditionally liberal conservative Helsinki received just 24 square kilometres of donated land when it was established. Today the city owns some 65 per cent of its over 200 square kilometer land area (Maanmittauslaitos 2023). The large land ownership in Helsinki's case is based on consistently leasing land and using the modest revenue to buy raw land for the land bank, i.e. active land policy (Virtanen 2000; Helsinki City Urban Facts 2013). The positive approach to public landownership by liberal conservatives in Nordic cities is a historical shared characteristic.

In the Nordic countries during the early 1900s the question of how to organise land ownership and what to do with land value increases were hot topics in the period's intellectual debates. Liberal-conservative public authorities began to stress their right to tax back to society the windfall gains of private landowners. The American land reformer Henry George's book *Progress and Poverty* was translated to Swedish, and it was widely influential for Nordic liberal conservatives. Inspired by George's proposals, municipal site leaseholds were introduced in Sweden as early as 1907, allowing land values to accrue in public coffers.

George's book *Social Problems* was translated to Finnish in 1908 by Arvid Järne-
felt, a notable Finnish dissident author who was introduced to Georgism through
the works of Leo Tolstoy. And in 1919 an influential Danish political party
called Retsforbundet was established, and it successfully advocated for a George-
inspired land value tax policy up to the late 1950s. During the early 1900s up
to 50 per cent of state revenues in Denmark came from land taxes (Silagi 1994).

As the welfare state developed, the rationales for public landownership
changed and the emphasis shifted from land value capture to public land development, from exchange values to use values of urban land for the dwellers of
cities, and on state regulation and intervention in the land market (Zetterlund
2022). A municipal planning monopoly, land allocation to private developers
by leasing instead of selling to prevent speculation, the use of rent revenue to
buy raw land for public purposes, and the allocation of land for free for public
services were considered indispensable tools for local authorities to ensure that
the public good was promoted in the development of the built environment
(Rasinkangas 2013; Virtanen 2000). These instruments remain appreciated
across the Nordic region in the present day. It is worthwhile to bear in mind,
however, as Clark and Runesson (1996, 206) remind us, that although in the
Nordic context these approaches are often perceived as closely tied to social-
democratic politics – the municipal leasehold in particular – "the original
legislation was forwarded by conservative and liberal politicians, inspired more
by Henry George than by Karl Marx".

In Finland the institutional framework of municipal land and real estate management based on active land policy – public ownership and leasing of land –
changed in important ways at the turn of the millennium. Previously municipal
land policy and real estate management were the responsibilities of public offices
that allocated spaces for the needs of public services. Public service providers were
not rent paying tenants of the city but were allocated land for free as needed and
their budgets were not restricted by concerns of rental payments. And municipalities subsidised affordable housing production by leasing land for housing
below market rent. Now public real estate is managed by so-called premises centres,[7] special-purpose public agencies, which sell and lease city premises and real
property for both the public and private sectors. The largest need for premises is
created by schools, day care centres, social and health services and libraries that
now must include rent in their budgets. By calculating rents, premises centres are
tasked with locating and getting rid of what is again seen as surplus land. This
surplus can then be sold off for instance to private corporations that are viewed
as more efficient users of land. And for housing production, municipalities are
increasingly inclined to sell the land or when leasing, extract market rent.

Under the premises centres and their new land disposal strategies, the old
methods of public land allocation are seen as wasteful and inefficient. In Helsinki
the leasing of premises to the city's own services is intended to "make the users

of premises more aware of expenses, which should be comparable to the private sector", The City of Helsinki Real Estate Strategy[8] explains. The rent that service providers pay to the City of Helsinki should cover all expenses arising from the use of space and the point of the rent is to make the city's expenses transparent and encourage different city actors towards efficient use of space. Efficiency means, again, that rents from alternative uses are calculated, and the difference between current and alternative rent is viewed as a public cost. This has also led to services losing their premises outright. A recent example of the outcome of such an approach is the moving of a local library in the East Helsinki neighbourhood of Laajasalo from municipal library premises to a new shopping mall owned by the Swedish real estate company Niam AB. Meanwhile the architecturally respected, old local library building was demolished, and the plot sold to developers. This comes after the city of Espoo to the west of Helsinki had already moved several of its libraries to shopping malls, where they now reside as tenants of the American real estate investment company Barings, Finnish real estate investment company Citycon and the pension company Keva.[9]

The Helsinki Land Use and Housing Programme (2008–17) explains that the goals of land allocation in Helsinki are affordability and diversity in housing. To reach this goal, the interviewed officials emphasised the importance of traditional instruments such as public land ownership and the leasing of land. These would ensure municipal control over the development of the built environment and predictability of rent revenue while avoiding driving up land prices. However, in Helsinki (but also Tampere and Turku), interviewed officials reported that since the corporatisation of land policy, the selling of residential land had increased. In Helsinki, land auctions have become more routine as the authorities attempt to maximise revenue from land. Yet auctions were not seen as good land policy by the interviewees; instead they were criticised for the increase in land prices they created. Contrary to the argument that private actors will be more efficient, interviewees thought the result had been poor-quality built environments that needed almost immediate repairs. A land use official in Helsinki explained: "Experiences of land auctions aren't very good . . . it is not the best land policy practised in Helsinki. Although we got a lot of money, the selling of land actually messed things up and the quality [of built environment] isn't very good."

Helsinki, Tampere and Turku all now have land sales goals, clear revenue targets regarding the alienation of public land. In Turku, where the corporatised real estate company manages not only real estate and premises but all real property, these goals steer land policy most obviously. Interviewees in Turku thought that land policy had become more "aware of expenses" since the corporatisation of the real estate department. The 2014–17 Housing and Land Policy Programme for the Turku region (4–5) states its central goals as being the strengthening of the city's position in competition between cities and the allocation of attractive locations to companies. The programme strings together housing and land policies with the development of urban competitiveness. An official interviewed in Turku explained how, after the establishment of the corporatised real estate department, the practice of land policy has changed from managerial activity to entrepreneurial activity: "It has become more business-like. Land development has changed its perspective from that of a civil servant's or an administrative perspective to a business perspective." David Harvey (1989) wrote about this type of change in the governance of the American city and called it a change from managerialism to entrepreneurialism. An entrepreneurial city becomes problematic if, for instance, the drive to maximise rent revenue surpasses the goals of citizens' welfare (Harvey 1989). As Artioli suggests, public authorities come to wear 'two hats', one as land salesmen, another as regulators of land allocation. In this Janus-faced role the "sale of public land as a financing instrument conveys a specific role for public authorities because their strategies as speculative landowners are prioritised over their role as land use regulators" (Artioli 2021, 9).

Land policy, practised as an entrepreneurial activity by corporatised departments, is a feature of a similar shift from managerialism to entrepreneurialism in Finnish local governance and real estate management. In Turku, the interviewed real estate official saw that the primary target of allocating land was money, whereas other targets such as organising housing for seniors, the disabled or students were secondary issues to be solved after securing revenues. As one official explained:

> allocating land should bring in euros and as a corporation that is of course what we are interested in. Then there are other objectives, housing production objectives, the city's growth targets and qualitative targets concerning some special groups, that is, are students or some disabled groups or seniors suffering housing shortages? So, then we can try to solve these.

The needs of residents are seen as secondary, something to be addressed only after the primary task of getting money out of public property is reached. Turku continues to be a large landowner and it practises active land policy in that the money from leasing land is used to buy raw land for future needs. However, the selling of land was predicted by interviewees in Turku to increase to support the municipal economy and maximise rents. According to recent segregation research (Saikkonen et al. 2018) looking at the period in question, the regional differentiation of the working-age population by income level was strengthened in the regions of Tampere and Turku between the years 2005 and 2014. The clearest difference between the regions is a stronger ethnic differentiation in the Turku region. Land use decisions are reflected in segregation via housing allocation. When the city sells land and attempts to maximise land rent, it will allocate land to the top end of the housing market where possible. Of course, it could also allocate land based on its use value as social housing for "special groups". But when comparing the three cities, Turku also stood out strongest with the regional differentiation of state-subsidised rental apartments (Ibid.).

Selling land has also become more commonplace in Tampere since the 1990s. In particular, prestigious sites in the city centre and plots that are planned for shopping malls have been sold in recent times. Selling land has contributed to the fact that today Tampere only owns around 24 per cent of its land. The reply of a land use official interviewed in Tampere, when asked about the reason for selling public land, was exceptionally unambiguous: "Money. The lust for money." And what do the officials hope to achieve with the money made from alienating public land? Interviewed officials in Tampere reported the primary goal to be increasing the city's attractiveness: "The revenue is of course a resource to be used to offer services, but more than anything it's a resource for developing the city and creating that attractiveness." One of the characteristics of an entrepreneurial city is that its activities are increasingly oriented towards succeeding in competition with other cities. The cities compete in their attractiveness to tourists, mobile professional workforce, and global capital investments. According to Nevalainen (2004) land use planning in Finnish cities has been tasked with succeeding in inter-city competition, while the development of the built environment has the functional role of attracting investments.

One feature of this type of built environment is the omnipresent shopping mall. Shopping malls in new development areas are a sign of revenue oriented public land disposal and development of urban space in partnerships between developers. A recent example is the Tampere Ratina shopping mall. The city sold the land at auction and received a large single payment. It also had public space around the mall developed with private investments, and most importantly, as the official explained, the project brought "growth and attractiveness". Now, Ratina has been sold off to the investment company Blackstone. Is the selling of a profitable retail space visionary urban policy? Firstly, a judgement can be made that the development of shopping malls creates a homogeneous city, a type of ubiquitous McSpace (Peck 2002), in which true public spaces are overrun by abstract spaces of consumption, an unequal urban realm under increasing surveillance, in which people are reduced to customers and their presence in public spaces justified primarily by their purchase power – even if the local library was renting out a space in one corner of the mall. Moreover, the selling of a shopping mall is just short-sighted from the real estate policy perspective. An example is the City of Helsinki selling the shopping mall of Kamppi to a private owner at a high price in the early 2000s. Helsinki lost its right to rent revenue from a mall that in its year of completion was visited by 30 million potential customers. Helsinki could have continued practising its active land policy and leased the land, collecting a safe annual rent revenue (Haila 2009).

Selling public real estate and leasing land for market rent are justified as returning money to the taxpayer. We saw the state's Senate Properties using this argument in land and real estate privatisation. The demand by economists and conservative politicians to 'return money to the taxpayer', or as one interviewee phrased it, to have "more money for services and less for walls", means that by doing away with public land and real estate that is seen as inherently wasteful, there is more money for the actual tasks of the municipality: welfare services. But since the establishment of municipal premises centres in the early 2000s and their rent maximising real estate, there is little evidence to suggest that the cutbacks in spending on walls would have magically turned to more money for services like libraries, day care centres, schools or health care. But not only is the conservative slogan ambiguous, much more importantly getting rid of "the walls" is also both poor social and fiscal policy. First, looking at public property through a policy lens that is focused merely on immediate budgetary expenses of surplus "walls" does not consider the social expenses resulting from a reduction in public properties. Early childhood education leaders for instance reported on negative pedagogical outcomes when spaces have been reduced (Kähkönen and Ritari 2020). And second, once public services are rent paying tenants, who is to convince the taxpayer that real estate values will never climb in the future? If the space rents in shopping malls increase, tax euros will be spent more on leasing "walls" from market actors, when the service could have operated in public premises.

The long-term problems with selling and alienating public land and real estate are not whether auctions have anticipated results, whether enough value is captured or if the buyer of a brownfield site builds according to expectations. It is that public property is privatised and commodified. Public land is transformed from an asset over which the public, through elected authorities, has strong control over and could regulate its use and allocation, to a private asset traded according to its exchange value and used to extract rents. In alienating public property, the state and municipalities are taking on the task of handmaidens to capitalist enclosure and dispossession. As Christophers and Whiteside (2021, 57) argue, designating public land as a "surplus" is a one-way street to privatisation. The more land in key urban areas sold off to private corporations, the more the profit-imperative of those corporations dictates who can access urban amenities like housing in the city centres (and thus who is excluded). In their contemporary roles, public real estate administrations are reliant on and emphasise the commodity form of land, and in doing so they neglect all those curious features of land that make it a troublesome commodity in the first instance.

Looking back at the changes of the preceding decade at the turn of the millennium, Haila's analysis of the newfound power of European cities was explicit:

> in this new era of increasingly autonomous and competing city states the task of urban planning is to sell the city (Ashworth and Voogd 1990) and market places (Kotler et al 1993) for investors, tourists and enterprises, and that there are other professionals who can do the job better than professional planners. Planning power was alienated to private sector consultants and public-private partnerships, and the modernist regulation, from above by professional planners, received a bad reputation as authoritarian and elitist. (Haila 1999, 177)

Two decades later, these observations still ring true in Finland. More recently Haila (2016, 117) went as far as to suggest that Finnish public landowners now treat land as a financial asset and prioritise rent revenue over everything else. However, as Christophers (2016, 67) aptly points out "she provides no analysis of this development" (Christophers 2016, 67). The truth of course is, that the treatment of public land by Finnish municipalities is much more nuanced. Social and environmental questions do still affect land use decisions, not merely rent maximisation. The city through its planning monopoly has the sole right to make decisions on what gets built and where. It is still generally the case that only after the city has decided on a project will it open it up for competitive bidding. The city may for instance decide on shares of affordable housing and only accept bids from developers that agree to build said shares. By placing conditions on land allocation, the city can very effectively steer urban development. However, as illustrated in this chapter, the power and control of local authorities has become increasingly challenged in recent decades. A final major change in public land policies I discuss is a legislative reform that has increased the power of private actors and landowners in urban development processes via the use of contracts and public-private-partnerships.

Contracts, partnerships and complaints

Legislation regarding land use in Finland has traditionally been based on the principle that cities should have the sole right to decide when and where urban planning and development take place. In other words, public land use decisions have had legal priority over private land use interests. However, according to the old land-use act of 1958, municipalities were also responsible for having their plans ratified by a state official (Mäkinen 2000). The purpose of this arrangement was that an impartial state official acting above the municipal level would reconcile conflicts of interest between municipalities. The new act omitted this requirement, and on the one hand significantly increased municipal autonomy. On the other hand, after the legal reform, private developers and real estate players have been able to put pressure on municipalities to make land use decisions that increasingly favour the private actors. How did this change come about?

Another reform concerning land use, introduced in the Land Use and Building Act of 2000, was the legalisation of land use contracts and development areas. These have, as we know, been used since the 1960s in the development of peripheral housing estates. But there was no mention of them in the old building act and so they were always legally a grey area. A development area was now defined as either a built or unbuilt area being developed in collaboration between the municipality and a developer who together form what is known as a development organisation (Land Use and Building Act 112 §). A land use contract is an agreement between a municipality and a private landowner, and it sets the terms for planning and the execution of the plans (Virtanen 2000). And since the land use contracts became legal, their implementation has also become more common. They are attractive for several reasons. Land use contracts are favoured as municipalities can pass the responsibilities over planning and development to developers. And with land use contracts, developers may be obligated to build public utilities and the city can roll over expenses to the private sector. Included in the legislation on land use contracts is a clause that the public must be informed about the use of contracts. According to the government at the time, the participatory opportunities of residents should not be weakened by contracts and that land use should remain transparent (Jääskeläinen and Syrjänen 2010). However, the legislation did not define precisely what aspects of land use and development could be negotiated with residents, nor at what stage of planning could contracts be signed and confirmed. Hence, the contents of city plans – traditionally drawn by public planners using the planning monopoly – were now legally more open to negotiation, and developers could, for instance, more easily lobby for development rights. Private interest in land use planning came to have a stronger say in urban development in Finland.

In Tampere, contracts are drawn up precisely to enable planning on land owned by large private landowners. However, drawbacks in land use contracts were reported by interviewed officials. One official from the City of Tampere, for instance, thought it questionable whether contracts had introduced any actual benefit from the residents' perspective. A traditional, key target of land policy has always been to moderate the housing market by allocating land for different types of housing tenures, including partly de-commodified social housing. For example, in the 2008–17 Helsinki Land Use and Housing Plan (2008), the very first goal of land and housing policies is stated as "housing production, improvement of living conditions and balancing of the housing market". But with contracts, this dominant public role has been weakened, because contracts also determine the shares of different tenures to be built. Now a developer may negotiate on the share of social housing in new development areas, and eventually affect the opportunities that working-class people have renting a home in newly developed areas. Land use contracts also favour large, powerful developers who are interested in developing vast tracts of land at once. As an official from Helsinki explained of the developers' new-found powers: "There are too few actors in the market. That is the big problem in Helsinki. There are no contractors, they are all developers. Their operations are such that the price doesn't give a cent. If apartments do not sell, they won't lower the prices, they just stop development."

Development contracts may weaken a city's planning monopoly and power to dictate the amount of social housing in a development area. In Helsinki, land use contracts are signed, for example, when brownfield sites are converted to residential use. Mäkinen (2000) proposed that housing estates developed with the use of contracts on private land in the 1960s and 1970s became dilapidated and socially differentiated for the very reason that contracts were used, and they weakened public oversight. When planning on raw land, interviewed officials from Helsinki explained that today the city does not sign land use contracts because of the weak control over development: "The reason is control. If you try to control with contracts, you're controlling indirectly. Like trying to control something with a string. But if the land is yours, then you can say straight off here is the plan we are drawing up and development begins now." However, development areas are used to enable the fast development of new neighbourhoods. In large development areas in Helsinki, conflicts between the city and developers have arisen. A developer calling off a new high-rise development project planned in the intensely redeveloping neighbourhood of Pasila is a recent example of developers' powers. The developer backed down from the project late in the planning process as it did not get development rights for the much larger buildings that were initially agreed upon. Instead of placing sanctions that would incentivise developers to meet their end of agreements, legislative reforms seem to have given them much more room to "negotiate" and make demands on the city for more development rights.

In the southwestern city of Turku, meeting the needs and requests of businesses are central goals of land policy. These goals are reflected in the land policy instruments chosen; land use contracts and public-private partnerships are routine practice. According to an official from the City of Turku, land use contracts have in fact been used since the 1980s. The new law did not bring a radical change to the city's land policy, and today Turku continues urban development of large areas on private land with the use of contracts. Land use contracts may save municipal expenses, but the increasing use of contracts may also prove unfavourable to the city in other ways in the long run. With contracts, the interests of businesses play a more significant role in planning, which could hinder the practice of active land policy. According to Mäkinen (2000) the risk is that responsibilities set for the builder, such as building utilities, could transfer onto house prices. In Turku, officials were aware of the weak control afforded by contracts: "Of course, we sign land use contracts and try to get infrastructure investments paid for, but the real control over development is weak, we [City officials] are sitting in the back-seat."

Public-private partnerships and contracts are emblematic of the coalitions between landowners, municipalities and developers that work hard to spur urban growth (Molotch 1976). Businesses naturally benefit from the growth of the city as the number of consumers increases. Landowners benefit from intensified land use as it increases land value and the rental yield. For the residents, the benefits of growth are – it is argued – that growth creates jobs. This as Logan and Molotch (1987) suggested, is an unconvincing claim. Urban growth does not so much create jobs as redistribute them. Yet, despite other conflicting interests, businesses, landowners and local decision-makers may then find a common interest in growth. Harvey Molotch (1976) described the capitalist city as a "growth machine"; as a city in which public functions are tied up with growth targets. The growth-machine city views a growing population as a sign of prospering business life and desirable growth in workforce and consumption. This is the argument made by contemporary urban age evangelists like Glaeser (2011), whose musings about triumphant cities I raised in the beginning of the book. Urban growth in these visions becomes an end in itself. The prioritising of new growth targets in the urban policy of Tampere can be explained by the downfall of industry that hit the city in the 1990s and 2000s. The number of jobs in this old manufacturing city decreased significantly and after the decentralisation of responsibilities and scaling down decision-making from state to municipalities in the 1990s NPM period, the city was forced to consciously market itself and think of ways to compete and be attractive to secure its growth.

A primary way to promote urban growth is the implementation of policies that prioritise corporate real estate requirements. According to an official from Turku, land use contracts were adopted as an instrument precisely to fulfil the wishes of businesses: "We created this mechanism that can cut some corners in planning, because we want to give positive answers to businesses who wish to locate here." Thus, land use contracts are used in Turku to take shortcuts around democratically decided plans so that businesses' requirements are met. These types of fast-track planning and tendering processes are more familiar in the Anglophone world, for instance, Australia (Berry and Huxley 1992), than in the Nordic context. The legal reform omitted the practice of ratifying plans with the state official, and Turku now applies land use contracts to fast-track the planning programme and allocate land quickly according to corporate wishes. But what about the increased opportunities in participatory planning; are residents able to oversee development projects and the plans of growth coalitions?

The Land Use and Building Act requires that the municipality organises the planning procedure so that citizens can voice their opinion on the plans in good time (Land Use and Building Act 62 §). But this clause has been criticised for its ambiguity. According to Mäntysalo and Nyman (2001), the most important planning decisions can still be made early, before the citizens have their input. On the one hand, new project-based development, in which a private developer and a municipality sign a contract, may diminish citizens' opportunities to have any say in the plan (Haila 2008). The promises of transparency in the planning system and a democratic means of urban development in the new legislation appear empty. On the other hand, the new law gives private individuals the possibility to complain about municipal plans in order to protect private property. Eranti (2014, 34), who has studied planning complaints, writes that "by enabling the direct participation of individuals the Finnish planning system gives ample room for vested interest politics". He investigated the opinions of residents who oppose infill development in Helsinki and found that many who left a statement felt their interests in protecting private property values against public development completely justified. It appears that in some instances the participatory planning intended by the Land Use and Building Act was reduced to not-in-my-backyard politics as homeowners concerned about the value of their property have hampered the development of affordable housing. In one case homeowners used the instrument to block the building of a care home for the disabled in their neighbourhood as they thought it would affect property prices negatively.[10]

Neoliberalism in public land management?

Corporatising municipal real estate departments and establishing state-run real estate companies were accompanied by changes in land use planning legislation and urban governance. This chapter asked how the changes brought about by the legal reforms and corporatisation of public real estate management influenced municipal land policy and land use. The focus of real estate projects and land use objectives shifted from qualitative social goals to quantitative goals of economic growth and competitiveness, image-building and city branding. As with any policy, land policy is the outcome of negotiation between competing interests and hence prone to contradictions in its objectives. Land policy can have as its objective the active prevention of urban inequalities like the differentiation of income groups, timely execution of city plans, reaching social policy targets, building affordable housing, safeguarding the conditions for industry and businesses or maximising revenues from the selling and leasing of public land. The strong autonomy of Finnish cities to use their planning monopoly and public landownership in support of the public interest in urban development is also the strong autonomy of cities to lighten their bureaucracy, utilise market mechanisms in land use, decrease regulation on development, and prioritise economic results of policies over their social targets.

In Helsinki the first order of business of the newly elected liberal conservative mayor Juhana Vartiainen was to introduce a new post in the city's organisation: the head economist. For this post the mayor appointed the ex-CEO of market liberal think tank Libera, Mikko Kiesiläinen. At the time of writing this Kiesiläinen is an economist at the employer organisation Confederation of Finnish Industries. His job in the city's organisation will be to "help civil servants make better decisions". In Kiesiläinen's own words, he hopes to make "reforms that promote efficiency".[11] His first task has been to find "economic inefficiencies" and "untapped potential" with the single purpose of increasing the profitability of the city.[12] Time will tell what advice the head economist gives the city and civil servants, but we might well expect the further downsizing of premises used for public services and maximising rent revenues to be on the menu. By competing with one another and marketing themselves, cities are encouraging businesses and workforces to move, while subjecting themselves to the risks of competition. Cities become ever more vulnerable. Neoliberal ideology has been important in legitimating the new "entrepreneurial city" (Peck and Tickell 2002, 393–4). What all this points to is not so much a withdrawal of the state, which has been a favoured argument of critical scholars. What we see rather is state recalibration to accommodate businesses and seek funds through privatising assets, commodifying land and attracting interest bearing capital. There is "a lemming-like rush towards urban entrepreneurialism, which itself would only serve to facilitate, encourage, and even publicly subsidize the accelerated mobility of circulating capital and resources" (Peck and Tickell 2002, 385).

Both the central and local states justify the selling and leasing of public lands with market rent with the notions of efficiency, shedding unwanted surplus land, and the good of the taxpayer. The selling of municipal land was practised in all the cities under discussion in the 2000s and 2010s. Its purpose is to increase the city's attractiveness, invigorate business life and to meet land sale goals. Land is sold for, for example, shopping malls, which enables the city to demand developers build public utilities and gives the city a great amount of money. Selling land may however be weak land policy, as the city gives up its right to collect predictable rental payments. Neoliberal urban policy encourages the development of homogeneous, privatised urban areas. In addition, the state real estate corporation Senate Properties manages its real estate in an entrepreneurial fashion. This has partly hindered municipal housing development and led to conflicts between cities and the state. For instance, the state no longer gives land for cities' social housing needs but attempts to maximise revenues from land, which increases land prices and the price of housing. Cities become vulnerable to the problems of neoliberal urban policy such as diminishing public space, weakening public services, increasing land and house prices, and differentiating neighbourhoods. Public authorities have become henchmen of privatisation and dispossession of public property. In many instances their land rent maximisation practices favour the corporate actors rather than the collective good. It is poor urban policy and comes to enforce segregation and the spatial differentiation of working-class and elite households. The next chapter introduces a case study that illustrates exactly these tendencies.

Notes

1. Kapiteelille 9 miljardin markan kiinteistöt (YLE 25.3.1999).
2. Blackstone offers $2 billion for Finnish real estate firm Sponda (Reuters 5.6.2017), Blackstone signs deal to buy Sponda of Finland (Financial Times 2017).
3. Valtion kiinteistöt 2023.
4. Government Resolution on the Government Real Estate Strategy 2030 (The Ministry of Finance 2021).
5. Usually, railways and transport facilities are managed by the Ministry of Transport and Communications. Now, another special-purpose agency, Senate Stations, has been established to develop and sell the train stations.

6. See Artioli (2021) for a sociological account of military land sales for high-end housing production in London.
7. In Helsinki, the Premises Centre was discontinued after this study was conducted. It is now part of the Urban Environment Division, which oversees service facilities and properties. It manages and leases real estate to public services and continues to calculate alternative rent.
8. Helsingin kaupungin kiinteistöstrategia (2019).
9. Ensimmäistä kertaa Helsingissä: Kirjasto avattiin Laajasalon uudessa kauppakeskuksessa (HS 22.11.2018).
10. "Asuntojen arvo laskee" – lapsiperheet vastustavat kehitysvammaisten nuorten tukiasuntolaa Kirkkonummella (Länsiväylä 14.6.2017).
11. Pormestari Vartiainen palkkasi Helsinkiin historian ensimmäisen pääekonomistin (HS 6.8.2021).
12. Juhana Vartiainen haluaa palkita työntekijöitä suoritusten perusteella (HS 19.9.2021).

CHAPTER 5

Entrepreneurial Public Real Estate Policy in Action

On 30 March 2004, the City of Helsinki Real Estate Committee (REC) decided to make a radical exception to the usual method of allocating public land for residential purposes. It digressed from the city's conventional practice of leasing land for housing, and decided instead to sell it for developers in a prestigious seaside location in south Helsinki. At the beginning of the 20th century, the area in question was nothing but a rocky shore of the Baltic Sea. From the 1930s until the early 2000s the location saw light industrial use as a wastewater management site and a city depot. But change in the land use plan was made in 2001, and the area was zoned for residential use. A stone's throw from the city centre and next to the bourgeois neighbourhood of Eira and the gentrified old working-class neighbourhood of Punavuori, Eiranranta bordered the most expensive residential neighbourhoods in Helsinki. The site had great potential – either for alleviating both the shortage of affordable housing in the city centre and segregation, or for tapping into tremendous land values.

A request for tenders for four sites was opened on 16 December 2004. The terms of the bidding competition stipulated that the highest offer would win. The City Council emphasised, however, that only offers made by companies showing "exceptional expertise and competence in building" would be accepted. The City Council minutes of June 2005 state that "the highest offer will not guarantee the sale, but the Council should be convinced that the company has extensive experience to carry out extremely demanding development projects in the prestigious area". With these reservations, the city wanted to make sure that the area would be developed following standards befitting of a waterfront development on the shore that is Helsinki's facade to the sea. With the authorisation from the City Council, REC decided to sell sites to four bidders who made the highest offers. How was this (at the time unusual) deal justified and did the public authorities consent to the transaction?

The previous chapter discussed how today the tendency of corporatised municipal real estate departments is to sell the land cities own and to charge their tenants the market rent. The aim of this policy is essentially to make a profit and it has introduced a market logic to the use of public land. As we saw, the new real estate policy began after the early 90s depression, and it has been justified by public authorities claiming that such a policy makes the use of real estate efficient, sheds off any surplus land, saves taxpayers' money and generates revenue for the public treasury. A key concern for public real estate entrepreneurs, supported by politicians, has been the amount of money tied up in public assets. This chapter investigates the real estate policy of selling public land in practice, and its consequences on the ground in Helsinki via a case study of the Eiranranta deal. I call this entrepreneurial public real estate policy.[1] This chapter asks how this new policy is justified and what the reasons are driving cities to adopt a business model for the management of public land. I explore the conditions that have enabled entrepreneurial public real estate policy and investigate what kind of built environment was produced by implementing entrepreneurial public real estate policy, as well as its ramifications for urban equality.

This chapter is based, first, on an analysis of policy documents, mainly the agendas and minutes of Helsinki City Council and Real Estate Committee meetings. The documents were analysed to answer the following questions: how was the decision to sell the sites made? Were there any disagreements or debates? Second, members of the REC who were in the Committee in 2005 when the sites were sold to private developers were interviewed. The REC is a politically elected body, whose members are elected by the City Council (that is, elected in municipal elections held every four years). The REC makes decisions and gives recommendations to the Real Estate Department and the City Council concerning the management of Helsinki's land and water areas, buildings, and facilities, including the leasing and selling of public land and real estate. The REC members were interviewed because, as a politically representative body, the REC is supposed to be a forum in which land and real estate policies are debated. Five out of its nine members were interviewed. The interviews provided insight into the nature of deal making and shed light on real estate policymakers' ideologies. Third, observations were made during several field visits to Eiranranta to describe the area and to answer the question: what kind of urban environment was produced?

In Helsinki, land policy had begun to change already as far back as 1993. The city began selling some of its landed properties, whereas previously the principal method of conveying land was leasing (Nurmi 2005). In 1994, the Real Estate Department was authorised to manage all the land and real estate owned by the city. Soon it began calculating so-called shadow rents, meaning that rents were not paid, but only calculated from the city's services and administration. The argument was that this was making the costs of public services more transparent. The Real Estate Department calculated the potential rent it could charge from leasing the properties on the market, compared it with allocating the land for free for public services and called it a "taxpayer expense". The Department was preparing for the market game. In 2005, the Premises Centre began charging its tenants the market rent. Just as the state's Senate Properties, Helsinki's Premises

Centre understands efficiency in public land management as the land being used in accordance with its highest paying alternative. One of the important reasons given by REC members for selling the land in Eiranranta was by appealing to the change of policy after the founding of the Premises Centre. One REC member explained:

> The city budget has been written so that part of the city's economy is balanced by writing in huge sales goals to the Premises Centre. So, we must sell land and real estate. Roughly ten years ago there was still thinking that the city should own [real estate]. Now the policy has changed.

At the time when Eiranranta was sold, the Deputy Mayor of Development and Building in Helsinki was Pekka Korpinen, who was in office from 1991 to 2007. Korpinen, who sat on the Board of Directors of the World Bank, is known for having brought in an economist's mindset to urban governance in Helsinki. REC members recalled the early 2000s as a time of drastic changes in land use and planning and Korpinen as an active initiator of many of those changes. For one, it was Korpinen who put forth the idea that the city would benefit by selling its cherished waterfront properties. The key arguments for selling were that Helsinki would receive money directly from the sale, but also indirectly by developing high-end neighbourhoods. The city would see growth in in-migration of highly educated professionals, individuals who would pay generous income tax to the city. Another REC member reminisced:

> Korpinen promoted the idea that the lands on the city's waterfront should be taken into use by selling them because shores are valuable areas. And they should not be used for social housing, but we should maximize our revenues from them. That's where the idea came from.

Today, vast waterfront development areas are found adjacent to the city centre in brownfield sites. The shores of the city have been actively taken to use.

REC members mentioned Eiranranta as a pioneer-case manifesting the new revenue-oriented land policy. The area was not called Eiranranta originally, but the new name was chosen deliberately to brand and boost the area by connecting its name to the old bourgeois neighbourhood of Eira (Eiranranta simply translates to Eira Beach). An REC member explained: "Even the name was changed to Eiranranta with marketing in mind. That was Korpinen's idea! He had this marketing mindset. And with the change the area became more attractive."

The state had shifted the authority over land use planning and the responsibility for providing welfare services to cities and made them compete for state subsidies. To answer these challenges, the City of Helsinki adopted a strategic approach, and land policy was seen as a tool to enhance the innovative capacity of firms. The adoption of this strategy was described by a member of the REC:

The City Councils of the 2000s accepted it and that's when the city began to be led by strategies. One was the land use and housing strategy. Another was the strategy for industry and trade. And these are always about coordination.

Coordination here means that land policy was regarded as an instrument to compete with other cities of the metropolitan area, not coordination in the old sense of settling conflicts and pursuing balanced development and equality, as in the time of the 1958 planning law and of regional policy. Civil servants and politicians in Helsinki had become worried that the neighbouring municipalities, Espoo and Kauniainen, which had developed detached and owner-occupied houses to meet the preferences of high-income groups, would attract the high-income households and Helsinki would be left to accommodate low-income households and special-needs groups (Haila and Le Galès 2004). REC members pointed out that inter-city competition was a key reason for selling land in Eiranranta. By selling land to be developed as an expensive, private residential area, the city aimed to attract more people it calls "good taxpayers".

But the land deal was not only seen as strategic policy to successfully compete with Espoo and Kauniainen, but also as a way of making the city more attractive to a foreign workforce and to compete with European cities. A wish to represent Helsinki as a global city was, at that time, one of the key drivers for replacing managerial strategies with entrepreneurial ones. REC members remembered Eiranranta as an important turning point in Helsinki's land use policy. Land was now seen as a strategically valuable instrument for competing successfully internationally. One interviewee recalled:

> At the time, there was a discussion about whether Helsinki was attractive enough compared to Copenhagen and Stockholm and Tallinn [. . .] Do we have the kind of city image that makes it worthwhile coming here? We didn't want people to think they were coming to some backwater place if their company sent them here.

REC members also talked about a new kind of pressure demanding that the city accommodate to the needs of both domestic and international corporations. Developers and companies had insisted that there was a demand for high-quality luxury housing and that the city should sell land to the developers to meet such a demand. Developers did not give the city any choice but to sell the land, otherwise developers would not build luxury housing and companies would locate elsewhere, as one REC member explained:

> At that time, at least, it [selling land] was used to attract companies that pay good corporate taxes to Helsinki . . . they do not want to lease land. Anglo-American companies tend to follow the policy that they will not move to a city if they are not allowed to own the land.

And so, with the selling of land widely agreed upon in the city council, in 2005, the bidding envelopes were opened. The bids hit a new record in Finland: €2621 per square metre, which would give the city altogether €54 million for the four plots. The highest offers were made by four companies: SRV, NCC, Tarkala and Apollo. The first three are large household developers in Helsinki. Apollo was a newcomer to Helsinki's development scene and took the city and other competitors by surprise. It is a small investment company, and it made the highest offer of all. A controversy flared up. The disputed issue was whether the site should be sold to Apollo. On the one hand, there was concern that an investment company without experience in construction would not be capable of carrying out a development project in accordance with the city's specifications for the valuable site. On the other hand, it was argued that the city should sell to the highest bidder. After all, Apollo had offered three million euros more than the other developers, whose offers were surprisingly close to one another. The issue was debated within the City Council, in the REC and even in the media. Information released by the City of Helsinki, including the bidding prices, tells of its efforts to make the costs on real estate transparent; or, alternatively, the record high prices released were meant to convince the public that the selling of public land would generate revenue for the city.

The agendas of the City Council and REC meetings reveal that the Real Estate Department had initially proposed to abandon the bid by Apollo, and sell the site instead to Skanska, another large international developer that holds a major place in the development game in Helsinki. The Real Estate Department questioned Apollo's experience. One REC member recalled how "there was a lot of talk among officials whether this was going to destroy the whole project . . . This was the one thing that divided people: should we accept this new developer or not." Real estate departments often have close ties with developers, and one would expect that might be the reason why Helsinki's real estate department defended the bid by an established developer such as Skanska in preference to the newcomer Apollo. However, only one of the five interviewees hinted that this was the case:

> Three offers were made by developers and the fourth one was a kind of wild entrepreneur, Apollo. And these others did not want Apollo to compete at all. First, it was offering three million euros more than the others, whose offers were quite similar. So, it seems likely there's a bit of a cartel. And there were all kinds of rumours that they have Russian illegal money and that they won't be able to finish the project and so on.

The Eiranranta apartments have been sold at €10,000, sometimes as much as €16,000 per square metre, and most likely made handsome profits for the developers. One might ask why Apollo, a novice in the Helsinki development market, offered three million more for the sites than the established developers. A plausible explanation for this is that the developers with experience in the Helsinki development market knew that it was possible to extract land rent from the city and get the value-increase created by development rights. However, the question that caused debate was whether Apollo was experienced enough to carry out the demanding development project. The opinions of the decision-makers were divided. The Real Estate Department argued that the site should be sold to the household developer Skanska, although Skanska made a lower bid than the three other bidders. Finally, the Deputy Mayor stepped in and argued in favour of selling the site to Apollo. More was at stake than the experience of Apollo. The Real Estate Department, which had a long-term relationship with traditional developers who were used to sharing the development market, wanted to exclude Apollo. The City Council and the Deputy Mayor proposed selling to Apollo. Whether to sell to the development companies with vested interests and a monopoly position in the market or let an investment company challenge these and penetrate the Helsinki market was a crucial question put aside in the debate about the experience of Apollo.

The interviewed REC members unanimously agreed that the selling of Eiranranta sites was a good thing. There was no questioning of or opposition to alienating public property. The City Council minutes show that only one councillor opposed the deal and brought a motion to overrule it. The motion received no support and was discarded. This suggests that the new entrepreneurial public real estate policy had already been accepted and viewed as natural not just for the REC but also in the City Council. The argument that the city should always sell its land to the highest bidder was repeated by REC members. And once the first deal is made, it is easy to continue with such a policy. As one interviewee proclaimed:

> Helsinki used to lease its land, but that has changed. Now we are more inclined to meet the buyer halfway. And in general, it's a politically acceptable way of doing things. We have seen that the greatest benefit is that [companies] locate here. That they invest and build here. Land ownership has become a secondary thing. [. . .] Those are the rules of the game today. If you wish to succeed, then city real estate policy must get with the programme. This isn't a politically divisive question.

The controversy blew over, and the development of Eiranranta began. But what kind of area was developed?

Eiranranta – not for social housing

The cities in the Helsinki metropolitan area have collaborated to deter the harmful effects of inter-city competition. The main objective of these joint efforts is to prevent segregation. The tool to achieve this goal has been to develop social housing in all municipalities and in all neighbourhoods, so-called tenure mixing. In Helsinki the requirement has traditionally been that a third of the housing in new residential developments should be affordable rental housing. The ideal is that in this way a social mix of income groups is created, and different groups are allowed to find housing throughout the city. Eiranranta was developed exclusively with one social class in mind –high-income professionals. It was developed for those who can afford to pay a high price for their living, excluding those who cannot pay. Was this compatible with Helsinki's policy of social mixing and the fight against segregation, agreed upon jointly by the cities in the Helsinki metropolitan area? Hardly. Eiranranta did not include any social housing and the housing prices were the highest in Helsinki. Nevertheless, REC members did not see Eiranranta as an exclusive, private residential area that would serve to exacerbate differentiation, but rather as a successful property development project that would meet the preferences of higher income groups. Any negative aspects or effects were denied. One interviewee pondered:

> I don't believe that the people who are incapable of buying their own homes or who require subsidized housing suffer if their home is not in Eiranranta, but somewhere else, wherever. I don't think this site was suitable for that purpose nor would it have been wise to develop it for that purpose. Not every place needs to be mixed; there can also be that kind of diversity. So, you can also have areas with only owner-occupied apartments.

Clearly then REC members did not regard expensive private market housing or a concentration of wealthy inhabitants living in their enclaves as problematic. They thought the differentiation between income groups was undesirable, but when prompted to explain why, it became clear what they regarded undesirable was a concentration of low-income and other "problem groups". They welcomed the social mixing policy – if it meant fighting against the concentration of social housing and its working-class tenants. The implications of this widely shared view in Finnish housing and land use policies are discussed in more detail in the next chapter. Meanwhile, the powerful discourse regarding the harms of problem neighbourhoods had reached the REC, and the familiar neighbourhood ghost of segregation was haunting their views on what the issue with spatial differentiation was. One REC member turned the discussion to neighbourhoods with what they saw as an undesirable concentration of social housing tenants to support the mixing policy in these areas:

> If you think of the other extreme – areas like Kontula, Mellunmäki, Jakomäki[2] – we should make it more so that . . . [it] does not become labelled as a social housing area. Because that can also be bad, so we need to have both [tenures: social and non-subsidized housing].

But REC members did not see that the building of exclusive, luxury areas contradicts the city's social mixing policy whereby the city should continue to prevent concentration of social housing. Another interviewee explained:

> Helsinki wanted to get rid of the Jakomäki-type [of development], so not too much social housing in one place. We must distribute tenures more evenly throughout the city. But this approach is not incompatible with some single sites being special

[Eiranranta]. So, it's been viewed as more problematic to have too much social housing in one place, especially the type that the people immediately think is somehow subsidised.

The REC members did not see that alienating public land to be developed for the sole use of one particular income group to the exclusion of other groups had anything to do with the differentiation in the city. What explains such an inability to spot the warning signs of segregation and urban inequality more generally? A plausible answer is the REC members' focus on real estate issues; they were either ignorant of, or negligent about, the social aspects of land use. They did not criticise rent-maximising, nor the concentration of the high net-income individuals in an exclusive neighbourhood. But they saved their criticism for the concentration of social housing and the concentration of social housing tenants. It is surprising that the REC as an elected body representing all political parties did not look at the Eiranranta project from the point of view of different income groups, and did not give a say to those excluded from the deal. Eiranranta was seen as a disconnected project, disconnected from the development elsewhere in the city. The Land Use and Building Act had made it possible to develop separate enclaves and the selling of public land realised this possibility. Finally, we turn to this matter and consider Eiranranta's exclusivity.

Eiranranta – a gated community?

Unlike typical neoliberal real estate projects, Eiranranta is not a large-scale urban development project (Swyngedouw et al. 2002), nor has it any eye-catching architecture. But it has gates and fences and its apartments are the most expensive in town. Can Eiranranta, then, be regarded as a gated community? Originating in the United States (Low et al. 2012), gated communities have become a popular form of urban development around the world. Although differing from country to country, gated communities can be understood as exclusive private residential developments with club services provided only for the residents. They may have fences, gates and private security guards, and the reason for developing them may be a demand for a sense of security or prestige and status. Whatever the reason, gated communities as exclusive developments diminish the contacts between social groups and exclude those who cannot pay – the precarious working-class tenants reliant on affordable housing. Exclusive gated residential developments have been absent in Finnish cities; where the municipality provides universal public services for all, residential differentiation has been small. Although Helsinki has some desirable private residential neighbourhoods (some may even have walls and gates), not until Eiranranta had there been any deliberate attempt to develop an area exclusively for wealthy homeowners protected by fences to keep others outside. In Eiranranta, fences and gates were included in the master plan,[3] which stated "the blocks are to be bordered with 1.2m high fences, which prevent visibility and the entrances are to be gated". In advertisements[4] for the Eiranranta apartments, the emphasis was on exclusivity and privacy:

> The apartments have also [. . .] alarms and gate phones with a camera. All the dwellings have separate space for housekeeping. Therefore, no common laundries are needed. From the car park, located below the buildings, there is a direct access to the residential floors. The apartment doors in the lit staircases are not too close to each other. The site is surrounded with masonry with an iron gate.

The fenced Eiranranta compound consists of eight apartment buildings. The architecture is nothing special: contrary to what one would expect from the housing at a prime seaside location it seems as if the area was designed to be inconspicuous. The buildings form small clusters with shared fenced gardens in each cluster. Entrances to the buildings are from the gardens. There is a public street that runs between the buildings. However, for a non-resident it is uninviting. The street is empty, offering little reason to linger or socialise. One REC member, an architect, commented on Eiranranta's streetscape, "you could walk between the buildings, but going there is in no way natural." Eiranranta sits by a popular public beach and a public park with exercise equipment, a skateboard area and other free recreation facilities. Next door, there was also a free needle exchange clinic. With children flying kites, skateboarders, dog walkers, patients using the needle exchange and workers coming and going, there is a vibrant buzz, compared to which Eiranranta is quiet and withdrawn.

Real estate brokers and developers pictured Eiranranta residents to be around 50 years old, "highly paid academics, option millionaires and corporate CEOs with no children". One REC member told us that Eiranranta was planned for "formula one drivers, investors and EU chemicals agency officials". Its housing was targeted at wealthy professionals with their distinct lifestyles. Eiranranta thus does not only gate out non-residents, but as Blakely (2006, 201) expresses it, "locks in economic position". Developers' and planners' deliberate attempts to meet the demand by upper classes led to a socio-spatial ordering that Swyngedouw and Kaika (2003, 12) characterise as "landscapes of power where islands of extreme wealth and social power are interspersed with places of deprivation, exclusion and decline". In a Nordic city like Helsinki, islands of extreme wealth as well as places of hopeless deprivation have been largely absent. Eiranranta was an anomalous development designed as an enclave for a homogenous group. Is Eiranranta, then, a gated community? The development of Eiranranta manifests what David Harvey has called "the neoliberal turn", restoring the class power to rich elites leading to "fortified fragments, gated communities and privatized public spaces kept under constant surveillance" (Harvey 2008, 32). Eiranranta also answers the expectations of wealthy homeowners and is an exclusive compound. Nevertheless, it is not strictly a gated community. Eiranranta may have club services and may be a 'privatopia' (McKenzie 1994; Flusty 2004) for its residents, however its residents do still pay taxes to the city, enjoy the public services it provides, and its fences still allow the right of passage through the area.

Selling the land in Eiranranta to private developers who developed the area for homeowners, the city gave up its requirement that an area developed on municipal land should include social housing. Selling the land to developers who managed to sell the apartments they built with record high prices, the city also facilitated the trend of excluding from the city those who cannot pay the market price for their housing. Finally, private fenced residential area exclusively for the high net-worth individuals that was developed on the privatised land introduced a new type of development to Helsinki. This chapter introduced the concept of entrepreneurial public real estate policy, and analysed its justification and effects. The case study of Eiranranta shows the variegated effects of neoliberal real estate policy and makes three contributions to the discussions on the political economy of urban land and neoliberal urban policies: first, by discussing land and real estate policies; second, by analysing property rights, particularly development rights; and third, by analysing the inequalities the entrepreneurial public real estate policy produces in a Nordic city.

As the state corporatised its real estate department, it gave an example for cities how to answer the challenges of 'saving' and using public resources 'efficiently', and made them "institutional laboratories for a variety of neoliberal policy experiments" (Brenner and Theodore 2002, 21). The state not only offered a model for cities to follow, but by launching new urban policy, by changing its rules for subsidising the municipalities and by enacting a new land-use planning legislation, the state pushed cities to see their public lands as strategic means to compete with other cities and to reap revenue. Like neoliberal urban policies elsewhere (Swyngedouw et al. 2002; Jones and Ward 2002), entrepreneurial real estate policy practised both by the state and cities had harmful consequences and created conflicts in Finland. What is perhaps unique in the Finnish case is that by establishing real estate companies and turning into just another player in the real estate market, the state lost its impartiality and therefore possibilities to intervene, "to manage the consequences and contradictions of such marketization initiatives" (Peck et al. 2009, 51). Unlike, for example, in the UK, where the state itself has not treated its land as a financial asset but has rather enabled such a treatment by selling its land to actors that do treat land in such a way (Christophers 2017, 81), the Finnish state through establishing state-run real estate companies became an actor treating land as a financial asset "according to the rent it yields" (Harvey 2006).

*

I suggested in the opening section to this part of the book that land tenure is important for how well we can tackle socio-spatial inequalities. For instance, if land is owned by the municipality, city officials have more room to decide how and for what purposes land is used and allocated. However, this chapter showed that public landownership does not directly mean that authorities will use the land in ways that deter urban inequalities. Instead, the case study here illustrated that public land can just as well be sold according to the highest market price and privatised. The case study of Eiranranta portrayed the City of Helsinki at an epoch-making moment; in 2005 the Premises Centre was founded and the city sold sites to private developers. These events mark a radical change in the city's real estate policy: from administrative allocation of land to entrepreneurial public real estate policy. The land rent maximising policy of the Premises Centre "monetized" (Soederberg 2017) the relationship between the city and its departments. Combine this with a development industry hungry to increase the role of private developers in zoning, privatising the municipal land also means privatising development rights. In the future it will be difficult for the city to implement its plans or address urban inequality in Eiranranta.

The Eiranranta controversy also revealed the contradictory effects of selling public lands at the market price. It may well be that Apollo – unaware of the possibility to extract land rent and the value increase from the city – simply calculated its bid based on the market value of the land. It is likely that the experienced developers, who bid less than Apollo, made no miscalculations, but were used to undervaluing the land costs when making the deals with the city to get land rent from it. Selling to Apollo, however, includes a risk. Welcoming an investment company into the Helsinki development market can turn out to become the beginning of a new phase in Helsinki's urban development. Selling to Apollo confused the vested monopoly interests of developers, but if one investment company is followed by more investment companies and Real Estate Investment Trusts (REITs), this may facilitate the deepening financialisation of land and housing, as well as the creating of liquidity out of spatial fixity (Gotham 2009). Eiranranta was an experiment by the city to test the upper end of the housing market. In recent years new, large waterfront development areas have been opened in Helsinki, boosting land values and attracting corporate investments. Urban political economists studying Finland and the development of its capital city have their work cut out in analysing the public real estate policies, their means and aims in new development projects.

The Eiranranta case showed the consequences of entrepreneurial public real estate policy on the built environment; it spatialised inequality. Eiranranta was developed as a neighbourhood for those who can pay a high price for their housing and excluded those who cannot. What explains the acceptance of such uneven development and differentiation by Helsinki's civil servants and politically elected REC members? It appears their primary focus on real estate business and seeing the Eiranranta project through successfully muted their worries over the dangers of urban inequality. They did not question the selling of public land, nor the development of an exclusive neighbourhood for the sole use of the wealthy homeowners. The "discursive practice" – to borrow Rachel Weber's (2002) concept – to sell the sites in Eiranranta was to introduce Eiranranta as an area with luxury housing with good taxpayers who would benefit the whole city.

One traditional means to tackle housing and urban inequalities in the Nordic welfare state has been housing policy and the mixing of tenures in developed areas. The entrepreneurial public real estate policy of the City of Helsinki that made the development of Eiranranta possible is in contradiction with the housing policy of tenure mixing. The lack of social housing in Eiranranta was not seen as problematic by civil servants. The welfare targets of urban development were buried by targets of a competitively organised system of urban development. Harvey (1989) observed some 30 years prior to this study how even the most progressive urban governments are hard-pressed to resist urban inequalities when targets of social responsibility and welfare provision are increasingly embedded in the logic of capitalist spatial development. The final part of the book explores how well contemporary Finnish housing policy is equipped to tackle urban inequalities in the face of such a logic, and an increasingly entrepreneurial land regime focused on revenues and growth.

Notes

1. This concept is introduced in Hyötyläinen and Haila (2018).
2. Well-known, peripheral housing estates in East Helsinki.
3. Helsinki 20. kaupunginosa, asemakaava (2016).
4. Eiranranta housing profile (2016).

PART III

The Inequalities of Housing Policy

Intricately linked to state land use policies and real estate management, housing policy – the state regulation, finance and allocation of housing – is, among other things, a crucial tool of the state to prevent and mitigate socio-spatial inequalities. In the context of the Nordic welfare state, the housing market was for a while understood as insufficient in ensuring an even distribution of quality housing and universal residential wellbeing. In the post-war era, Nordic welfare states' various housing policies were implemented to provide correctives to the housing market's pervasively unequal outcomes (Bengtsson 2001). Housing was partly de-commodified and provided as affordable, high quality social housing for both working- and middle-class households. Sweden and Denmark had their own, vast social housing development programmes. In Finland, social housing construction boomed in the 1970s. As discussed in the opening to Part I of the book, during the development of social housing estates in Finnish cities, more than half of the total of 600,000 units built over the decade were state subsidised. However, there has been a significant shift across the Nordic region regarding the thinking on why and how the state should intervene in housing provision.

Today, housing provision in the Nordic context is guided by the notion that houses should primarily be treated as commodities bought, sold and rented on the private housing market (Tranøy et al. 2020). And, in the Finnish policy context, it is no longer the housing market as such that is seen as an inadequate means of housing provision, creating a plethora of housing related inequalities and hence being in need of state correctives. Instead, housing problems are viewed as affecting individuals who are unable to satisfy their housing needs on the market due to some specific personal reasons, such as disability, old age, or substance abuse problems. Instead of developing social housing as a more universally accessible alternative to fully commodified housing, the role of the state housing policy is increasingly to serve those who are seen as market incapable. This approach follows a wider European trend. Beyond a targeted social service for the needy, housing policies across Europe are characterised by government decisions to withdraw from supply-side programmes, encouraged by debt-based owner-occupation, deregulation of the development sector and a stock-transfer of public housing units to the market (e.g. Aalbers 2015).

In the two following chapters I explore how housing policy transformations are linked to urban inequalities in Finland. I pay specific attention to the retrenchment of the social rental housing sector and explore two key issues in this process. First, I discuss the targeting of social housing to so-called 'special groups' and the deliberate recoiling of social housing from general welfare provision to a special social service. And second, I analyse the ongoing, large-scale stock transfer of social housing units to the private market and its violent consequences for social housing tenants. Over the next two chapters I build a historical trajectory of Finnish housing policy and the political-economic changes that have led up to social housing cutbacks. I argue, that instead of offering a robust, regulatory framework and accessible alternatives to the housing market, state housing policy now tries to navigate and negotiate with the market in its attempts to answer residential needs and well-being. I discuss the ramifications of policy retrenchment for urban inequality and use case studies to illustrate them more particularly. Because of the weakening role of housing policy, instead of tackling urban inequalities, policy has come to exacerbate and even produce urban inequalities by the way it problematises, represents, frames, and operationalises housing issues; sets agendas; and finally by the way it is implemented (James et al. 2022).

Although my focus is on housing policy, I concur with Aalbers and Christophers (2014, 389) who note that it no longer makes sense to "cede housing analysis either to economists who ignore or reduce the importance of power, politics and the state, or to a separate field of housing/social policy where the wider political economy is equally invisible". I wish to understand Finnish housing policies' connections to the wider political economic context. In Chapter 6 I take a historical perspective on the development of housing policy in Finland and study how social housing is slowly reduced into an ambulance service for special groups. Drawing on the sociology of territorial stigmatisation (Wacquant 2008) I argue that housing policy itself now divides residents based on tenure. Policy narrative feeds a stigmatising discourse about social housing and its tenants as abnormal, further cementing the dominant idea that under any 'normal' circumstances, homes are acquired and treated as commodities. This narrative works in favour of developers and landlords, but also motivates paternalistic and class-antagonistic social mixing policies that aim to demolish social housing in working class estates and replace it with owner-occupied and private rental units. These are all part of a revanchist project that aims at bringing housing firmly back into the process of capital circulation and accumulation. In Chapter 7 I analyse transformations of the non-profit housing sector and the dependence of state housing policy on so-called non-profit companies for affordable housing production. These companies have in recent years converted into institutional real estate investors and rentier landlords. They used to develop social housing for the workers, but now displace their working-class tenants and transfer hundreds of thousands of social housing units to the market for higher income tenants. But before all that, a few words on Finnish housing policy in general are in order.

On housing policy in Finland

Let me begin by making very clear my normative position on what I think the purpose of housing policy should be: a home is a universal, basic human need, not merely an economic demand, and it follows that the fundamental purpose of housing policy should be to guarantee that everyone has a home. Not, mind you, that everyone owns property, but that everyone is housed and enjoys a home as a complex bundle of interconnected use values contributing to personal autonomy, providing secure shelter, privacy, and social and family space – a home embedded in local, physical communities or as a safe access point to virtual ones. A home that contributes to a sense of reliability and predictability over their personal life trajectory, or what sociologists call ontological security (Giddens 1984). Some prerequisites for autonomy, home as part of a community and ontological security to be obtained through housing are, for example, housing affordability; adequacy of dwelling size and fitments for household needs; the location of the house; and a guarantee one will not be evicted or displaced. I argue that the successes of housing policy should then be assessed not merely based on whether people have a roof over their heads, but on the wider outcomes for the residential wellbeing of dwellers. I concur with Clapham (2018, 11), who takes a similar stance, which he justifies with the simple value judgement that "the sole objective of housing policy is to improve the situation of dwellers and not, for example, to enable developers and landlords to make profits".

Finnish housing policy has historically been informed by various other objectives than promoting progress in the wellbeing of dwellers as it relates to the bundle of use values that is home. Marked by periods of consistency, Finnish housing policy in the long term has been sporadic, and its instruments have been applied as short-term solutions to social crises and housing problems, and as counter-cyclical economic policy at times when private housing finance and development have stalled. Housing policy has been characterised by incremental changes, implemented according to the decisions of whomever happens to hold political power at a certain juncture. The state role in housing provision has waxed and waned; it has been accentuated in one period and withdrawn in the next, making for an undulant policy that lacks long-term vision (Juntto 1990; Haila 2015).

According to housing scholars Bengtsson and Ruonavaara (2011) the purpose of housing policy across the Nordic welfare states has traditionally been to address the failures of the housing market. I argue that Finnish housing policy no longer, in a sustained way, addresses the deep-seated failures of the housing market. Instead, the Finnish system of housing provision primarily relies on the commodity form of housing and this reliance has only intensified in recent years. Residential property was the most traded property sector for the second consecutive year, accounting for 29 per cent (€2.1 billion) of the total volume in 2022, according to the independent real estate market research company KTI Benchmarking.[1] Institutional investment companies and foreign investors have taken on a growing role within the Finnish regime of housing provision. Over half of all apartments sold in recent years have been sold to investors.[2]

When houses are treated as commodities, they inherently serve purposes that contradict the improvement of many dwellers' wellbeing and the use value of houses as homes. They serve the primary function of accumulating wealth for their owners. In the contemporary configuration of rentier capitalism (Christophers 2020), these owners are more often interested in houses merely as assets, used to maximise profits by extracting payments from the user of those assets. Housing policy has not been motivated by a systematic and surgical de-commodification of housing. Instead, cosmetic policy instruments have been used to address the symptoms of commodification and housing market failures. Meanwhile, a home-owner ideology has prevailed, building on cultural norms of a successful housing career and social expectations for households to eventually fulfil their housing needs on the market and buy into owner occupation. Ruonavaara (1996) has conceptualised these norms and expectations as traits of a "homeowner society", which is an outcome of a historical "home ideology" that was an essential aspect of nation building and attracting the able factions of wage-labour to join the propertied class to quell any revolutionary sympathies (Nurmi 2010).

The state has financially supported the homeowner society by subsidising first-time buyers in the form of tax-deductibility of interest payments on mortgages.[3] But even with state subsidy available for mortgages, for many urban working-class households, saving up for down payments and buying into owner occupation in the city is well beyond their reach and so their primary means of acquiring a home is the rental market. Also, in support of tenants, who again especially in major urban areas struggle with skyrocketing rents, the preferred housing policy instrument is the demand subsidy. This is paid by the Social Insurance Institution and social services in the form of different housing benefits and allowances to lower effective rents. Today, the housing allowance is the key form of state support for housing in Finland. There has been a significant increase in housing allowance payments over the past decades, especially after the global financial crisis. In 2000 the state paid €1.15 billion in housing allowances and in 2022 it had already reached €2.3 billion, making housing allowances are one of the largest forms of income transfer in Finland. Of its recipients, 97 per cent live in rental housing (Kela 2023).

The purpose of allowances is to improve the situation of the dweller and support their housing consumption by reducing the effective rent of the dwelling, thus leaving more money for other consumption. However, as Viren (2012,

1498) notes, housing allowances affect not only the income of the tenant, but also the income of the landlords, rents, labour supply and housing production. Demand subsidies are a housing policy instrument widely favoured by landlords, economists and liberal conservative politicians, who argue that demand subsidies allow for transparency of alternative costs, for house prices to find equilibrium according to supply and demand, and hence do not distort the market.[4]

But when extensive housing allowances are paid, are rents really set based on supply and demand or do allowances create anomalies in this and push up rents? Regarding the Finnish system, economists have reported different results. Kangasharju (2010) found that in the private sector, every additional euro of housing allowance to a tenant increases the rent they pay by 60–70 cents. In the social housing sector, no increase was found. And based on their findings Viren (2012) was convinced that a part of the housing allowance is shifted to prices, their conservative estimate being one third, but noting that it could be as much as half. Whether demand subsidies push up rents or not, and while demand subsidies may help some households pay for the suitable housing that the market fails to provide them, they are also without a doubt a transfer payment from the public treasuries to private rentiers. Demand subsidies guarantee that landlords have no requirement to lower current rents to answer the housing demand of those who cannot pay market price. Furthermore, we also know that the favouring of demand subsidies across Europe has led to the sharp rise in recurrent expenditure for governments on individual housing assistance. Consequently, there has been a substantial decline in the production of social and affordable housing in many countries – including France, Austria and Finland (Lawson and Ruonavaara 2019). Demand subsidies ensure that houses are commodities traded according to their exchange value and financial assets that catch the market rent and circulate on global financial markets.

When it comes to supply subsidies, the Housing Finance and Development Centre (ARA by its Finnish abbreviation, which I will use from here on) is the responsible government branch in Finland. ARA is governed by the Ministry of the Environment. ARA subsidises housing supply and controls and supervises the use of the so-called ARA housing stock. Today, there are three types of developers that are eligible for ARA subsidies: municipalities, non-profit organisations and limited liability companies in which one of the above has a dominant role. State subsidies are granted for the development of rental housing, owner-occupied housing, and also so-called intermediate housing (Juntto 1992). State subsidised rental housing has traditionally played a big role in housing provision. Roughly half of all rental units in Finland have been built with state subsidies. Their share is the greatest in cities and they are the only part of the rental housing stock with regulated rents. An example of intermediate housing are so-called right-of-occupancy apartments, where the resident pays roughly 15 per cent of the market price of the apartment and a monthly user charge. The right-of-occupancy is for life and it can be passed on as inheritance. When moving out, the original right-of-occupancy payment will be reimbursed. Helsinki had its own intermediate housing tenure called HITAS, which was a price regulated model of owner-occupation intended for middle-income households.

However, the idea that middle-income households might live in anything but fully commodified houses has become unacceptable to conservative politicians and the economists who inform their policies. Hence, due to years of conservative pressure and stirring of moral panic over misdirected subsidies, Helsinki recently ended its HITAS model. This reflects a wider trend of cutbacks in subsidised housing supply. The largest, non-profit developers of social housing have been turning into rentier landlords and privatising social rental units. Meanwhile, municipal housing offices lack the power to provide enough affordable housing to make up for what is privatised. The social housing sector is in a state of deliberate retrenchment. The Finnish regime of housing provision is increasingly penetrated by market logic and commodification. This reflects a worldwide trend. Globally, we face what Madden and Marcuse (2016) call a "hyper-commodification" of housing under a tripartite process of intensifying deregulation, globalisation and treating housing as a financial asset.

Deregulation means the removal of restrictions on housing as a commodity, the weakening or abolishing of rent regulations and the loosening of customs and rules regarding housing size, to give several examples. In Finland, a steady increase in both professional buy-to-let and mom-and-pop landlords is seeing the private rental market mushrooming. Related to this is the so-called "financialization" of the housing sector (Aalbers 2017; Lilius and Hirvonen 2021) which has seen various actors such as pension companies – discussed in more detail in Chapter 7 – produce profits from real estate through buying, selling, financing, owning and speculating with securitised mortgages, housing stock and bond. These actors are far removed from the occupants of houses and the use values of houses as homes. They are merely interested in the prospects for capital accumulation offered by real estate. With private rental housing in cities becoming increasingly expensive due to lack of regulation, a growing number of people see a major share of their income spent on rent, never mind young people and single person households in cities being able to save the down payments required for a mortgage and move to the idealised tenure of owner occupation.

Globalisation in this instance means that housing markets become more responsive to global economic signals and less responsive to local social needs. Extreme market liberal contexts, such as London, serve a harrowing example. In recent decades London has seen a surge of displacement of inner-city households and working-class communities and growing numbers of homeless people. Meanwhile, foreign investors have been found buying London homes suitable for first-time buyers, using them as buy-to-let investments and storing profits in off-shore tax havens (*The Guardian* 13 June 2017). We tend to think of such examples as endemic to the neoliberal Anglophone world, but the deregulated Nordic policy context increasingly leaves room for housing's commodification, if not hypercommodification, subjecting urban dwellers to the many predicaments and inequalities that arise from treating land and houses as assets in a global financial market. In Chapter 7, I explore so-called non-profit housing companies that have transformed into institutional real estate investors with diversified portfolios. These companies used to develop social housing for working-class tenants, but they now compare their domestic direct investments with indirect overseas real estate investment. State housing policy allows the privatisation of a dwindling stock of social housing, and these companies have displaced their working-class tenants to make a better yield on their direct investment.

But first, in Chapter 6, I discuss the historical trajectory of a retrenching social housing sector. The story told by neoclassical economists – that supply subsidies are a misdirected expenditure of taxpayer money and taxpayer money is lost if alternative costs are not calculated – rests on the simple assumption that houses can be nothing else than market commodities and that the most important information we can possibly have about them is the exchange value. Because this story has effectively crowded out alternatives to housing provision, state subsidised social rental housing is today increasingly intended for distinct individuals who belong to so-called special groups. Unfortunately, leaving social housing seemingly no other role than as an ambulance service for special groups has fed a noxious, stigmatising narrative about social housing and its market-incapable tenants as abnormal, further cementing the dominant idea that under any "normal" circumstances, homes are acquired and treated as commodities.

Notes

1. KTI Benchmarking – Finnish Property News (2023).
2. Statistics Finland (2020).
3. This policy was in full use until 2011. Since then, this subsidy has been incrementally weakened and it will be completely abolished in 2023. But traditionally it has been a one housing policy tool to motivate households to buy into owner occupation.
4. For example, The Finnish Landlord Association (2018), economists Saarimaa and Eerola (2015), and the liberal-conservative National Coalition Party (2022) all favour demand subsidies over building social housing.

CHAPTER 6

The Specialisation of Social Housing

Referring to the gap in research on the production of territorial stigmatisation (see Chapter 1), in this chapter I build an account of how social rental housing within the Finnish regime of housing provision has been rendered a tenure for the marginalised, become shorthand for social problems and finally contributed to the creation and maintenance of a blemish of place for the tenants of social housing neighbourhoods. I do this from a historical explanatory perspective, unearthing how and why the notion of "special groups" in state housing policy was adopted. Although I briefly illustrate how stigma works on a neighbourhood level at the end of the chapter, I am not focused here on its direct, experienced effects on the populations of the defamed and neglected neighbourhoods. To truly understand the symbolic contamination of urban areas, we must exit those areas and scrutinise the role of state and market institutions and actors in their production and reproduction (Larsen 2014).

Historical periods of housing policy

Nordic housing scholars have distinguished different historical periods of housing policy to help make sense of its development. Anneli Juntto's (1990) history of Finnish housing policy runs from 1858 to 1988 and she divides it into three periods. The first period she calls philanthropy (1850–1918), an era marked by subsistence agriculture and low housing standards in the rural areas, and the important role of employers in providing housing for labour in the cities. Juntto calls the second period in her analysis functionalism (1919–39), a time when Finnish architecture was renowned, when the ideals of the modern home developed and when private developers assumed a big role in urban housing markets. Proper housing, and bourgeois notions of proper domestic life, were enjoyed by the urban elites during this period. Meanwhile housing conditions remained poor for workers as the 1918 civil war had violently silenced the labour movement and with it any calls for public housing. Finally, the post-war period, which Juntto calls the welfare state (1945–88), saw growing acknowledgement of the housing problems faced by labour and the increasing prevalence of the state in overall housing provision.

Later, Bengtsson and Ruonavaara (2010) introduced their four periods of housing policy. Although the Finnish system of housing provision has its curiosities, according to these scholars in all Nordic countries housing provision can be seen developing through the same four ideal-type periods. The first period Bengtsson and Ruonavaara call the introduction or establishment phase, and this is when housing becomes a political issue and state interventions in the housing market are introduced. Second, is the construction phase and here the policy emphasis is on volume and the elimination of the housing shortage by producing as much housing as possible. These first two periods can be read as overlapping with Juntto's welfare state period. The third period they call the administration or management phase, when attention shifts from production to the maintenance and management of the existing housing stock. Renewal of the housing stock, the quality of the environment, resident participation in planning and tackling social segregation become major issues in this period. In Finnish cities such concerns grew throughout the 1990s and early 2000s. Finally, the fourth period is one of housing policy retrenchment. Now, the policies and institutions introduced in the previous periods are questioned and even discarded, while the responsibility over housing provision shifts from the public sector increasingly to the market (Ruonavaara 2017).

My account of housing policy development in Finland does not necessarily deviate from these illustrations. But it is worth emphasising that the field of housing studies in general has been dominated by an evolutionary and undialectical "modernization" framework regarding historical transformations in housing policy (Hodkinson and Mooney 2013). In my account of housing policy's historical trajectory, I try to avoid an uncritical path dependency approach – adopted by some European housing scholars – that simply argues that history matters. I concur with Aalbers (2016), who notes that calling something an explanation because it follows an apparently stable trend does not qualify as an explanation. Instead, I hope to contribute to a historical account by emphasising and contesting a missing element in these histories, that will help in unpacking the role of the state in the production of urban inequality and territorial stigmatisation. The provision of social rental housing is increasingly targeted at people who Finnish housing policy documents call special groups. My interest is in when and why, precisely, did this expression enter housing policy language, who belongs to special groups and who has the power to define the groups?

In what follows, I reflect critically on Finnish housing legislation and housing policy language and the implications of labelling social housing tenancy a "special need". I suggest that the symbolic defamation of social rental housing plays a major, yet largely neglected part in territorial stigmatisation in Finnish cities. And I suggest that the labelling of social housing and its tenants as special, feeds largely into both this defamation and urban inequality more generally. It is also a mechanism that accentuates the normalisation of housing commodification and fits well the dominant ideology of housing privatisation and deregulation. In short, to use the denomination special of one group, presumes that there is another, "normal" group whose housing needs and demands are answered in some other way. This naming of individuals and groups by housing policy documents and authorities is an exercise of symbolic power. It builds a power-ful narrative and implies that housing inequalities are a result of the differences between people and wilfully ignores any structural dynamics at play. I discuss the implications of categorisation of people based on tenure in housing policy. These revolve around the symbolic differentiation of tenures, but materialise as the very real differentiation of people.

Paupers and poor laws

Until the early 1900s the rural population in Finland lived under subsistence agri-culture and individuals were responsible for their own welfare, including housing (Waris 1962). Those who could not fend for themselves – a landless population consisting of the disabled, elderly and poor – were viewed as a homogeneous group of paupers. Homelessness was common, and poor people were dependent on the benevolence of private households for temporary lodging and food. They lived from hand to mouth, with some casual or seasonal earnings and begging as a significant means of subsistence (Haatanen 2017). In the cities, the industrial proletariat was taking shape, but it had become evident in the early 1800s that it was impossible for the urban working class to meet its housing need under the wage relation (Juntto 1990). Private landlords extracted sweet rents in Helsinki; meanwhile in Tampere, private landowners refused then, just as they do today, to give land for the city's development needs. Suffice to say, urban housing con-ditions were abysmal for all but the bourgeoisie. Paternalistic industrialists and businessmen – hoping to demonstrate their philanthropic tendencies to work-ers, but also to cut back on labour costs – established housing companies in the mid-1800s which provided affordable rental housing for their employees (Juntto 1990). Later, skilled workers and liberal reformists – those with the required capi-tal and ideological interest in ownership – founded their own housing companies, where the ownership of shares gave one a right to a unit. These were the early version of a very particular, Finnish style condominium or housing company[1] that is the main format of owner occupation today (Ruonavaara 2005).

Social care for the non-working poor and the homeless remained weak. Municipalities maintained a hard-line approach, and scanty assistance was pro-vided only for those who were deemed wholly unable to work. No distinction was made whether incapacity was due to physical or psychological disability, old age or something else. Were a person to depend on social assistance the munici-pality would take custody and place them in alms-houses. Some municipalities even auctioned off destitute people to households that made bids on who would charge the least for taking a pauper under their roof (Social Insurance Institu-tion of Finland 2018). Gradually the attitudes toward the poor, elderly and dis-abled began to change and by the early 20th century, social care was replacing the approach of pauperism. Separate fields of care – health care, childcare and care for the disabled – were slowly being introduced. The Poor Law,[2] which was passed in 1922, obliged municipalities to provide targeted care for the children and the elderly, and for those suffering from different psychological and physical disabilities respectively. This law, the first to give certain individuals a subjective right to social assistance, is largely regarded as the foundation on which social care would develop in the Finnish welfare state (Waris 1962). And the understanding that people have various disadvantages that require different kinds of care and assistance was followed by the idea that different types of care should be provided in different places. The Poor Law required municipalities to get rid of alms-houses, which had merely provided immediate shelter for the paupers, and develop specialised municipal care homes, which would provide both shelter and care for distinct groups (Rintala 1995). Although the Poor Law changed attitudes, the general thinking persisted that people are primarily responsible for their own welfare, including housing.

Housing and urbanisation

In the post-war years Finland's housing provision was in crisis. The ravages of war and territorial concessions had cost some 120,000 units of housing and thousands were again left homeless (Kuusi 1968). As developers lacked the funds to build, the state established the Housing Construction Delegation or Arava[3] to provide interest-subsidised construction loans to developers (Tulla 1999). The developers entitled to state subsidies were non-profits and municipal housing companies. Between 1945 and 1957, they built up to 70 per cent of all housing (Juntto 1990). Housing was subject to regulations on rent and price. During this time public intervention in housing provision was initiated throughout the advanced capitalist world, more so than in any other period. Rent controls were introduced in many places to guarantee housing affordability. Building standards were regulated and overseen by public authorities and a strong urban planning paradigm was implemented to meet social and environmental targets. Social housing was built to the extent that housing in Europe became partly de-commodified.

In Finland, Arava continued to provide low-interest-rate construction loans for all developers. In the 1950s and 60s state subsidised housing development increased, and it reached peak annual volume in the mid-70s when some 37,000 subsidised units were constructed per year. More than 300,000 housing units were built during the 1970s with state financing (Ruonavaara 2017). A period of universalism in housing policy prevailed, social housing was regarded more as universal public good than a social service for the needy. This was both rental and owner-occupied housing, built in the housing estates outside the city centres. Both working- and middle-class families could, with a state loan, now afford an owner-occupied apartment from the new housing estates. State loans had a loan to value ratio of 40 per cent, so most loans were granted to households capable of making the required down payments. Arava legitimised the new housing model that prioritised families with the idea that developing new housing for them, their previous homes would become vacant and "filter down" to the lowest-income groups (Juntto 1990). However, unsurprisingly, housing never "filtered down" to those on society's lowest rung.[4] Homelessness was common especially among war veterans, traumatised single men often suffering from alcoholism and other addictions. As Arava, the primary objective of which was to house families, did not provide housing for the homeless, the task was left to the Ministry of Social Affairs and Health. Homeless veterans, who also suffered from manifold physical and psychological problems, were housed in institutions – such as psychiatric hospitals – where patients were divided into groups based on the type and urgency of assistance and medical care they needed. In the 1960s the ministry had begun calling them "special groups" (Taipale 1982).

Women were now entering the workforce to meet a growing demand for labour. Family sizes had been getting smaller throughout the early 1900s (Statistics Finland 2022), and children would now move out sooner. For elderly people these changes were dramatic – family members were no longer staying home to care for them. Authorities grew aware that it was both socially and economically important to develop senior care outside the home and it slowly became accepted as a long-term, public responsibility to develop old-age homes (Kuusi 1968). Higher education was possible for a growing amount of young people, and students were also seen as a new group who needed special attention in housing provision during this period. Helsinki's housing programme of 1975 is the first housing policy document to mention these two groups – the elderly and students – as targets of special housing intervention (Taipale 1982). In the late 1970s a major reduction of institutional care was also implemented. Many who previously had been thought of as in need of round the day institutional care, were now seen as perfectly capable of living on their own, given sufficient assistance was made available at home. Institutions were closed, and patients were discharged. Deinstitutionalisation saved direct costs of care, but patients now needed homes to live in. The Ministry of Social Affairs and Health introduced the idea of developing what it called *social housing for special groups* (Ibid.).

In 1979 the ministry carried out a research project looking for the groups "most in need of social care". A report was produced in which these groups were not limited to students, the elderly and the deinstitutionalised, but the following groups were also mentioned: families with children, large families, single parents, visually impaired people, the lowest income quintile of all households, war veterans and the indigenous ethnic minorities of Finnish Roma and the Sami (Halla and Kyrö 1979). Curiously the Ministry of Social Affairs and Health report lumped all these people together under the category of special groups. As housing officials then became responsible for organising accommodation for those previously cared for by the social care sector and housed in institutions, the term special groups travelled from the language of social affairs to the language of housing policy.

The transformation of the social housing sector

In the 1980s the Nordic countries looked to the west for a model of economic growth. The pinnacle of neoliberal restructuring in Europe was of course the UK. Thatcher had risen to power advocating for the Right to Buy policy – an infamous programme of public housing privatisation. The Right to Buy policy enabled tenants to purchase their council apartments and become homeowners. The weight of UK housing policy shifted from subsidising housing supply to subsidising housing demand. As Ball et al. (1990, 72) wrote at the time,

> the growth of housing allowances has to be seen in the broader context of attempts to change the role of social rented housing, to target it on low-income households and to reduce overall support for this tenure with lower levels of building, degressive construction subsidies and rent levels linked to current market costs. Governments introduced these changes at a time of economic growth when most sections of the population had rising real incomes. The belief was that, as income growth continued, the state obligation to social housing could be reduced.

In hindsight we know that by 1989 over a million units of the highest quality public housing stock were sold off and discharged to the private market. By 1997 the number was already 1.7 million. What remains as social housing is poor quality public housing in peripheral housing estates (Forrest and Murie 1983; Harloe 1995). We also know that Thatcher's policy has led to severe housing shortages for people of low income, initiated a national house price bubble and led ultimately to what is commonly recognised as the displacement and gentrification of many working-class communities.

But at the time, UK housing policies were seen as exemplary. As other European countries reformed their policies in similar ways, international housing scholars conceptualised what was going on as a trend of extensive housing policy 'modernisation' across Europe. Social housing became regarded an anomaly of the post-war period and responsibilities for housing provision were being rolled over to the individual (Hodkinson and Mooney 2013). Other regulatory policies were discarded as well. In Finland strict rent controls had been implemented in the post-war years and after a brief period of deregulation during the 1960s, reintroduced in 1968 (Kettunen and Ruonavaara 2015). Rent controls ensured that rents in the private rental sector – including rental housing transferring from the social to the private sector – remained affordable. Tenants were also well protected during this era, and for instance evictions were illegal (Kettunen and Ruonavaara 2015). But during the late 1980s such state meddling in the housing market became increasingly frowned upon.

Importantly, the financial sector was deregulated in Finland in the 1980s. Financing opportunities for banks grew, and it became easier for working-class families to take out a mortgage from a local savings bank and purchase residential property. Instead of providing loans to prospective homeowners, the state's role

in housing provision was reduced to subsidising social rental housing development and handing out housing benefits (Ruonavaara 2017). This arrangement
resonated better with the market liberal beat of the 1980s and the ideas of Finnish
decision makers of the era, according to whom individuals should be responsible
for their own housing and buy their homes on the market (Juntto 1990). Public
monopolies in general were seen as harmful, therefore public housing production was also to be minimised. State subsidised housing provision was increasingly
regarded as little more than a social service for those unable to acquire housing
on the market. The system of housing provision was split more distinctly into two:
the deregulated private housing market, and a regulated and means-tested social
housing sector. Using Bengtsson's (2001) concept, Finnish housing policy changed
into a "selective policy". In 1987 the dismantling of rent control was set as a housing policy target, and in 1991 it was included in the government programme. As
Juntto (1992, 50) writes about the 1980s housing policy in Finland in general:

> by 1988, the state financed only eight per cent of all housing production. The housing
> demand was estimated to be mostly satisfied. Housing policy had 'done its job' and
> would in the future be needed only for special groups and for minor adjustments.

Picking up where Juntto's analysis left off, Ruonavaara (2017) marks the beginning of the Finnish housing policy retrenchment phase in the early 1990s. First,
the deep economic depression called for state intervention. Thousands had been
left unemployed and lost their homes to banks as mortgages turned to bad debts.
Social rental housing was required to answer the housing needs of unemployed
Finns but also to sustain work in the construction sector. The state stepped in
again to finance social housing production as a countercyclical regulator and to
ensure effective demand during the depression as private developers froze their
projects. However, social housing of the era had none of the 1960s universality
principles nor architectural ambitions. It was built as affordably as possible from
prefabricated materials, often in or close to the post-war housing estates, and
allocated based on strict income limits.

Second, the depression hardened attitudes towards state regulation. As private rental supply had stagnated, rent control and policies that protected tenants
were blamed. The depression blew the doors open for deregulation and marketisation in public policies. In Part I, I discussed the neoliberalisation of the period,
reflected in the introduction of NPM and Finland's integration into the European free market community in the early 1990s, all of which intensified the trend
of welfare policy retrenchment (Niemelä and Saarinen 2012). Housing policy
reforms of the time reflected a larger public sector transformation. Rent control
was completely terminated in 1992 and rental contracts revised to weaken tenant protection – terminating contracts became easier and landlords were free to
set the rent. Once rent controls were removed, more private rental housing was
available. However, the rent levels started to diverge aggressively, and rents in

the private rental sector were significantly higher than in the social rental sector (Kettunen and Ruonavaara 2015).

Through the 1990s social housing was being transformed into a social service for the unemployed and special groups. Tenure and residential location on social housing estates now disclosed one's social and economic status more than before. Stark cultural and economic divisions between housing tenures are not a specific trait of the Finnish housing system, of course. According to Larsen (2014) the state in Denmark for instance has played a key role in creating a dual housing market: the private sector governed by market principles and the regulated non-profit sector. This dual market favoured owner occupation and made it, for those who could afford it, economically sound and preferable compared to renting. The effect of this was, according to Larsen (2014, 1395):

> the removal of large sections of the middle and working classes from the non-profit housing sector and, just as importantly, a move away from collective forms of housing as a cultural institution that sustained the pride and (re)production of the working classes.

Private and social rental tenures began to differentiate drastically in similar ways in Finland. Social housing tenants were now chosen based on strict criteria. The three key eligibility criteria required of tenants who are allocated social housing are low income, low wealth and the urgency of housing need. Furthermore, in 1991 housing authorities announced that thousands of people were still housed in institutions, such as psychiatric hospitals, because they did not have a home and that they should be accommodated in social housing. In assisting people to acquire a dwelling, the benevolence of authorities met with the demand to save on institutional costs (Vesanen 1992, 23–4).

At the same time, public perceptions of social housing were changing. The more social housing was allocated exclusively to special groups, the unemployed and deinstitutionalised, the more it was connected to marginalisation and per-ceived as a form of social assistance on the one hand, and a drain on dwin-dling public funds on the other. Social housing was becoming a shorthand for social problems. In 1997, Finnish housing researcher Korhonen wrote about the attitudes towards social housing: "the general understanding is that many social problems concentrate in social housing [. . .] Social housing is feared to bring about disturbances, insecurity, criminal subcultures and to lower the mar-ket value of apartments" (Korhonen 1997, 210). Meanwhile, a powerful narra-tive about problematic and deviant residents of social housing estates was forged in the media throughout the 1990s (Roivainen 1999). Problems with peripheral housing estates were discussed as early as the 1970s. Back then, however, the major issues were the lack of services, the geographical disconnect from the city and long commuting times. Residents were seen as the victims of poor plan-ning and sometimes unsuccessful urban development decisions. But by the late

1990s the tone had changed. It was now the people who lived on social housing estates who were the problem (Roivainen 1999; Junnilainen 2019). The narrative about problematic social housing estates continued to be built in the early 2000s. In Chapter 2 I explored how this narrative has been constructed in descriptive research literature on segregation and circulated in the media and in policies.

Today, the notion of social housing problem-estates is common in public narratives (e.g., Van Aerschot and Salminen 2018). Authorities link social housing to social problems, and this is reflected in policies. An interviewed land use official from Helsinki talked about the deliberations that go into deciding how the city allocates land for social rental housing:

> We discuss how much social rental housing can be allocated in different areas. Like, how resilient the areas are, meaning how many higher-income people there are. And how much an area can shoulder the placing of challenging folk in that area.

The very approach of the city to social housing allocation, this official suggests, is based on the notion that introducing social rental housing in an area is the same as introducing "challenging folk". Tenure today prescribes the status of the resident as the majority of new-built social housing is social housing for special groups. Since 2004, the proportion of "normal rental" out of all new social housing development has been lower than the proportion of housing for special groups – I return to the fate of the "normal rental" sector in more detail in the next chapter.

The term special groups was also officially added to housing legislation and policy in 2004, with the introduction of The Act on Subsidies for Improving the Housing Conditions of Special Groups (FINLEX). The act defines special groups as groups with "special needs". According to the act, these are people: 1) whose housing conditions are bad and income exceptionally low; 2) who require more support services than usual; 3) for whom, in addition to support services, the provision of housing requires significant spatial or technical arrangements in the building or apartment; 4) whose substance abuse, mental health issues or other comparable problems have caused long term homelessness; or 5) whose handicap sets the building or apartment exceptionally challenging or expensive requirements. Furthermore, the Finnish Environmental Administration (2018), which is responsible for guiding and developing land use policies and housing policies, including policies on social housing, also distinguishes the following special groups who should be allocated social housing: the homeless, refugees, students, people with substance abuse and mental health problems, the disabled and those elderly people who suffer from memory disorders or weakened physical condition. Clapham and Smith write about the extensive use of the concept of special needs groups in the UK: "the precise groups considered to have 'special needs' varies considerably and can include almost everyone" (Clapham and Smith 1990, 194). Similarly, the Finnish authorities list so many people under special groups that it becomes easier to define who does not belong to a special group. The officials and civil servants understood the term special in terms of its opposite, what they called "normal". And normal, it turns out, is not too difficult to define.

In the City of Tampere interviewees reported that about 70 per cent of their state subsidised housing development is for special groups and only 30 per cent, in their words, for "the normal people". An official in the Housing Department of Tampere explained:

> The developers building for special groups get a much larger subsidy from the state, free money for building. There is not the same kind of interest in developing state subsidized, normal rental housing [. . .] because the state subsidy for normal social rental housing is so low, it doesn't bring a competitive edge.

Similarly, in the City of Turku, interviewed officials explained that developers who build normal rental housing seemed to have disappeared. The non-profit associations have begun developing housing for special groups instead of rental housing: "It's a fact, there hasn't really been any development of basic, afford-able social rental housing in recent years. It has been mostly these special groups' sites that are developed." The goal of Finnish housing policy is not to extend the provision of partly de-commodified, affordable social rental housing to those who are not deemed special groups. The comment of an official from Espoo, the second largest city in the Helsinki Metropolitan Area, makes clear that social housing exists as a social service for the needy:

> The number of people on waiting lists for social housing has grown in recent years. But it's likely so that if we had unlimited supply of affordable housing then there would be an unlimited number of people coming in. And it's not meant [for all], it's meant for those who need it.

An official at the Real Estate Department of Espoo emphasised the distinction between people who live in private and social housing:

> We have focused on three groups: young people, immigrants and the elderly. These are the large groups that the city needs to pay attention to and guarantee a good life and a good community for. Then you have the normal, working popula-tion who take care of themselves. They don't need public assistance.

Normal is the designation used to define people who can pay the market rent, or "take care of themselves". The 19th century distinction between the normal working person and the pauper has returned. Included in this distinction is the contrast between responsible owners or private sector tenants, and those depen-dent on social benefits, or as the official from Helsinki put it, "the challenging folk". As in the UK and Australia, there is a tendency in Finland's housing policy rhetoric to promote a "narrative which stigmatizes social housing as 'not for nor-mal people'" (Fitzpatrick and Pawson 2014, 612).

Just like under the Poor Law of 1922, in today's housing policy "normal working people" are expected to house themselves. Social housing is seen as a social service for special groups, people without "market competence" (Haila 2015, 285). Even government papers repeat this rhetoric. Reflecting the stigmatising public narrative is a recent housing policy report by the parliament's Audit Committee (Antikainen et al. 2017) which calls people who cannot afford market rent in Finnish *asuntomarkkinoiden väliinputoajat*, a nonsensical term which directly translates to "those who fall between housing markets". A more accurate translation would be housing market drop-outs, as the Finnish term implies it is not the housing market as such that is flawed and a source of serious housing related inequalities, but that flawed individuals who cannot support themselves will drop out of the normal housing market and into social dependency.

On the stigmatisation of social housing and its tenants

Finnish housing policy acknowledges the existence of residential problems but casts them as the special concerns of individuals who are ill-housed due to some personal reason in the context of an overall housing system that is held to be functioning well. Housing policy language emphasises problem-people instead of the structural problems with the housing market. The focus is on the characteristics of people imagined as exceptional. In the Helsinki Metropolitan Area, social housing has been disproportionately developed in peripheral housing estates. As I explained in the introduction to Part I of the book, many housing estates have become severely disinvested over the decades, lacking needed repairs and upgrading. Services were poor and declined even further when higher income groups moved out. Some of the social housing stock from the 1990s was so poor in quality – and after periods of disinvestment and neglect – it has become hopelessly dilapidated and today is being demolished as local authorities find it cheaper to build all new houses than renovate the old. As a result of such uneven development of the built environment, some of these demographically heterogeneous neighbourhoods became increasingly working-class, as middle-class residents left soon after the investments did. Socio-spatial unevenness was aggravated by uneven development of urban land and selective housing policy that concentrated unemployed and marginalised households onto these same housing estates. In Chapter 2 I discussed the production of territorial stigmatisation of suburban social housing estates in descriptive research, media narratives and policy papers (see also Juntto 2010). I devote the last pages of this chapter to illustrate how territorial stigma operated in a social housing estate in east Helsinki and how it was closely entangled with the stigma of social housing tenure.

The neighbourhood in question is located on the north-eastern border of the municipality of Helsinki. The oldest residences in the area are small owner-occupied apartment buildings constructed in the 1950s and early 60s. Much of the neighbourhood, however, was built in the 1970s using development contracts with construction companies. The plan for the area was finished in 1967 and gave two developers development rights for apartment buildings of up to seven stories. One company built rental housing with state subsidies and the other owner-occupied private flats closer to the older, smaller apartment buildings. By 1975 the neighbourhood was home to 5,500 residents. Infill development throughout the 1990s and 2000s and the extending of the subway line to the area in the late 1980s attracted more people, and today it is home to roughly 10,000 residents. In 2013 I worked in the neighbourhood and was involved with local residents, neighbourhood association actives and business owners. I had noticed the residents distinguished between what they called the New Side and the Old Side of the area. It was clear that the Old Side was used to refer to the area with owner-occupied apartment buildings constructed since the 1950s. The New Side referred to an area on the south side of a major highway, and the area around the local subway station with more recently built, denser housing. However, the distinction appeared to be loaded with other information besides simply referring to the period of development of the areas.

My job in the neighbourhood ended, but I was intrigued by the divisions the residents had made regarding the neighbourhood. So, through my contacts at the resident association, I returned to the neighbourhood and began interviewing residents about it. The interviews turned into a study and the study into a thesis (Hyötyläinen 2013). The key finding of my thesis was that in this neighbourhood residents would distinguish social micro-locations. And among the fourteen people I eventually interviewed, the main line of distinction between these locations was one drawn along housing tenure. Tenure, however, was used as shorthand for differences between people. Across the board, people living in social rental housing were held to deviate from the "normal" owner-occupiers and private tenants. A shared opinion prevailed in the neighbourhood that the people living in specific social housing areas were the key reason for inactivity in local matters, bouts of social disorder and the general poor reputation of the neighbourhood held by outsiders. Tenure was heavily linked in discussions to a territorial categorisation of the active, original Old Side of homeowners and the inactive, problem ridden New Side of social housing. My findings reflected those of Wacquant's (2008), who noted that for their residents, French housing estates are not monolithic entities. Instead, residents distinguish sub-units and micro-locales which centre on buildings and even different stairwells inside a single building and are used to organise daily lives.

In the neighbourhood of my study, housing tenures on both New Side and Old Side were, in fact, mixed. There were detached houses, row-houses, apartment buildings and different types of tenures. People used the same services and children went to the same schools. The entire neighbourhood was near the sea and forests, features which were highly valued by interviewed residents.

However, my interviewees all shared the same view of clearly distinguishable areas. A young woman, who lived with her family in social housing on the New Side explained:

> The areas are very clearly different. They are distinguished by money. And when people come out of the subway you can assume which side they live on. And the Old Side has noticeably more elderly people. So that's the biggest thing, you have those buildings constructed in the late 1950s and people who moved in at that time. And these ones [municipal social housing units] were built 1989 so there you have it. The ones built in the 1950s are better than these prefabricated houses which they [ARA and the city of Helsinki] built for us in a terrible hurry.

For this social housing tenant, the differences between micro areas are not merely physical and between buildings but living on either of the two sides of the neighbourhood also discloses the socioeconomic status of residents and vice versa.

A homeowner also living on the New Side spoke about the differences between tenants and owners. According to them social housing tenants are people who deviate from "ordinary" homeowners:

> I want to say no, but the truth is that, well, [social] rental housing is inhabited by people who are different. There's social housing right next to us and quite often the police pay them a visit [. . .] I'm not saying it's the only reason, but you notice that the neighbour's house is paid a visit by the police more often than ours.

This homeowner made a distinction down to the level of specific buildings, and their residents, based on their tenure. The homeowner also brought up a single individual who was causing disturbances in the area. The problems brought on by social housing were generalised from the deviant behaviour of an individual neighbour who was known to be living in social housing, then represented as a trait endemic of all social housing tenants. Naming can be a form of symbolic distancing which then becomes personified in residents of the same neighbourhood. In Wacquant's (2008) study of the French banlieue, residents would go to great lengths to distance themselves from neighbours on the north and south sides of the same neighbourhood and even in adjacent stairwells.

A young homeowner living on the Old Side talked about his perceptions of the neighbourhood. He lived with his family in what he calls the "hilltop" on the Old Side. Having previously lived in social housing in another part of Helsinki, he talked very openly about growing tired of it. He chose to move to the neighbourhood for the peace and quiet and natural surroundings and the lack of social housing close to where he now lives. He described the neighbourhood as its "own little world". But, like most interviewees, he was clear that it is not the same throughout the area:

> The closer you go to the metro station, there you have municipal [social housing] apartments. You have the owner-occupied housing on top of the hill here and

then there's the town-house area. But they [disturbances] are small for that kind of concentration of city apartments. I know these addicts and drunks, they won't climb the hill!

This former social housing tenant wanted to now distance himself from the social housing and its residents in the neighbourhood, reflecting what Wacquant (2007, 68) suggests:

the acute sense of social indignity that enshrouds neighborhoods of relegation can be attenuated only by thrusting the stigma onto a faceless, demonized other – the downstairs neighbors, the immigrant family dwelling in an adjacent building, the youths from across the street who 'do drugs' or are engaged in street 'hustling', or the residents over on the next block whom one suspects of illegally drawing unemployment or welfare support.

As spaces and territories come to be known as deviant, a noxious narrative about their residents enters the everyday discourse and is soon widely accepted. Slater (2015, 5) develops this notion and writes:

it is not only policy elites and upper-class voyeurs who recoil at, mock, or slam a small set of notorious urban districts; it is also the citizenry at large (many of whom have never visited them), and sometimes even the residents of those districts.

In the neighbourhood of my study tenure was playing a strong part in symbolic distancing, but also of mocking social housing residents. Furthermore, Wacquant (2008) suggests that territorial stigmas have the tendency to turn into a type of self-fulfilling prophecy. When a neighbourhood becomes socially disreputable, its residents will develop coping mechanisms. They will find symbolic and material ways to distance themselves from their neighbours who are viewed as the causes of those social problems. This is symbolic power at work. It breaks working-class solidarity in the face of structural inequality and drives people to point at one another for the reasons to their predicaments. Social atomism, disorganisation of the community and cultural anomie then easily ensue from that public taint or stigma which was supposed to only record them.

Finally, there was a distinction made between the level of participation and activity in neighbourhood matters between owners and social housing tenants that drove a wedge between the two. It has become commonplace for policymakers to call for more participation in neighbourhoods, to build a sense of community, and to activate the residents to revitalise neighbourhoods (Junnilainen 2019). Successfully revitalised neighbourhoods with for example wide participation rates in local associations are then held as exemplary in media reports and policy papers. For some of my interviewees this comparison between neighbourhoods had left them feeling shame regarding their own neighbourhood's inactivity. They blamed social housing for it. A homeowner from the Old Side explained:

people in East Helsinki in general are like this, incapable. And this estate now has plenty of these municipal [social housing] apartment buildings. I don't know how many, but probably so that there are now fewer owner-occupied apartments. So, when you go to the New Side, it's all social housing. People there are even less, or they are not active in their own neighbourhood. Because they have their own problems. The New Side has all sorts of people living there. Starting from alcoholics to regular families with children who can't afford to live any other way. But they don't bother [participating] in anything, it's one of the difficulties of an eastern housing estate.

Junnilainen (2019) explains how calls for more neighbourhood community-building are made top-down, even when locals might feel that they already have a meaningful and vibrant community. And De Decker and Pannecoucke (2004) have studied the formation of an image of the "incapable tenant" in the context of Flanders, Belgium. They analysed policy documents, reports, news articles and other media sources and discuss how the public definition of the "incapable tenant" has been created very much apart from what residents themselves might have to say. De Decker and Pannecoucke (2004, 305) write:

> all in all, the discourse evolved from a local and dispersed theme to a broad consensus on problem tenants, problem estates and the mechanism causing the problems. In all this, the press has served as a megaphone, publishing sensational headlines, front-page scandals and cliché photos.

De Decker and Pannecoucke chart the formation of this label using as their back-drop a study which shows that residential satisfaction among social tenants is relatively high; residents feel positive about their neighbourhood and have no intention of moving out in the near future. Despite the results of such studies, which according to De Decker and Pannecoucke (2004, 294) most importantly prove that there is no liveability problem in the social rental sector, social tenants are nevertheless labelled as "[. . .] deviant, noisy, dirty, dependent, ungrateful and above all, incapable of living together with other people".

Although the findings of my tentative study are from nearly ten years ago, more recent, extensive ethnographic work on the territorial stigmatisation of two social housing estates in Finland has reached similar conclusions. The findings of Lotta Junnilainen (2019) in her brilliant, meticulous studies confirm that the most significant social distinction being drawn in neighbourhoods is the one based on tenure (Junnilainen 2019, 164). Those housing estates where social rental housing is the predominant tenure are today affixed with powerful notions of otherness. Living in a social rental housing area stigmatises the resident. Finland continues to be a homeowner society, where tenancy in a municipal rental flat is an unavoidable symbolic marker of failure and market incapability. Because rental housing is synonymous with problem housing, in the comparatively het-erogeneous urban fabric of the Finnish city, entire neighbourhoods in which social rental housing exists easily receive the stigma of abnormality. The symbolic othering may be internalised by the residents, bringing about sentiments of guilt and shame that ultimately hinder the development of a sense of community or local solidarity (Wacquant 2008).

Using tenurial stigma to justify gentrification?

The purpose of this chapter's historical account of the development of housing policy in Finland was to explain and illustrate how social housing became treated as a separate strand of housing provision. As housing policy has been reformed to give more room for and support the private housing market instead of intervening in it, social housing has been increasingly made into a social service. Housing policy now views housing problems more as the problems of heterogeneous market-incapable individuals who belong to so-called special groups. This view disregards the general systemic failures of the housing market to provide decent, affordable homes and conceals them all under a collection of distinct problems of distinct individuals. In the process, housing policy comes to blame the victims of housing related urban inequalities for their problems (Madden and Marcuse 2016).

I explored how residents who cannot afford to pay the market rent are singled out and labelled "special" as opposed to the "normal" people who manage to buy or rent housing on the market. The legal definition of special groups diverts our attention from housing inequality to individuals. The term renders the inability to cover the market price of housing a special condition of an individual, when in fact the problem is the unbearably high housing cost caused by the commodification of housing, land rent maximising behaviour of speculative developers (Haila 2016) and entrepreneurial public real estate policies of municipalities (Hyötyläinen and Haila 2018). The rationale of social housing is deliberately reduced to that of alleviating the symptoms, not fixing the actual problems. Social housing is provided only to those who are incapable of buying or renting on the market and the social housing itself is regarded as a social service. Such a categorisation is a useful myth that works in favour of the propertied class who benefits from the normalisation of the commodity form of housing. By individualising the housing question into a personal responsibility, housing policy hides the fact that the housing question is a class question. Urban inequalities related to housing stem predominantly from the fact that there is a capitalist rentier class extracting and accumulating wealth from housing assets, buoyed by state legal and policy frameworks that defend property and property values, and backed up by a credit and finance system that maintains private demand.

This chapter argued that housing policy now differentiates people according to tenure. I conclude the chapter by noting a particularly urgent research gap in the Finnish context. What warrants further investigation is how the specialised role of social housing and the concentration of working-class households, people who are unemployed, marginalised groups and language minorities is then used to justify contemporary, paternalist and class-antagonistic housing policy decisions. Today, a major housing policy goal for the city of Helsinki is to disperse concentrations of social housing in the name of social mixing and the ambiguous notion of social cohesion. There is a painful irony in that public authorities first purposefully target social housing for the low-income and marginalised households, and now accuse social housing of concentrating those same households. That concentration, or segregation, is then used to justify developing more owner-occupied units on social housing estates. What has been paid very little scholarly attention to in research on urban inequality in Finland, is how and to what degree social housing tenure stigmatisation is used to justify the state-led gentrification of social housing estates. One recent preliminary study regarding the planned redevelopment of the social housing estate of Meri-Rastila in East Helsinki sheds some light on this (Kukkonen 2022).

In Kukkonen's study regarding the justifications and plans for redevelopment in Meri-Rastila, they found the city planning authorities repeatedly brought up the area's social housing, which was explained to have a direct impact on the population and image of the area, as well as the scarcity of housing types. As the housing estate is predominantly made up of social rental housing, the city considers the area's demographic structure too unbalanced. Working-class households, those belonging to special groups and people of immigrant background are, in the city's view, over-represented in the area. Kukkonen's analysis shows the city of Helsinki's redevelopment plans to be driven less by a hope to improve the lives of those living on the estate and more by an urge to attract more middle-class households to the area. The redevelopment of Meri-Rastila is largely justified by the fight against segregation. The area is seen by the city as socio-economically weak, segregated and as having a poor image. The area is expected to strengthen socio-economically and image-wise with the demolition of social housing units and the development of owner-occupied apartments. The City of Helsinki Urban Planning Office documents, as cited in Kukkonen (2022), note:

> the problem is currently the lack of demand for owner-occupied housing in the area. The area is not perceived as attractive, presumably because of its reputation for being dominated by social rental houses. This can be seen in the low price-level of old owner-occupied apartments and low transaction volumes.

A situation of low housing prices is viewed as lowering people's economic perceptions and therefore as having a negative influence on the urban economy at large (Aalbers and Christophers 2014, 378). The city hopes to allow for social housing estates to be penetrated by housing market rationales. Neil Smith used the concept of revanchism to discuss such state policies that force affordable, working-class residential spaces back under the umbrella of capital accumulation and circulation. Here is what the City of Helsinki Urban Planning Office (2012, 27) wrote a decade ago about Meri-Rastila:

> In terms of the housing market, a seaside area close to nature next to the metro station is attractive. Meri-Rastila's housing stock is dominated by small social rental apartments. It can be changed to a more balanced one by building larger apartments and increasing the proportion of owner-occupied apartments in new production. This may also affect the population structure of Meri-Rastila and promote regional equalisation.

This approach is writ large with class-antagonistic revanchism. It is state-led gentrification masquerading as an urban policy promoting urban equality and social mixing. But gentrification is not a policy solution to segregation. Both are socio-spatial processes that reflect the same deep-seated urban inequalities and class struggle in the city. More critical studies are needed in the Finnish context to uncover the political economy of state-led gentrification projects in the future.

*

In this chapter I have addressed the research gap regarding the production of territorial stigmatisation and explored primarily the historical and structural dynamics of social housing retrenchment and stigmatisation in Finland. These processes work in favour of those who profit from housing commodification. They legitimise the social rental housing retrenchment, justify not-for-profit housing associations and statutory corporations turning into rentier landlords – the topic of the next chapter – and leave municipalities as the sole providers of social housing. This blinds us to the innate inability of the housing market to provide decent housing for all and depicts this as a special characteristic of certain individuals who should then be assisted by housing policy. Further studies on the qualitative effects of social housing retrenchment, how social housing is perceived and increasingly stigmatised, and how that feeds into both symbolic and physio-spatial expressions of urban inequalities may hopefully build on this discussion. The next chapter turns the focus on the retrenching stock of so-called normal rental housing and illustrates the consequences of housing commodification for working-class households.

Notes

1. Fin. asunto-osakeyhtiö.
2. Fin. köyhäinhoitolaki.
3. Known today as the Housing Finance and Development Centre, or simply ARA by its Finnish abbreviation.
4. The filtering theory, a kind of trickle-down economics for housing, finds its contemporary advocates especially among neoclassical economists. Today their argument is that the state should relax regulation on the top end of the housing market and let developers build expensive, luxury housing. Ultimately, increasing supply at the top end will

bring prices down and as the wealthy move into the new luxury stock, their old houses will open for the lower income households (e.g., Brotherus HS 6.7.2019). Filtering theory has been shown time and again not to work in favour of low-income people who in a deregulated housing system will eventually be forced to live in the worst of the housing stock (see e.g., Boddy & Gray 1979). Finnish economists (Bratu et al. 2021) recently published a report showing scant evidence in favour of filtering. What they failed to explain was that their own research clearly shows that the quickest, most affordable way to provide high quality housing for the working-class and low-income individuals is in the highly regulated social housing sector, built on public land.

CHAPTER 7

Locking Out Use Values

In September 2019, Sara, who works as a radiographer in a public hospital in Helsinki, received notice of a registered letter to be retrieved from her local post office. The letter was from her landlord, the Finnish pension provider and non-profit housing company called Keva. Sara did not think much of it, and only went to pick up the letter several days later while running errands with her partner. At the post office she opened the envelope and read the opening line: "Keva is terminating your rental contract within six months of retrieval of this letter." The letter was signed by Keva's Real Estate Portfolio Manager and Keva's Housing Secretary. Stunned, Sara and her partner walked back to the apartment that for 15 years had been their home, but which they were now being forced to leave. The question that haunted Sara, and the one that I seek answers for in this final chapter, is why would a public sector pension company that boasts being a reliable, long-term landlord, resort to displacing its working-class tenants, many of whom worked in the public sector? Keva had developed the block of 56 affordable apartments in the central working-class neighbourhood of Sörnäinen in 1999. ARA had helped finance the construction by subsidising the interest payments on Keva's construction loan – provided that Keva would rent the units out affordably, below market rent. During the last two decades, Sörnäinen has undergone noticeable, accelerating changes, not least in real estate values. In fact, the greatest increase in housing prices in Helsinki during the past ten years has happened in Sörnäinen. The hikes in rent have been just as phenomenal. In 2015 the average rent in the neighbourhood was 17 euros per square metre. Only four years later it was 24 euros per square metre (Marttinen 2019). Considering these changes, coupled with the overall retrenchment of social housing described in the previous chapter, it is safe to say that the need for affordable social housing in this heavily gentrifying neighbourhood has only been accentuated.

The question why a non-profit housing company would terminate the contracts with its working-class tenants must be unpacked by explaining the historical transformation of non-profit companies, their new operational logic and their role within the Finnish system of housing provision. In this chapter I do this in three parts. First, I return to the general problem of housing commodification mentioned in the opening to the third part of the book. I articulate and connect the commodification of social housing and displacement using David Harvey's (2003) concept of accumulation by dispossession (ABD) and emphasise the role of the state in this process. A brief overview of well-known international experiences of privatisation of social and public housing illustrates how ABD in housing violently undermines the residential well-being of working-class and marginalised households. Second, I discuss the transformation of Finnish non-profit housing companies into for-profit, institutional landlords. These landlords no longer have an interest in developing social housing and instead are exercising an all-out stock transfer of state-subsidised units into market commodities. I will argue that the contemporary project of social housing privatisation – a project best understood as a case of ABD – is abetted by the inconsistent, sporadic and precarious nature of Finnish state housing policy that refuses to tackle housing commodification. I thus bring the state into the analysis of ABD. Third, I introduce Keva, the non-profit housing company and discuss the changes in its operations as a landlord and how these changes lead to the displacement of Keva's tenants. In the fourth and final part of the chapter, I illustrate the consequences of housing commodification for urban equality through interviews with Sara and representatives of three other households that Keva displaced before renting out their affordable homes with the market rent.

Public housing privatisation as accumulation by dispossession

Marx's concept of primitive or original accumulation describes an essential process in the birth of capitalism. It entailed the enclosure of common land and the dispossession of peasants from their traditional livelihoods and their eventual proletarianisation. These events amounted to nothing less than a historical transformation in social relations in which the producer is divorced from the means of production, while the social means of subsistence are transformed into capital, and the producer is left with nothing to sell but their labour. According to Marx (1990/1867), from this "original sin dates the poverty of the great majority who, despite all their labour, have up to now nothing to sell but themselves, and the wealth of the few that increases constantly, although they have long ceased to work" (873). The notion of accumulation by dispossession is David Harvey's recalibration of primitive accumulation, a process he argues essentially to never have ended. Instead, labour continues to be the subject of insidious arrangements of dispossession that open new spheres for capital accumulation. Accumulation must be understood not only as a feature of an early "primitive" stage of capitalism but an ongoing process under the complexities of advanced capitalism (Harvey 2003).

ABD, however, is being applied to discuss not only the continuous divorcing of labour from the means of production, but a wide array of contemporary enclosures, privatisations and appropriations of collective and common resources in order to spur accumulation. Here, "privatization, in myriad forms, is one of the crucial ways in which capitalists have been able to 'actively manufacture' new realms for proletarianization and private appropriation of public property, even within the global core" (Harvey 2003, 141). One of these myriad forms and events reoccurring in the capitalist city is the appropriation of working-class residential space and its tearing open as a frontier of accumulation. And gentrification, or the eviction of working-class tenants and the commodification of their partly de-commodified, affordable homes in order to maximise land rent, is a classic example. Historically perhaps the most widely known housing privatisation programme in Europe is the right-to-buy policy in the UK discussed in the preceding chapter. Thanks to this policy introduced in the late 1980s, to this day housing associations in the UK are known to stimulate homeownership via social housing privatisation (Van Gent 2010). In the process of commodifying the social housing stock, many vibrant working-class communities have been displaced as housing estates have become utterly gentrified (Watt 2009).

Housing associations are important stimulators of gentrification also in the Netherlands (Teernstra and Van Gent 2012). There, non-profit housing associations turned into private companies as early as 1995 and were able to generate great profit by selling off social housing, converting social housing stock vital for the residential wellbeing of the working class into privately rented housing and promoting the constructing of owner-occupied housing. In Amsterdam, for instance, the privatisation of social housing is concentrated in inner city neighbourhoods where ongoing gentrification processes are greatly intensified. Hochstenbach (2017, 399) in his research on the Amsterdam case argues that such transformations must be analysed indeed by illustrating the policy context and writes:

> local policies increasingly focus on catering to the preferences of middle-class households, while welfare state restructuring and national austerity measures push policies that cut back on social rental housing. Thus [. . .] the demise of social rent has accelerated under conditions of market-oriented housing restructuring, and increasingly occurs in high demand neighbourhoods where current housing policies push gentrification.

In Sweden, housing associations invite residents to collectively buy their social housing units in old working-class neighbourhoods. As apartments thus enter the market fully commodified allowing for wealth accumulation, the share of social housing has gone down in said neighbourhoods, leaving less and less chances for lower income households to find housing there in the future (Andersson and Turner 2014).

Such processes raise questions about housing on the one hand as a basic need and social right – essentially, urban residents' right to stay put in their homes and neighbourhoods – and as an increasingly liquid asset used for speculative purposes on the other. Yrigoy (2020) has studied the evictions of a staggering

600,000 families in Spain in the aftermath of the financial crisis and housing market crash. Articulating the process via ABD, Yrigoy insightfully emphasises the role of the state in the analysis. ABD is a solution to the problem of over-accumulation faced by capital. Accumulated capital needs a place to be invested. So, for example, by releasing assets from regulation, the state can unlock new frontiers of investment and accumulation. For urban scholars what is of relevance is the increasing use of the built environment, particularly working-class residential space and housing as loci of intensifying accumulation.

Indeed, the state is often mentioned as a central dynamic in not only allowing for, but orchestrating capital accumulation. But how exactly it does this, what state instruments are used (and not used), should also be illustrated. An important research gap in ABD literature is identified by Levien, who suggested that the role of the state in dispossession has remained under-studied (Levien 2013). In the next section, I explore this in the case of the transforming Finnish system of housing provision. A second important research gap which I address is indicated by Hodkinson and Essen (2015), who argue that "there remains little sense of how the theorised predations of accumulation materialise on the ground as forms and experiences of dispossession in the everyday places and lives of ordinary people – how have they experienced dispossession?" Instead, we face a "neglect of how dispossession is experienced on the ground (Hodkinson and Essen 2015, 73–4). I address this in the final part of the chapter when I turn to analysing interviews with displaced tenants.

The roll-back of the social rental housing sector

A restructuring of housing policy and reorganisation of housing provision, reminiscent of the abovementioned cases from the UK, Sweden and Netherlands, is underway in Finland. But we are only beginning to understand the consequences this has for urban inequality, and housing scholars working on Finland must pay close attention to the process. Since 1949 over one million state subsidised apartments have been built in Finland. 445,000 are owner occupied, 555,000 are rentals and roughly 50,000 are so-called intermediary tenures, rental units that in time will turn owner-occupied (Ahola 2021). All of these are or have been subject to some form of regulation, whether regarding their allocation, tenant selection or rent. Social rental housing is developed by private developers, municipalities and non-profit companies. First, private developers are usually required to include some social housing in their projects if they wish to lease land from the city. Between 2018 and 2020 the biggest private developers built 44 per cent of all ARA subsidised housing in Helsinki. However, less than half of these were normal rental housing for working-class households and the majority of their projects were housing for special groups and intermediate forms of housing for the middle-class (Ahola 2021). Second, municipalities are significant developers of social housing and they play an important role in ensuring that some housing is provided below market rent. For instance the Helsinki municipal housing company Heka, the biggest landlord in Finland, owns and operates some 50,000 units and rents them out considerably below the market rent. In 2019 in Helsinki the average monthly rent per square metre in private rental units was €20.52, while in Heka's units it was €11.68.

Finally, the so-called non-profits. There are roughly 600 non-profits who develop and provide social housing in Finland. These can be divided into two groups. The first are small, locally based non-profit organisations founded to defend the rights of an interest group such as the elderly or the disabled, and that have at some point also applied for the right to provide so-called sheltered housing.[1] According to the Finnish Environmental Administration,[2] sheltered housing is intended for people who need help in their everyday lives but who do not require institutional care. Sheltered housing covers both the apartment and the related services. In general, these organisations are interested in providing housing as use values for their residents, without an interest in speculating or seeking to maximise land rent. Their role in overall housing provision is marginal. The same cannot be said for the second group under the non-profit developer category. The second group of "non-profit" companies consists of large housing developers that were granted non-profit corporation status and are eligible for state subsidies. The four biggest non-profit corporations – Avara, Sato, TA, and VVO – were all established between 1940 and 1970, mainly by labour unions, as either cooperatives or social housing corporations intended to solve the housing crises of those periods and develop affordable social rental housing, especially in cities.

The state assists the construction of social housing by subsidising the interest payments on construction loans for non-profit companies. Concerning rental units in particular, statutory limitations apply to their use and handover as determined in the Act on Interest Subsidy for Rental Housing Loans and Right of Occupancy (2001). This act demands that the rent must be costs based and affordable, i.e., below the market rent, and the developer may generate only moderate profits for its shareholders. The purpose of these limitations according to ARA is to keep the homes in rental use for a sufficient period of time and to maintain their cost at a reasonable level.[3] The rent stabilisation is lifted after a period set by ARA – as long as the developer has paid off the construction loan – after which the owner may discharge the houses into the market as commodities (Ruonavaara 2005, 2017). The stabilisation period varies. The "sufficient period" has commonly been set at 40 years for normal rental homes. However, there have even been attempts to attract developers back into social housing production by shortening the rent stabilisation periods. In 2016 a short-term interest subsidy with merely a 10-year regulation period was introduced by ARA.

Two important changes have taken place since the establishment of the non-profit developers. First, even the short-term subsidy no longer attracts developers to build social housing to the extent that they used to. The role of state financing in housing has waxed and waned since the 1980s. As the financial markets were liberated in the 1980s the share of private investment in housing development started to grow. In 1993 the housing committee was discontinued, and housing finance was moved to ARA. ARA no longer received funds for construction loans directly from the state budget. Instead, it would receive funds from amortisations of outstanding loans and by securitising and selling its loans on to third parties, typically overseas investors (Tulla 1999). After the early 1990s recession, private housing finance was lacking and ARA subsidies maintained the construction sector. However, the potential for profits in the private rental sector soon became more attractive for developers and shareholders as the rent controls were removed in the early 90s (Kettunen and Ruonavaara 2015). By the late 90s there was again plenty of private construction finance to go around, with attractive loan-to-value ratios and no strings – like rent stabilisation – attached. By the year 2000 it had become clear that the numbers of new production of affordable rental housing by these so-called non-profit companies had significantly decreased.[4] Since then the production of state subsidised rental housing has been on the decline, only making up some 15 per cent of total volume, focusing on housing for special needs groups (Ahola 2019).

Second, by around 2010 many of the non-profit developers had paid off their old interest subsidised construction loans and were now free to rent their stock of old apartments on the private market. The annual number of deregulated units varies greatly, as the units built and the terms of the loans have also varied. In the 1970s some 30,000 units were developed per year, but in the mid-2000s the number dropped to under 5,000. Rents in many of the seventies-built units have now been deregulated. Meanwhile, the key developers of social housing have radically changed their business strategy by turning into listed companies. The main task of these companies today is to redevelop their old units of affordable rental housing in growth centres and rent the units out to more affluent, middle-class tenants. They are also focusing their development of new housing on private rentals. The building of new social housing does not keep up with the number of older units that are released from rent controls. Between the years 2000 and 2017 the shares of non-profit units in Turku and Tampere went down 12 and 17 per cent respectively. In the three biggest cities of the HMA, Helsinki and Vantaa have seen a three and four per cent respective decrease during this period, while in Espoo the share grew by one per cent. Meanwhile, the shares of private rental housing units out of these cities' rental stocks have increased tremendously. The shares have gone up by 30 per cent in Helsinki, 84 per cent in Espoo, 93 per cent in Vantaa, 82 per cent in Tampere, and by 43 per cent in Turku (ARA 2019). In the Helsinki metropolitan region, some 22,000 apartments altogether will be freed from rent stabilisation in the next decade. Researchers must keep a close eye on the process, as it is highly probable that a great deal of these units will be fully commodified.

What we are witnessing is nothing less than a stock-transfer of old social rental housing units to the housing market. Since the year 2000 some 140,000 housing units have been freed from restrictions. In relation to the population, the share of affordable rental units has gone down the most in large cities. Predicting the fate of social rental housing, housing scholar Juntto (1992, 54) wrote decades ago:

> [r]ental flats are securely preserved as a non-profit housing stock only for the duration of the state loan. However, these loans have been shortened. Between 1949 and 1971 the loan time was 45 years, then it was shortened to 25–27 years. If the Government does not reach an agreement of prolongation of the restriction times, there is a risk that an essential part of the already insufficient stock of social housing will be sold in the 1990s.

Currently, only less than 13 per cent of Finnish housing stock is so-called ARA housing stock and subject to use and transfer restrictions. The number of regular ARA rental apartments has decreased significantly in the 2010s, due to the number of properties exempted from restrictions being greater than new production (Hietala et al. 2021).

Framing these changes with the notion of ABD, three important matters need to be emphasised. First, social housing stock is privatised and its working-class tenants dispossessed of affordable homes to spur the potential to make profits through housing. Meanwhile, any residents that possibly can are urged to arrange their housing on the private market, financed either by bank credit or state housing allowances, which permit finance institutions and landlords to expand capital accumulation and wealth extraction. This is ABD in action. And second, the role of ARA, the state housing finance institute, is being intentionally rolled back. It was state housing finance that enabled statutory limitations on the use and costs of housing, both of which were essential for the residential well-being of working-class tenants. But because of the short-term nature of the subsidy, they functioned as state assistance in capital accumulation rather than protection of the well-being of tenants. Now, developers too would rather seek credit-backed financing for their private housing projects. As Harvey (2003) writes of this process of ABD,

> the power of the state is frequently used to force such processes through even against popular will. The rolling back of regulatory frameworks designed to protect labour and the environment from degradation has entailed a loss of rights [. . .] The umbilical cord that ties together accumulation by dispossession and expanded reproduction is that given by finance capital and the institutions of credit, backed, as ever, by state powers. (Harvey 2003, 148–52)

Finally, as relates to the accumulation project, the third thing to highlight is the question of who owns the old non-profit housing companies. Perhaps the most well-known of the above-mentioned developers of subsidised housing that completely turned around its operations is the housing co-operative VVO. VVO was established in 1969 to alleviate the housing shortage as Finland was seeing unprecedented urbanisation. It was started by a construction company called Haka, originally owned by labour movement organisations and progressive co-operatives. In the 2000s several pension companies bought VVO. And in 2015 VVO decided to begin selling and renting on the market its stock of formerly rent stabilised units, turning a great profit from the apartments that had been developed with inexpensive state loans. In 2017 VVO changed its name to Kojamo, floated its shares on the market, and it now operates as Finland's biggest private real estate investment company. The majority ownership of Kojamo is shared between numerous Finnish labour unions. On the one hand, labour union bosses have been under heavy criticism for collecting handsome bonuses from Kojamo while the working-class union members struggle with hiking rents. On the other hand, the state-driven roll-back of social housing – retrenching of subsidised housing into a social service discussed at length in the previous chapter – means that unions no longer view it as their task to provide social housing, as it is intended for the unemployed and other special groups. The workers' housing question is primarily to be addressed on the housing market and logically that is where the non-profits have switched their operations.

Kojamo alone owns 147 apartment buildings across Helsinki. A search of the company's listings in August 2022 shows that in Kallio, Sörnäinen and the adjacent new Kalasatama development area, it owns 16 apartment buildings with altogether 1,079 rental apartments (Kojamo 2022). Today, it rents these out under its 'Lumo-houses' consumer brand. The real estate holdings of Kojamo used to consist of affordable social rental housing for the working class. Now the company's sole interest is to make great profits for its shareholders by privatising the stock, renting it on the market and investing in new private housing projects to spur further accumulation. A third of the shares in Kojamo are owned by overseas investors. This is a trend across European cities where in recent decades international finance capital has been recycled through the built environment (Rolnik 2013, 1059). Kojamo's biggest individual shareholders are the Swedish real estate investment company Heimstaden Bostad, and Finnish pension companies Ilmarinen and Varma.

The role of pension companies in the Finnish housing regime is curious. The very origins of Finland's pension system can be traced back to an arrangement called *syytinki*, a type of life annuity. *Syytinki* guaranteed the continued use right to a property for its original owner even after property ownership was transferred. This centuries-old system was basically a guarantee of the right to stay put for a senior person even after they sold their house and land or transferred its ownership to their descendants (Hedman 2022). Today, pension providers such as those investing in the operations of Kojamo described above, are portfolio-managing real estate investors and landlords who have little interest in tenants' right to stay put, but a great interest in using real estate assets to maximise land rent. Finland's regime of housing finance is increasingly dependent on actors whose primary functions are something altogether different from housing provision and for whom real estate ownership is merely an auxiliary instrument to fund those primary activities such as investing pensions profitably. The example I use in the rest of the chapter is Keva, the public sector employees' pension company that used to also operate as a non-profit housing company.

Keva

Keva administers the pensions of local government, state, Evangelical Lutheran Church and National Social Insurance Institute employees in Finland. Formerly known as the Local Government Pension Institution, Keva is responsible for the pensions of 1.3 million workers and is Finland's largest pension provider. It is an independent body governed by public law and its operations are based on the Public Sector Pension Act and the Keva Act. Keva is supervised by the Ministry of Finance, the Financial Supervisory Authority, and the National Audit Office of Finland. What has driven this public sector workers' pension provider and affordable housing provider to transfer its affordable units to the market? Following the onslaught of neoliberal ideology in Finland in the 1990s, the idea that the public sector should also make use of the perceived advantages of the institutional investment management industry gained popularity. These principles were ultimately ingrained in the legislation on public pensions. And as Finland joined the EU in 1995, investment opportunities grew and pensions savings could now be mobilised as interest-bearing capital to be circulated in the international market, including the financialised real estate market. A pension fund with a real estate portfolio could now invest not merely in domestic properties, but much more easily also in international REITs and real estate funds. The former is called direct investment and it involves ownership of the land and its improvements. The profit on investment is made in land rent. The latter is known as indirect real estate investment. The profit is made in the form of derivative rents where land is the underlying asset (Haila 2016). The job of real estate portfolio managers is to explore direct and indirect real estate investment opportunities and find the most lucrative option for pension instalments.

Keva's pension fund is ruled by an act. According to the Public Sector Pension Act, Chapter 9, §135, the pension instalments are to be partly transferred into a fund, from which Keva invests them to be responsible over the "credibility, profitability, monetisation and diversification of the portfolio". An increasingly credible and profitable area of investment for pension companies is real estate and real estate finance. The Act on Keva (66/2016) lays down that "Keva, in its capacity of managing local government pension funds, is a long-term investor and as such it must ensure the security of and return on investments". Keva is, then, by law required to invest the pension payments of its clients in ways that secure long-term returns on those investments. The pension liability covered by Keva extends decades ahead. In 2019 the total market value of Keva's investments was €56 billion. Keva's real estate portfolio consists of direct investments in Finnish and Nordic real estate and real estate shares as well as indirect investments in Finnish and foreign real estate funds. Its real estate funds account for 25 per cent of real estate investments. The market value of Keva's real estate and real estate shares at the end of 2019 was €37 billion, while it possesses a total lettable area of around 870,000m^2. At that time, there were some 4,200 leases in place generating a net rental income of €103 million (Keva 2019).

Keva has published two separate documents that outline its investment principles, titled *Keva Investment Beliefs* and *Keva Responsible Investment Beliefs*. The former document is in essence a justification for why Keva should take on investment risks as the objective of its investment fund is to generate investment returns to long-term pension liabilities under the Act on Keva. Although the latter document talks about environmental, social and governance (ESG) criteria in investments, a careful reading of the documents reveals that in truth they are also mainly used to assess investment risks, not to guide investments based on environmental and social targets. The document states that the "starting point to Keva's definition of responsible investment is its basic task to manage its cross-generational pension liability [. . .] ESG criteria for investments create a framework for assessing long-term risks and opportunities" (Keva, 2017). Keva's Portfolio Manager is responsible for investing the pension's savings of Finnish public sector employees as lucratively as possible. Because residential real estate is an increasingly lucrative investment opportunity, Keva now tends to look at its real estate portfolio also in a new light. It is no longer first and foremost an affordable rental housing provider. Instead, it will assess how to put the affordable rental housing it manages to its highest and best use.

But would not having their pensions invested in real estate and stocks and shares the world over make workers the majority shareowners in many companies, also real estate? As real estate is now an ultimate object of investment for public sector workers' pension funds, are those workers great real estate owners? This arrangement prompted Drucker (1976) to declare "pension fund socialism" in the United States as in his analysis it was working-class shareholders who operated and owned companies. Drucker's claim was but an exercise in hyperbole. As Clark points out, what we are rather witnessing is a "pension fund capitalism" which "is a further stage in the evolution of capitalism rather than a profound break with the past" (Clark 1998, 139). Pension funds are dependent on the performance of markets for capital accumulation. As Clark (Ibid.) continues:

> Their assets are the product of the employment relation, and agency relationships with the investment management industry. The concentration of financial assets in pension funds coupled with the fact that trustees and their investment advisers have considerable autonomy from plan beneficiaries is analogous to the separation of ownership from control characteristic of modern corporations.

For the very same reason, workers are in no way in control of the real estate their pensions are invested in. They are controlled by professional portfolio managers. The people whose pension payments are invested in real estate are utterly detached from the actual use decisions regarding that real estate.

What is more, from the perspective of the working-class, there is a painful paradox in the actions of companies such as Keva. The lucrative investment of one worker's pensions in residential real estate may come to mean the dispossession of another worker from their affordable home. While attempting to invest the pension savings of an ageing working-class profitably, in its rent maximising real estate operations Keva comes to hurt that very same faction of labour. There is the danger, as Rolnik notes, that the "crucial participation of workers' pension funds in the financialization of housing [is] also central in breaking the political coalitions which sustained the old welfare state" (2013, 1064). Indeed, new insidious forms of ABD are eroding any remnants of the notion of a universal housing policy characteristic of the Nordic welfare state. At the same time it might be suggested that the dispossession of the working class from their affordable homes and the investment of workers' pensions in real estate are part and parcel of the disintegration of workers' class consciousness, pitting the interests of workers as tenants and workers as pensioners against one another. From the perspective of trying to solve urban inequality and promote housing justice, this begs the question, should housing be an investment vehicle for companies and organisations that clearly are not housing providers first and foremost? And should the state give such agents short term subsidies that secure affordability only temporarily? The experiences of displaced tenants, which I turn to next, provide answers.

Locking out use values in Sörnäinen

One of the reasons displacement is so complex to study is that from an empirical standpoint it is often challenging to detect. Unless we are talking about an all-out, planned demolition of a social housing estate, "slum clearance", or other comparable large-scale and visible displacement, there are few tell-tale signs of where urban displacement might happen next. Events such as that which transpired in Sörnäinen are difficult to anticipate. Where people have been displaced, often no indicators of their presence remain since by definition the displaced no longer live in their previous home (Atkinson 2000; Watt 2009). The process of displacement has then been described as both invisible and silent. First, urban displacements are invisible as they tend to go uncounted by state officials. There are no national statistics tallying up the displaced. Clark (2011, 2) suggests that the reluctance to register instances of displacement is "rooted in the condition that these acts of violence are commonly sanctioned by the state and inflicted upon undesired minorities and marginalied low-income communities". This invisibility is aggravated by the disregard with which mainstream urban research treats the experiences of the displaced. This is part of a wider neglect of the working class, which contemporary research tends to simply avert its eyes from. Instead, mainstream urban research (including studies on gentrification) choose to be blind to working-class displacement and focus their sights on other matters, such as the housing preferences of the middle classes or the positive effects of urban renewal (Wacquant 2009).

Second, while the precarious housing situations of displaced people exist outside official registers, the lack of public interest and attention in their lives is muted. Very little is written or talked about regarding housing displacement in the media in Finland. Recently, mainstream commentaries regarding housing issues in Helsinki for instance have focused on how Helsinki has offered a leading example of doing away with street homelessness, or how well housing production targets are being met. This self-congratulatory narrative has worked to crowd out any discussion of how many people are annually forced to leave their homes due to rising housing costs, caused in no small part by stock transfer and housing commodification. Finally, those rare times when someone does attempt to track them down, displaced people are, understandably, not necessarily eager to be interviewed about their experiences (Baeten et al. 2017). Displaced people may also keep silent and fear protesting displacement as resistance poses many risks and is taxing on personal resources. In the neighbourhood of Sörnäinen there are entire blocks of flats that have been converted and rented out to new tenants. But it is difficult if not impossible to verify the scale, details and experiences of displacement post-event – the displaced are long gone. Having said this, when I caught wind of the termination of rental contracts by Keva I knew I had to act fast if I was to interview people living in the building. In my attempts to contact Keva's former tenants in Sörnäinen for interview purposes, I received answers from four households who then willingly shared their painful stories of displacement. Despite the small number of replies, these interviews work as a most important heuristic device and shed light on the phenomenological, experienced aspect of encountering the violence of dispossession (see Elliot-Cooper et al. 2020).

In 1999 Keva built a rental apartment building with state subsidies in the neighbourhood of Sörnäinen. For 20 years it provided social housing in 56 units for working-class households. During this time residents settled in and grew attached to the neighbourhood, started families, built friendships, enrolled their children in local schools and hobbies, got used to the local services and the short commuting times for those working in the inner city. As market rent in the area gradually climbed, Keva continued to offer much-needed, rent stabilised and affordable housing in the neighbourhood. Paula, a university student, and her partner had been tenants in the building since 2014. Their child was born when they lived in Sörnäinen. Paula talked about the relevance of the neighbourhood and community for her family. It was where they had made their home, as Paula discussed:

> There were people that invited us along for events when we moved in and after that we were basically part of the community of families. You felt safe to leave your kids to play outside, there was always an adult around. We organised birth-day parties for kids in the building together and visited. We spent midsummers together. There were people from very different backgrounds. But maybe more like hairdressers, social workers. People working in local organisations. Couples where one of them might be unemployed.

On paper, Keva appears to appreciate such residential communities. It organises workshops with tenants with the aim of building "community spirit" and "tenant participation in the development of their housing".[5] A document titled *Responsible Investment Beliefs* presents some of the corporate social responsibility elements that steer Keva's investments. The document states for instance that Keva is "continuously stepping up integration of the ESG perspective with regard both to the assets we manage ourselves and those where management is outsourced [. . .] there will also be *a wider benefit from the operation for communities*, the environment and financially via the more sustainable practices of the entity invested in" (Keva 2017, author's emphasis). But after the end of rent stabilisation period, and the increase in the potential rent to be made through housing in Sörnäinen, it is quite clear that Keva became wholly indifferent to the community spirit of its tenants and lucrative investment beliefs were prioritised over any semblance of social responsibility.

The suggestion that Keva would be open to tenant participation in the development of its housing was also disrobed for the utter fabrication that it was. In its eviction letter to tenants, Keva did not mention the end of rent stabilisation, but justified its decision by courtyard renovations during which the building would be uninhabitable. However, the tenants had been requesting the courtyard renovation for years, a major concern being that it had become hazardous for children to play in the yard due to poor maintenance. And for years, Keva had neglected their requests and participation, refusing to improve the yard for the current tenants. Paula explained:

> During the last year in particular, the management and maintenance did not work that well. They wouldn't take care of the repairs. The courtyard was in a poor shape. It felt negligent on their part. We asked for them to fix the courtyard.

For two years they told us they would do it, but then they always backtracked. The swing-set was in a bad shape. This kid was on the swing, and I told him we should try to get a new one. The kid replied and said "don't, they will just take the old one away". And he was right, they eventually did, just took it, and never replaced it!

Contrary to its responsible investment beliefs, in Sörnäinen Keva failed to "step up in integrating social responsibility in managing its asset" and failed to "benefit the community" that tenants had built. Instead, the potential rent to be made by disintegrating the community and renting the units on the market to boost the profit on pension investments was too attractive. It was only when Keva assessed that it was now profitable to close the rent gap by making a small injection of capital in maintenance that the company decided to carry out the yard renovation, ultimately to the displacement of the original residents. Sara's partner Matti, a writer, described his frustration, ending with a figure of speech that even when translated from Finnish conveys well his view of Keva's speculative action:

> The eviction notice said the reason was courtyard renovation. Then later they informed us that the flats were being done up and they needed to get people out. But no official reason. The flat we lived in was in its original condition, it was in an unbelievably good condition. That's when we suspected that maybe the 20-year rent control was ending. And it was exactly so! They had been shining their shoe all along, just waiting to kick us out!

In Germany, a similar system of short-term state housing finance was used in the past, and Balmer and Bernet (2015) appropriately characterise it as "social housing as temporary occupation". They write "considering that the subsidized units are destined from the outset to revert into regular, commercially rented homes in this type of arrangement, it offers at best a temporary barrier to the commodification of housing, while breeding its own brand of speculation" (Balmer and Bernet, 2015, 184–5). While, according to Balmer and Bernet (2015), the short-term subsidy system was criticised for corruption and ineffectiveness and terminated in 2001 in Germany, the policy continues to be used in Finland. ARA explains that the objective of the short-term interest subsidy, where developers are bound by only ten-year restrictions, is "to increase affordable housing production in areas that have long-term demand for rental-housing. The financing method supports the possibilities of low- and middle-income households to find affordable housing solutions especially in urban growth centres."[6] However, it is debatable whether ten years meets the definition of "long-term". In this time residents will have had enough time to settle down and make the house a home, build a life in the area. The short-term interest subsidy allows the units to be released to the market as private rental units. In Keva's case, it led to the termination of contracts and displacement of residents.

One question raised by the tenants, like Matti above, concerned the justification of the displacement with renovations. Polanska and Richard (2019, 2021) have used the concept of "renovictions" to discuss renovations as a way of justifying evictions. In their work on the large-scale renovation of the Swedish social housing stock built during the Million Programme, Polanska and Richard (2019) show how behind the renovations and evictions are housing associations looking to maximise land rent. They write how "emotions and lived experiences of renovation processes are systematically being excluded from the public debate on housing and Swedish housing policy" (Polanska and Richard 2019, 143). Keva's justification for the termination of rental contracts was that it would be impossible to live in the building during renovations. This was also what the Portfolio Manager referred to in their short refusal to my request for an interview. But the interviewees felt that Keva's justification was poor and did not warrant the termination of contracts. Kirsi, a nurse by occupation and working two shifts, had lived in the building with her partner for 12 years. She talked about how Keva had sent inspectors to see about the condition of the apartment but found little to call for actual renovations. She explained how her neighbours had similar experiences:

> We had a hunch that something was going on when they came around to inspect the bathrooms. They had a peek in from the door and took a few photos. There was nothing wrong with our bathroom. No need for renovations. And neither did anyone else in the apartments in our stairwell! They came and inspected the flats; they checked every corner. But if they are going to do big renovations, why would they do that? Really makes you think.

The purpose for inspections might have been that Keva had in fact been using the apartments as short-term rentals before the beginning of renovations.[7] It wanted to profit from the end of the regulation period as soon as it was possible, getting rid of old tenants just to get three months of market rent out of short-term tenants before beginning the renovations. Although impossible to verify as Keva's representatives refused to be interviewed, it is likely that the check-ups were done to see which apartments were ready for short-term tenants to move in quickly. After the renovations the apartments would be rented out again with market rent, which today in gentrifying Sörnäinen is the highest in the city (Statistics Finland 2021). The interviews portray a landlord uninterested in the emotions and lived realities of its tenants. Keva would only make improvements on the property once it became clear that higher rent could be extracted. Keva's interest in renovating the building overlaps with being freed from rent control. Keva saw the potential for profit with a small injection of money into refurbishment and renovation as substantial, as market rent in the gentrifying area keeps on climbing. In the framework of the rent gap theory, the difference between actual and potential land rent had grown substantially (Smith 1979). Of course, it is impossible to say whether Keva would have kept the units as social housing had the neighbourhood not been undergoing gentrification. But the potential of tapping into the value increase of the neighbourhood made Keva ditch any remaining interest in the provision of affordable housing.

Newman and Wyly (2006) argue that "those who are forced to leave gentrifying neighbourhoods are torn from rich local social networks of information and cooperation (the 'social capital' much beloved by policy-makers)" (51). Kirsi discussed how the termination of rental agreements and a forcible uprooting from her home and community affected her daily life. Much of the social capital she might have acquired in Sörnäinen disappeared along with her lease agreement. She had to move out of Helsinki, her hometown, to Vantaa, a city sharing a border with Helsinki to the north-east, to find suitable housing that she could afford:

> I was taking out the recycling when the neighbour came to talk and asked if I already received the letter. I said, what letter? She told me they are terminating everyone's rental agreement. That's how I heard about it first. And then I of course did receive the letter. They gave six months' notice. I moved to Vantaa, but the rent is higher. The commute to work is much longer. I lived in Helsinki for 30 years, so it has taken getting used to.

Previous research of similar cases in Sweden discusses how tenants whose displacement from affordable housing was justified by renovations tended to be forced to move to neighbourhoods in which rents were higher, meaning that they would come to depend on state housing benefits. But even though the rents were higher, tenants would move to neighbourhoods where households had lower average income levels and poorer educational outcomes, implying a link between housing dispossession and segregation (Baeten et al. 2017). Amidst policy-accentuated spatial reshuffling of people that sees the working-class displaced and increasingly pushed out of and excluded from central urban areas, policy narratives that promise to prevent segregation and improve social mix come off as little else than hot air. Paula discussed the effects of community displacement on individuals and explained "many have been completely devastated by this. It was their home, their kids were in schools close by, the children might have lived there their whole lives. Think about what it does to friendships and everything like that."

Coupled with Keva's complete disregard for people's attachment to place illustrated by Paula's comment above, another particularly painful aspect of the displacements in Sörnäinen was how many of the tenants were completely blindsided by Keva's actions. They had lived under the impression that a public sector institution would be a reliable landlord. The tenants explained how they had been under the impression that Keva would provide them with long term, predictable tenancy. A major part of the shock of being displaced, as expressed by interviewees, was due to this breach of the trust they had placed in Keva.

The company's aggressive manoeuvre was unfathomable. Sara had lived in the building for 15 years. Matti had moved in with her a few years ago. For 50-year-old Sara, it was the longest period she had lived in the same address. As they explained:

> Sara: "We thought Keva was a reliable landlord, that they would never have a reason for this kind of speculation. Even their marketing slogan is something like 'safe housing for everyone'. . . ."
> Matti: "Yeah, they brag about being this reliable landlord!"

The issue was also raised by Tanja, who works at a vocational school. She was one of the first tenants to move into the building when it was finished in 1999. Prior to Sörnäinen, she lived in the city centre, renting from a private landlord. Tanja explained how she had already once experienced losing her home abruptly, as the private landlord had suddenly decided to move into the apartment and terminated the rental contract with Tanja. With Keva as landlord, she thought she was safe from similar experiences being repeated:

> I always felt like it was my own home. That no-one would push me out of there. I had settled there. These kinds of situations where you don't have ownership and you can be so easily let go; it shakes up your sense of basic security. I hope to never experience this again.

The very moment of displacement is an obvious major experience of disruption. However, it can also profoundly transform one's sense of security over their place in the city in the long term. Stabrowski (2014) suggests that displacement may lead to "a radical reduction of place-making ability for low-income, working-class, and minority residents" (798). As capitalism colonises working-class life-worlds, individuals and communities are subjected also to the speculative temporality of capitalism. Displaced individuals are left uncertain about settling down again. What if I make my home elsewhere and am driven out yet again? Giddens (1984, 375) wrote about the notion of ontological security as a "confidence or trust that the natural and social worlds are as they appear to be, including the basic existential parameters of self and social identity".

And more recently the concept of housing precarity has been used to explore uncertainties in residential experiences (Clair et al. 2018; Listerborn 2021; Waldron 2021). These recent discussions reflect what Peter Marcuse (1985) in his classic work on the different forms of housing displacement called displacement pressure, including the various uncertainties and anxieties that residents will experience. As profit increasingly drives urban development, the displacement pressure felt by residents grows, leading to a growing sense of uncertainty in one's residential prospects. My interviewees spoke of how they had begun to see themselves as much more vulnerable after the shock of having their trust in social housing broken. Kirsi pointed to the inadequacy of Finland's housing policy and the outrage of allowing working-class people to be displaced from their homes:

> I thought Keva was a stable and reliable landlord, that if I ever moved out it would be out of my own choice. This was a rude, shameless thing to do. We were all working people. How can you have housing policy like this in Finland? Not everyone can afford to own their place and I think renting is just as good an option as owning.

Paula shared a similar growing suspicion over housing security and recalled many in the building having placed their trust in Keva as a landlord:

> For a long time, we wanted to rent, we thought that renting is a good thing. And with Keva, I remember how many in the building would say that 'this is a trustworthy landlord because it's not some private landlord, you can live there for as long as you like'. There was no incentive for us to get on the housing market.

I discussed in the previous chapter the historical production in Finnish housing policy of a stark division between tenures. This division was now reflected in how interviewees considered owner occupiers to be much more protected from displacement than social housing tenants. But they also questioned why social renting should not provide similar protection, which especially in heavily gentrifying neighbourhoods would be essential to ensure the current residents' right to stay put. The tenants in Sörnäinen knew that their neighbourhood was undergoing transformation. They discussed how years ago the area had still been the inner city's hinterland and carried a dubious reputation. As Paula described "There are people who truly think that there shouldn't be affordable housing in Sörnäinen, this expensive area. It has even become socially acceptable to sell those units off."

One great injustice in gentrification is that when investments in the form of property renovations and infrastructure development are finally made in a disinvested neighbourhood, they are seldom done in favour of the original residents. When capital is looking to revalorise through investment in the built environment, it is looking to extract greater profit in the form of land rent. The tenants had grown very aware of the skyrocketing price of housing in the area, as Sara expressed: "It was a bit on the outskirts of the city when I moved in. Today it's really central. It became clear in recent years that we are living affordably comparing to the market rent in the area. I thought I'm never leaving here!"

When Keva invests indirectly in overseas real estate funds the yield comes from land titles securitised together with, for example, mortgages. Indirect investments operate in a global financial market, they are diversified and dispersed as far and wide as possible. The rent maximisation imperative behind indirect investment will accelerate very similar processes of land use change, gentrification, and displacement as direct investment did in Sörnäinen. However, as titles to landed assets are globally spread across owners and distances, it becomes increasingly difficult to tell from the outside who owns land and buildings. As forms of wealth, they are made invisible. The owners of securitised real estate titles and mortgages, and how much derivative rent is accumulated from property, cannot be immediately seen (Haila 2021). As indirect investments work at a distance, they also blur, disperse and rescale lines of responsibility (Fields 2017). With titles to land and buildings diversified among multiple investors, accountability for displacement, for instance, becomes increasingly difficult to locate. "This operation of distance" writes Fields "may represent an obstacle to the articulation of grievances and formulation of demands by urban movements" (Fields 2017, 6). In Sörnäinen, the culprit behind displacement was well known and the line of responsibility clear and visible. Was it then easier for tenants to voice grievances? Were demands formulated and presented to Keva? Hardly. Tenants in Sörnäinen did report having deliberated protesting the displacement. Eventually, however, all had felt that challenging Keva would have been too demanding on their personal resources. They were not, as Tanja discussed, willing to take such a big personal risk:

> I remember thinking whether it was possible to somehow let Keva know that I do not accept their reasons for the eviction. But then it would probably have ended up in a legal dispute and I did not want to spend all my resources on that.

Another daunting aspect that suppressed the voicing of grievances was the size of Keva. A large national institute and landlord, the tenants felt it was a lost cause to try to criticise Keva. Paula for example talked about how she understood Keva's actions to be legally in a grey area – renovations, she thought, are not a sufficient reason to terminate a rental contract – but that due to the size of the company, they knew that individuals would not mobilise to criticise them. She explained "they (termination of rental contracts) were legally questionable, but as a big actor they could use their position to their advantage, knowing that no-one would challenge them".

In their study of gentrification in New York, Newman and Wyly (2006) found that tenants under displacement pressures such as increased rents would not challenge landlords as they were afraid, for example, of harassment from the landlord. In Puerto Rico, residents resisting gentrification-led displacement were concerned that campaigning would make their ability to find alternative housing more difficult, particularly single mothers, for whom "the gendered trope of the irresponsible lone parent was projected by the press to legitimise demolitions (Arrigoitia, 2014)" (Elliot-Cooper et al. 2020, 501). And in Sweden, "conflicts between tenants and housing companies regarding renovations are solved in a special tribunal. Tenants are often aware of the minimal possibility of winning at the tribunal and thus fear ending up in court in the first place" (Polanska and Richardson 2019). In Helsinki's Sörnäinen, Keva's tenants feared that they might still one day depend on Keva as a rental housing provider and did not wish to cause conflict. Tanja, who already had once experienced displacement and the precariousness of housing as a tenant, discussed:

> The tenants did not want to make a fuss about the evictions. I think it might be about people not wanting to question Keva in a very visible, public way. There is a fear that you might have to apply for housing from them again at some point.

The individuals and families whose lives are disrupted by gentrification often lack political and economic power, resulting in a situation where they are not only easily exploited but unlikely to mobilise and resist local government encouraged gentrification (Beauregard 1986, 50). This is not to perpetuate a "damage-based" view of displaced tenants and their neighbourhoods or to belittle their efforts and struggle (Thurber et al. 2021). But without an infrastructure of dissent such as radical housing organisations that would take on the state-led deregulation of the social housing sector, it is hard for individual tenants to mobilise. Resistance is complex and uneven, and necessities such as work, or caring for family members and other dependants, can make protest risky and burdensome. There is also a lack of mobilisation from the civil society and organisations and urban displacement cases largely remain under the radar of mainstream debates in Finland. The case of Keva's evictions was reported in just one short newspaper article. Displacement in Helsinki remains largely invisible and silenced. As thousands of affordable units will transfer to the private market in the coming years, urban scholars and activists will need to pay close attention to how this affects the residential well-being and right to stay put of working-class tenants.

*

International research literature is rich with stories of evictions, displacement and other violent infringements of the right to housing experienced by urban dwellers. The perpetrators are found in private actors: greedy private landlords, private property owners, speculative private real estate investors and faceless, global rentier capitalists. This chapter told the story of a well-known public sector pension company and affordable housing provider, which not only failed to secure the right of 56 households to stay in their homes in the gentrifying, working-class neighbourhood of Sörnäinen in Helsinki, but adopted novel strategies to treat land as a financial asset and accumulate capital by dispossession. Because of the increasingly precarious and subdued or entrepreneurial roles of individual public agents – namely the impotence of the state housing finance and development centre ARA, the increasingly entrepreneurial real estate policy of the City of Helsinki and the rentier capitalist motives of the public sector pension company Keva, the transforming and retrenching public sector enabled the displacement of tenants in Sörnäinen.

The chapter highlighted the role of land in the displacement and criticised the short-term interest subsidy for its inbuilt, speculative element. Whether Keva was speculating on future appreciation already 20 years ago when it built the apartments with state subsidies is impossible to say. What became clear however in this study is that Keva has been waiting to unlock the value "trapped" within the rental property (Teresa 2016). As the two-decade restriction to keep the rent below market rent closed in 2019, Keva moved swiftly to get rid of the original tenants and rent out the flats with a market rent in the area. The outcome is nothing less than the accentuation of the ongoing class transformation of the neighbourhood as working-class tenants will not be able to afford the market rent in yet another block of flats. Keva's objective of a "sustainable community structure" was put to one side. In unlocking the exchange values, Keva simultaneously locked out the use values of its units for working-class residents. What the case shows is the inadequacy of Finnish housing policy to protect the right to stay put for people and communities. Instead, the multidimensional disruption of their life worlds was built into the very housing policy instrument of short-term subsidy.

Furthermore, the tenants had lived, many for the better part of two decades, under the impression that a non-profit housing company would be a reliable landlord. The landlord broke the trust of tenants, jeopardising their sense of predictability in their housing, or what sociologists have called ontological security (e.g., Giddens 1984). Finally, the interviewees discuss how they had internalised a notion that they should suppress any thoughts of dissent. Individual tenants found it daunting to mobilise their resources to protest the actions of a large institutional housing company and did not want to ruffle any feathers as they feared they might depend on Keva for housing in the future. Its actions now pit the interest of public sector pensioners against those of working-class tenants, breaking up old coalitions that maintain the Nordic welfare state. This suggests the hazards of giving such actors major responsibility over national housing provision. On basis of the judgement I made in the opening to this final part of the book that housing policy should be evaluated from the perspective of the dweller and the affordability and security of their housing, pension companies are not a socially sustainable way to finance housing. Such an approach seriously questions short-term subsidies as a housing policy instrument, as the risk of housing precarity and urban inequality are built into the policy. Finnish housing policy aims at ensuring the right to housing and social sustainability of residential space (ARA). Gentrification represents the type of urban inequality produced in the housing market that policy is supposed to tackle. And yet we find the short-term interest subsidy to allow affordable housing producer Keva to maximise potential rents and profit from gentrification by displacing tenants. As I suggested, the contemporary housing policy of a Nordic welfare state merely tries to navigate the housing market and apply cosmetic treatments to the market's inherent inequalities. The refusal to provide robust alternatives to the market and de-commodify housing are leaving housing policy itself precarious and unequipped to protect working-class residents' right to their homes, neighbourhoods and communities.

Notes

1. For example, Sininauhasäätiö, which provides sheltered housing and services for over 1,000 people affected by homelessness, drug abuse, mental health problems or who have a criminal history.
2. Housing for special groups (The Ministry of the Environment 23.10.2013).
3. Käyttö- ja luovutusrajoitukset (ARA 6.3.2023).
4. Sato, VVO ja YH ajavat alas valtion tukemaa vuokra-asuntojen tuotantoa pääkaupunk-iseudulla (HS 25.8.2000).
5. Asukastoiminta Kevan kodeissa (6.3.2023).
6. Lyhytaikaisen korkotuen ARA-vuokra-asunnot (ARA 13.2.2020).
7. Confirmed in Keva's listings during the time of conducting the research for this chapter.

Coda

This book explored the links between the changing means and goals of land and housing policies and urban inequality in Finland. As discussed at length in Chapter 2, research on urban inequality in Finland has been predominantly focused on the spatial differentiation or segregation of different groups. A descriptive research methodology drawing on the urban ecological notions of succession and concentration of income and ethnic groups, and on the neoclassical economic assumption of rational consumer choice as a guiding dynamic of the urban form, have left the task of explaining urban inequalities unattended. There has been a great deal of description of the differences between neighbourhoods and their residents. The use of unanalytical and even colloquial language to discuss these differences in research publications has been common. Meanwhile analyses of the structural dynamics of urban inequalities have been omitted. Applying Loïc Wacquant's (2008, 2009) sociology of territorial stigmatisation, I illustrated (Chapter 2) how segregation research has contributed to the symbolic devaluing of working-class and immigrant neighbourhoods. Segregation, I suggest, is merely one spatial expression of the deeper inequalities inherent to the urban process under capitalism. In this book I have argued in favour of embracing wider optics on the matter and I have used the concept of urban inequality to allow for discussing various processes of housing dispossession, territorial stigmatisation, residential displacement, gentrification and segregation, to move beyond a narrow focus on the last. I analysed the changing institutional landscape of the Nordic welfare state, the tensions between the state and municipalities after implementation of neoliberal public management practices, and the changing land and housing policies.

In the Finnish welfare state configuration, land and housing policies have traditionally been key instruments that keep in check some of the harsh urban inequalities of capitalism and its uneven urban development. While these policies do little to tackle the inherent class exploitation and marginalisation of labour in a capitalist economy, they have traditionally smoothed out some of its most violent spatial expressions while aiming at evenness in urban development. In this book I presented some of my research over the last ten years regarding how land and housing policies in Finland have been revised to allow for the penetration of land use and housing provision by market mechanisms and rationalities on the one hand, and the withdrawal of some of these policies' important equalising mechanisms on the other. By way of concluding the book I wish to look to the future. As noted in the introductory chapter, the international left and liberal commentators tend to think of the Nordic welfare model as exemplary in keeping at bay the harsh inequalities of neoliberal capitalism. Reflecting on some key insights from the preceding chapters, I discuss how well equipped the land and housing policies of the Finnish welfare state are to tackle urban inequalities in the future, specifically in the capital city Helsinki.

The new market rationalities of municipal land policy

On 2 February 2022, the Helsinki City Council accepted several reforms to the city's land policy.[1] The first of two key reforms was that the city would thereafter only allocate land for residential development by leasing it with long-term contracts of 80 years. As we know, however, leasing land itself is not a radical change to municipal land policy in Helsinki. The city has always leased land. A much more radical change was implemented in the early 2000s, when Helsinki and several other cities began experimenting with the selling of public land to developers – a process studied in Chapters 4 and 5. Chapter 4 explored the justifications of three big cities – Helsinki, Tampere and Turku – to sell public land and real estate. These included answering the requirements of businesses to own land, inviting private investments to cities, spurring urban growth and making profits from public land in the form of large single rewards. The social benefits from land sales were, however, seen by interviewed authorities as dubious. Chapter 4 discusses how in alienating public land the cities had ceded land use powers to private developers, how private interests in the exchange value of land had in some cases been prioritised over public use values and how the possibilities to deter urban inequalities had weakened. And Chapter 5 analysed this change using the concept of entrepreneurial public real estate policy, illustrating the negative social outcomes of said policy via a case study. The study explored how the selling of land had seen to the development of an exclusive neighbourhood for the wealthy in the city centre of Helsinki. The project was carried out in complete neglect of a key urban inequality, that is the shortage of affordable, working-class housing in the urban core, and only contributed to segregation.

The return to land leasing in Helsinki was understandably favoured by left-wing council members, as it means that public property is no longer alienated, or sold off and privatised.[2] The city now potentially maintains a stronger control over planning and land use and will not attempt to reach highest possible single yield on land by selling it to such exclusionary projects. Instead, it now has the mechanism to generate predictable, long term rent revenue for the public treasury. Furthermore, as land remains in public ownership, speculation by private landowners and developers may better be deterred. Throughout Part II of the book, I discussed how public landownership ensures the conditions for more equitable urban development. The use values of land such as accessible housing and evenness in the development of the built environment may be prioritised over quantitative private interests. Critical urban scholars are largely in agreement that private property in land is at the core of major urban inequalities (e.g. Harvey 1973; Haila 2016; Christophers 2018), however, public ownership of land does not directly do away with said inequalities. It is a condition to develop the city in an equitable manner and to emphasise the use values of land. As a landowner, though, the city may also choose to emphasise other goals (Zetterlund 2022).

Like the first, the second principle of the revised land policy in Helsinki is not particularly new. Nevertheless, the reform may have a major fiscal impact and once implemented land use is projected to bring in significant revenues to the city coffers. The second principle is that the leases on public land will now be set on the land market based on competitive bidding. Until now, the city's land leases for residential uses have been based on plot-specific leasing principles and individual agreements between the city and users of land from different periods. Many old land-lease contracts were signed decades ago, and land values and potential land rents have seen great increases since then as the city has grown. The city authorities now wish to cash in on these land value increases. With the update to land policy, the annual leases for new contracts will be set at three and a half to four per cent of the market price of the land determined through auctions. Importantly, in the future, land leases will be periodically checked throughout the 80-year lease period and updated to reflect current market values. This explains why the liberal conservatives who have always held the majority of the seats on the Helsinki City Council also vehemently backed the land policy reform. It incorporates a market rationality to land allocation and promises to offer a potential way to increase public revenue without increasing local taxes (Loikkanen and Laakso 2019).

In Part II I also discussed how public land has become increasingly viewed by state and municipal authorities as a fiscal asset, allocated to its uses via competitive bidding to maximise rent revenue. Helsinki's new land leasing policy reflects the intensification of this approach. The authorities of the growing capital city in the centre of a flourishing metropolitan region have come to realise that, in the coming years, updating the leases upon the renewal of contracts will potentially bring in hundreds of millions of euros in annual rent revenue. The Land Use Chief of Helsinki lamented in an interview with the Finnish public broadcasting company: "The value of land has gone up quickly and the leases have been lagging."[3] Land leases were in the past not as strictly tied to market rents nor renewed to reflect current rents. This, according to Mayor of Helsinki, economist Juhana Vartiainen, speaking to the Helsinki City Council in wake of the city's land policy reforms, has "weakened the transparency, predictability, and efficiency of leasing land. Helsinki is a growing city where the land values will go up due to that growth." And after the mayor's speech, council members then took turns to congratulate one another and the mayor about the new policy. One councillor[4] served penance for past mistakes:

> we are responsible for something that is the collective property of the people of Helsinki, we should take really good care of it. We have not taken very good care of it so far. We have allocated land at discount prices, and this is very poor land management.

The arguments in favour of auctioning off land leases seem awfully familiar. The authorities are hoping to achieve what they call transparency, predictability, efficiency and that the city does not allocate land at discount prices. The management of "collective property" as the councillor called municipal land, is evaluated predominantly from an economic perspective.

First, contemporary land policy is steered by the neoclassical fiction that there is some true and correct market price for each plot of land, but because the land market has not been allowed to operate fully and freely, this price is left opaque. Transparency means making visible the market value of each plot of public land through auctions. Second, predictability refers to the predictability of future land rents for both the municipality and developers. We know from urban political economy and rent theory that bids for land are based on the potential for future land rents (Harvey 2006). The bids will be based on predictions – how much the developers, investors and landlords can expect to profit from housing development for the decades to come. And as the mayor explained, Helsinki is a growing city where land values are predicted to keep climbing. As it pertains to residential land, the reason for the mayor's confidence in this is, most likely, that he understands houses are and will in the long term continue to be expensive commodities and financial assets. And when houses are commodified and assetised, traded in the financialised housing market, it is house prices that determine land rent, not vice versa (Haila 2016). Predictability is key to assure the developers and investment companies that apartments can be sold and rented out with great profits.

Third, the owners, investors and developers of residential space expect to extract profits from their assets in a growing city, allowing them also to bid more for land. The city now wants to use its land policy to treat land as a fiscal asset to profit from the high price of housing and maximise land rent. Taking good care of collective property from the perspective of market rationalities means the city should calculate potential rent from alternative uses. When authorities grieve allocating land for 'discounts', what they mean by discount is the potential revenue from an alternative land use calculated as a cost. But the assumption about a true land price is an ideological and political construct, and the narrative that not maximising land rent is poor management of collective property scaffolds this construct. That this new, rent-maximising policy saw no opposition from the left shows that in agreeing to the reforms, the left of the Helsinki City Council bit a sugar-coated bullet. The sugar-coating was the leasing policy – a good decision in its own right, a policy that potentially deters privatisation of and speculation with residential land. But the bullet is having land rent now and in the future be set in the land market. While extracting maximum land rent revenue from private developers might appear sound urban policy, it poses several challenges.

Underpinning urban land rent are the capitalist relations of class exploitation and the commodification and monopoly control over residential space. In Chapter 1, I discussed Harvey's criticism of the von Thünen and Alonso-Mills-Muth economic models of land use and location theory that portray how different groups and land uses find their positions in the city based on competitive bidding for rent. Harvey's (1973) insight on urban inequality – at the time the question of ghetto formation – was, that if we are truly concerned with spatial differentiation of groups in the city, then we should be concerned with the reality that gives truth to the Alonso-Mills-Muth model. That reality is the competitive bidding for land. A land policy that is based on competing and bidding for land is encouraging development that allows the highest possible return on real estate. The result of this "efficiency" is the exclusion of those who cannot bid: low-income households and small businesses from centrally located and easily accessible spaces. In Chapter 7 I explored the very real consequences for urban inequality of putting housing to its most economically "efficient" use as the working-class tenants were displaced from their homes and replaced with higher earning tenants by a real estate company thirsty for potential rents in a gentrifying neighbourhood.

The argument of Finnish land economists is that hanging land leases on the market rent would boost the economy. For instance, Loikkanen and Laakso (2019), who are strong advocates of Helsinki's adopted land policy, explain how extracting the market rent will motivate developers to be efficient; to develop and redevelop plots as land values go up. A logic of use value in land allocation decisions is replaced by conferring losses on the user if she is not using land in the most efficient way. This is to promote the highest-and-best type urban development, where land is expected to be redeveloped to meet its market value. But is the value of urban land for the residents of Helsinki merely in the price it can fetch on the market? Obviously not. The value of urban land is in the uses that the city allocates the land to, such as affordable and good quality housing, evenly distributed healthcare centres, good schools, libraries and swimming pools. As Haila (2015, 288) wrote "the simple truth is that the benefits of land use accrue from land use, not its market price". And in 2016 (117–18) she returned to the question of what the value of public land is, explaining "there is no 'natural value' for public land. Rather, the value depends on the role the city and the state assume as landowners, their point of view and whether they count alternative costs."

The reason Helsinki's land policy is troublesome for urban equality, is that when the land leases are set on the market at auctions, those with the most win.

The liberal formulation of maximising and then distributing the profits made in land rent happily leaves in place the system where land and houses are treated as commodities and traded and allocated with a priority on profits. The city leases most of the land to private developers and investors and as was illustrated in Chapter 4, these actors now also have more room to negotiate on planning and land use questions than previously. In Chapter 4 I analysed how land use contracts and planning partnerships allow these private players to affect city plans, negotiate for more development rights and stall projects when they feel their wishes are not granted. Developers who will sell the apartments they build to transnational real estate investors and corporate landlords interested more in the bottom line and less in the well-being of residents, are inclined to place bigger bets on the land than, say, small domestic companies or housing co-operatives (Charlesworth and Hyötyläinen 2023).

To repeat, public ownership of land is a crucial, necessary condition to ensure that urban land is used in a way that deters urban inequalities. Public authorities can use their landed property to encourage evenness in urban development. But they can also try to maximise what Haila (2016, 216) called "fiscal rent". Haila also noted:

> States can use their land resources like private enterprises, and today, when governments face pressure to cut their expenses and find alternative sources for collecting revenues other than increasing taxes, they are increasingly tempted to sell their landed properties and charge the market rent for the use of their land and real estate.

To quote Heather Whiteside (2019, 508), Helsinki's new land policy rests on "privileging exchange value over use value and turning qualitative values into quantitative calculus through the monetization of public property; land is treated as a financial asset whether sold for revenue or retained as 'public' land for rental income." There is, however, one form of housing that prioritises the qualitative value of houses as homes and has the potential to contribute to urban housing justice and a more socially sustainable urban future.

The missed potential of social housing?

The political decision to link the leases of land to its market price is not entirely in the hands of the City of Helsinki and its authorities. Finnish municipalities are bound by EU and national legislation regarding market-based land valuation when allocating land for private development. They essentially require land prices to be set in the market to allow for transparency of prices in competition and to deter hidden land subsidies that might tweak the process in some companies' favour. Partly the justification for Helsinki's reformed land policy is that it merely renewed the policy to answer to EU and national legislation that supports and safeguards the operations of a competitive land market. However, even in the face of these legal requirements and market rationalities, there is a way for the city to allocate residential land in a way that prioritises its qualitative aspects. An important exception to the rule for setting rent on the market is land allocated for social housing. This has traditionally included social rental housing, Helsinki's own subsidised, non-profit, owner-occupation model called HITAS in which prices are set according to building and maintenance costs, and different types of intermediate forms of public housing – such as the right of occupancy housing – introduced in more detail in Part III. The City of Helsinki provides land for these social housing tenures below the market rent. In different forms of state subsidised housing development, the land rent of the plot is granted a relief according to the requirements by the Housing Finance and Development Centre (ARA). This relief is temporary and valid only as long as the units are used as social housing. A way to release significant amounts of housing from the inequities created by housing commodification is to increase the amount of social housing development and to do it on a long-term basis.

In Chapters 6 and 7 I explored how well social housing in Finland is geared to address urban inequalities and the potential to develop a system of more extensive, affordable social housing provision. The findings were not encouraging. Newly developed social housing is retrenching in numbers and increasingly targeted as a social service only for special needs groups. I argued that this specialisation of social housing is lending to the growth of tenurial stigmatisation of social housing estates and their residents, as social housing becomes viewed as an "abnormal" tenure of those seen as market incapable compared to the "normal" market tenures of those making their way on the private housing ladder. Meanwhile paternalist tenure mixing practices do little to alleviate the noxious reputation of social housing and even in mixed neighbourhoods social housing is known as synonymous with social problems (Junnilainen 2019).

This targeted and recoiling role of new social housing is coupled with an aggressive enclosure of the existing stock of affordable social housing. In Chapter 7 I explored how the social housing stock in Finland is subject to a process of accumulation by dispossession in the form of social housing stock transfer, as so-called non-profit companies have turned into listed investment companies. They are in the process of selling off and renting on the market vast amounts of affordable units built with state subsidies since the 1960s. This is enabled by a housing policy based on short term regulation of subsidised units. Once state subsidised construction loans have been paid back and the regulation period of ten to 40 years closes, developers may do with the units as they wish. I illustrated the ramifications of this via interviews with evicted tenants in Helsinki's gentrifying neighbourhood of Sörnäinen. The public sector pension company Keva had offered affordable, state subsidised housing for the working-class in 56 units. In recent years the potential rents had become too appetising. As the 20-year regulation period ended in 2019,

Keva terminated all rental contracts, evicted the tenants and doubled the rents. Unlocking the exchange values in land thus meant the locking out of use values of houses as homes for low-income households.

Such events speak about the commodification of housing and its growing treatment as a financial asset according to the rent it yields. As of now, most plots are reserved for private developers and the only substantial producer of social housing is the City of Helsinki's own housing company Heka, which still owns and operates some 60,000 units. The targets on state subsidised housing development set by the City of Helsinki (2021) in its *Implementation Programme on Housing and Related Land Use 2020* have not been reached in recent years. According to the programme, the share of state subsidised social rental housing in Helsinki should be 25 per cent of new production, but since 2021 has only been 16 per cent of total production. The target for intermediate tenures was 30 per cent, but only 18 per cent has been realised. And the share of private market housing provision is supposed to be 40 per cent but has been up to 66 per cent.[5] Meanwhile, when looking at housing financing, we can see the growing role of institutional investors and private landlords in the housing market (Lilius and Hirvonen 2021). Investors include real estate investors like Kojamo, institutional investors such as insurance and pension companies like Keva, and private individuals who invest professionally. Individuals with an income from rents in Finland grew between 2006 and 2016 from 241,391 persons to 317,852 (Alho et al. 2018). In Helsinki such actors increasingly profit from and enjoy the skyrocketing housing prices.[6]

Housing policy is not suited to de-commodify housing. It is in fact doing the exact opposite, by increasingly linking the social housing rents to market rent on land. As discussed in Chapter 6, HITAS is being slowly driven down. According to Helsinki's new land policy principles new HITAS housing will no longer receive land below market rent. In 2017, as if getting ready for its new real estate policy, the City of Helsinki also introduced a new model in its housing policy it calls "rent adjustment". This means that the rents in social housing units will be updated to reflect the market rent of the area they are located in (Heka 2017). Under the bid rent paradigm, market rents vary between different neighbourhoods, and now also social housing rents will follow this variation more closely.

This change in Helsinki's housing policy was justified by Anni Sinnemäki (2018), at the time acting as both Chair of the Board of Heka and as Vice Mayor of Helsinki, who argued that it increases "spatial justice".[7] The notion of justice held by the vice mayor leans on the idea that the market is a fair and just way of dictating land and house rent based on locational advantages, and hence even social housing should be priced based on the particular area's market rent. But from a more critical perspective on socio-spatial justice the competitive bidding for land based on unevenly developed locational advantages drives urban inequalities. The new model means that the lowest income households living in social housing will in the future find their apartments where all rents are the lowest. This goes against the traditional goals of developing residential space in a way that allows for people of different means to find and access housing across the city and runs a risk of increasing segregation. As market rents on housing continue to grow in Helsinki, binding social housing rents to market rent has already harmed social housing tenants who are seeing considerable rent increases.[8] Such rent increases in the municipal housing production combined with non-profit companies' stock transfers (Chapter 7) give reason to believe that the new market rationalities adopted in municipal land and housing policies make answering the working-class housing question more and more difficult, exacerbating a plethora of urban inequalities. However, it appears that the high price of housing is not high on the list of concerns for public authorities nor the economists who give policy advice to authorities.

Land economists Loikkanen and Laakso (2019), and the economic consultancy Forecon (2020) hired by the City of Helsinki to produce a report on reforming the index-basis of land rent, gave strong support for fixing the land rent on the housing price index, so that the rent is periodically checked and readjusted to reflect the market level of house prices. Adjunct Professor of Economics Heidi Falkenbach at the Aalto Economics Institute is another public advocate of the new policy. She is the principal author of a report titled *On the allocation of residential land in Helsinki* (Falkenbach et al. 2020), which provided further guidelines for the newly adopted policy. The report instructed the city to always strive to sell residential plots at the market price, meaning according to the highest bid. It argued that auctions are a transparent way of land allocation, and that they promote the competition between developers and the city's income from land (Ibid., 15–16). In an interview, Falkenbach made clear her concern regarding the housing question in Helsinki. It was indeed not that housing is too expensive in the capital city, but in her words "some people in Helsinki have been living in their apartments for too cheap for too long".[9] Prominent Finnish urban economists tend to share the logic behind this strange view, that land allocated below the market rent is a subsidy. Instead of allocating land below market rent and building social housing, they advocate for leasing land on the market and only subsidising housing demand through the state's housing benefits (Falkenbach et al. 2020; Loikkanen and Laakso 2019; Saarimaa and Eerola 2016).

But demand benefits merely allow for houses to continue to function as instruments of capital accumulation. As Madden and Marcuse (2016, 204) point out, "the power of private capital in the housing system comes from the fact that the public role has been reduced to facilitating private action". Two billion euros are paid annually in demand subsidies by the National Insurance Institute and 15 per cent of Finns receive housing benefits. Even middle-class residents in Helsinki are increasingly dependent on state housing benefits to bare the excessive market rents on housing in the city. As Lilius and Hirvonen (2021) aptly point out, there is an urgent need to also investigate to what extent housing benefits are a state instrument fueling what they call the financialisation of rental housing. Housing benefits do not de-commodify housing nor do they tackle the cause of housing costs, they merely address the symptoms while allowing for houses to be treated as financial assets. The contemporary land and housing policies do not appear to be guided by social questions of urban equality. Instead, they allow for the increasing penetration of urban development by market logic and using public resources as financial and fiscal assets. Consequently, there is less room to confront the inherent inequalities of capitalist urbanisation via said policies. As the economic perspective becomes increasingly dominant, what room is left to consider the social and qualitative rationalities of urban development?

Toward a more equitable, transformative urban land and housing nexus

I began the book by referring to two major structural dynamics of urban inequality. First is the enduring, global exploitation of the working class that today manifests in various insidious, intersecting forms of domination, precarity and marginalisation. The Nordic welfare state continues to hold a cathartic role in western left and liberal views for keeping at bay the violent inequalities of neoliberal capitalism. The wide dissemination of singular policy successes like Finland and Norway practically doing away with street homelessness support this view. However, in this book I have discussed how the welfare state has gone through marked transformations of decentralisation, privatisation and policy rollback. The liberal formulation of the Nordic welfare state never did away with class conflict, and although for a period it did work to smooth out the rough edges of a class society through redistribution and universal welfare policies, as noted in the Introduction and in Chapter 3, wealth and income inequalities are again on the rise, while the working class consists of precarious individuals in part-time and gig work, facing penalising workfare policies and challenges to union protection. These processes now meet with intersecting forms of domination of repressed groups and marginalised minorities.

And second is the uneven development of capitalist urbanisation that gives the hierarchies of a class society its spatial characteristics, or a division of the city into enclaves of wealth and prosperity and concentrations of disinvestment and marginality. My concern in the book has been with this second dynamic. The book focussed on the transformations in the key policies of the Nordic welfare state that have traditionally worked to deter the most violent urban inequalities such as displacements, housing dispossession, gentrification and the segregation of socio-economic classes, processes underpinned by uneven urban development and accumulation. Today, to refer to Bourdieu's (1999) framing of the issue, the welfare state's "right hand", corresponding to budgetary and fiscal functions, has overpowered its "left hand", which has traditionally controlled the social purposes, such as spatial equality (see Artilio 2021). I have argued that due to transformations in land and housing policies, we are allowing for the deepening of urban inequalities in the future. In particular this book has discussed the weaknesses of urban land and housing policies and their growing reliance on market rationalities in Finland. The interests of urban authorities in designing these policies are today intensely aligned with those of private companies, developers and investors.

And as we learnt in Chapter 4, in Finland like elsewhere in the advanced capitalist world, it is growth that the coalitions of urban managers, elites and corporations strive for. The interviews with local authorities in Finnish cities (Chapters 4 and 5) attested to growth having become an end in itself, even surpassing the traditional welfare goals of the cities. This idea of the desirability of urban growth is justified by a trickle-down economics that assumes growth will eventually benefit even those on the lowest rung of the capitalist class-hierarchy; that it will bring jobs and prosperity even to the working-class and marginalised. However, over the course of this book I have discussed the numerous ways that an urban policy approach dominated by the market rationalities of economic efficiency and competition for growth, coupled with deregulation, withdrawal of protective policies and privatisation, allows for urban inequalities to intensify. If we instead wish to bring the use value considerations of urban life centre-stage, an alternative approach to social and spatial justice and equality in the city clearly needs to be adopted. How then to begin thinking about alternative, equitable housing and land policies that start not from a purely economic rationality of growth and efficiency but from a social rationality that prioritises qualitative aspects of urban life for all?

If we are interested in doing away with inequalities and their spatial expressions in the differentiation between classes into their own enclaves, the gentrification of working-class neighbourhoods, the displacement of their residents and the vexed housing question, then it is not enough for the city to own the land simply to then lease it to the highest bidder and capture as rental payment a percentage of the market price. Neither is it enough to allocate social housing as a retrenching social service and leave a large part of the population reliant on housing benefits that merely allow the owners of housing commodities to reap great profits while the wealthy retreat into exclusive, expensive urban enclaves and core areas. In such formulations, the city continues to be unevenly developed. The social conditions through which land use is determined must be radically changed from competitive bidding to giving more emphasis to allocation according to the collectively and democratically defined needs of residents. Land and housing policies of the central and local states must be brought into closer collaboration. "The state is clearly part of the problem, and yet it is absolutely necessary for any solution" write Madden and Marcuse (2016, 198). Some steps that the state could take to get closer to that solution include:

- Understand how the housing question is a land question. Device land and housing policies in tandem.
- Understand that gentrification is not the solution to segregation. Both are socio-spatial processes of inequality, pivoting on uneven development and class conflict.
- Empower and extend the role of existing social housing companies ran by local government bodies and funded by the central state.
- Make social housing viable and attractive for all, not a means-tested, specialised service for the few.
- Increase drastically the share of social housing from all new production and build it in central areas close to employment, transit, schools, services and cultural amenities.
- Remove housing from its role as an instrument of fiscal revenue for the local state.
- Support the collective use value of urban land and housing financed by the central state through taxation and redistribution and organised by local social housing companies and cooperatives. This means more collaboration between different levels of government and administration.
- The current, temporary rent restrictions written into state subsidies allow for a speculative element in social housing production and we are now seeing its consequences in the stock transfer of social housing units to the private market. The possibility for the types of terminations of rental contracts and displacements of residents illustrated in Chapter 7 must be eliminated.
- Increased state regulation of urban development to protect residents and the environment from urban development run amok.
- Develop an alternative urban policy based on collective ownership of land, robust public planning, universal social housing and allocation of land based on use value, not exchange value and competitive bidding.

The ultimate point should of course be to address the cause of urban inequalities, which is urbanisation undergirded by an economy based on accumulation and exploitation of the working class and an uneven urban process that pivots on profits on investments. As a transitional policy, Helsinki's decision to maintain strong public landownership and only lease land for users is excellent. But to tackle urban inequalities would also need stronger public land use planning and land allocation where developers are not given room to lobby for development rights via land use contracts and partnerships. Capturing and maximising land values for public treasuries still means that rent is paid and that the highest bidders will succeed in acquiring land. Any socially sustainable urban future will require a vastly expanded, universal social housing sector where residential space is allocated based on democratically defined social need. Ultimately, the goal must be to de-commodify land and its residential improvements and to not have homes and the land they are built on – universal human needs and matter of existence – continue to be abused as instruments of accumulation.

Notes

1. Asuntotonttien sekä asumista palvelevien tonttien maanvuokrauksen yleiset periaatteet (Helsingin kaupunginvaltuusto 2.2.2022).
2. Helsingin maapolitiikka, tonttivuokrat ja asumisen hinta – mistä on kyse? (Helsingin vasemmisto 11.2.2022).
3. Helsinki haluaa jatkossa vuokratonteistaan markkinahinnan (YLE 2.2.2022).
4. Minutes of Helsinki City Council meeting 2.2.2022.
5. Helsingissä valmistui jälleen yli 7000 uutta asuntoa vuonna 2021 (STT 14.2.2022).
6. Asuntojen hinnat nousivat useilla Helsingin alueilla räjähdysmäisesti vain yhdessä vuodessa (HS 21.2.2022).
7. Helsinki korottaa vuokra-asuntojensa hintoja (YLE 4.6.2018).
8. Jopa satojen eurojen vuokrankorotukset uhkaavat lukuisia Helsingin vuokra-asukkaita (HS 10.2.2021).
9. Helsinki haluaa vuokratonteista markkinahinnan: Uusi malli nostaisi asumisen hintaa monilla alueilla (HS 20.10.2020).

References

Aalbers, M. B. (2011). The revanchist renewal of yesterday's city of tomorrow. *Antipode*, 43 (5): 1696–724.

Aalbers, M. B. (2015). The great moderation, the great excess and the global housing crisis. *International Journal of Housing Policy* 15 (1): 43–60.

Aalbers, M. B. (2016). *The Financialization of Housing: A Political Economy Approach*. London: Routledge.

Aalbers, M. B. (2017). The variegated financialization of housing. *International Journal of Urban and Regional Research* 41 (4): 542–54.

Aalbers, M. B., and Christophers, B. (2014). Centring housing in political economy. *Housing, Theory and Society* 31 (4): 373–94.

Adisson, F. (2018). From state restructuring to urban restructuring: The intermediation of public landownership in urban development projects in France. *European Urban and Regional Studies* 25 (4): 373–90.

Adisson, F. and Artioli, F. (2020). Four types of urban austerity: Public land privatisations in French and Italian cities. *Urban Studies* 57 (1): 75–92.

Ahlqvist, T. and Moisio, S. (2014). Neoliberalisation in a Nordic state: From cartel polity towards a corporate polity in Finland. *New Political Economy* 19 (1): 21–55.

Aldén, L., Hammarstedt, M. and Neuman, E. (2015). Ethnic segregation, tipping behavior, and native residential mobility. *International Migration Review* 49 (1): 36–69.

Alho, E., Härmälä, V., Oikarinen, E., Kekäläinen, A., Noro, K., and Tähtinen, T., et al. (2018). Vuokraasuntosijoitusalankannattavuus, kilpailutilanne ja kehittämistarpeet. *Valtioneuvoston selvitys- jatutkimustoiminnan julkaisusarja* 9/2018.

Alonso, W. (1964). *Location and Land Use: Toward a General Theory of Land Rent*. Cambridge, MA: Harvard University Press.

Andersson, R. and Bråmå, Å. (2004). Selective migration in Swedish distressed neighborhoods: can area-based urban policies counteract segregation processes? *Housing Studies* 19 (4): 517–39.

Andersson, R. and Turner, L. M. (2014). Segregation, gentrification, and residualisation: from public housing to market-driven housing allocation in inner city Stockholm. *International Journal of Housing Policy*, 14 (1): 3–29.

Anttonen, A. and Sipilä, J. (2000). *Suomalaista sosiaalipolitiikkaa*. Tampere: Vastapaino.

Arbaci, S. (2019). *Paradoxes of segregation: Housing systems, welfare regimes and ethnic residential change in Southern European cities*. Chichester: John Wiley & Sons.

Arbaci, S. and Rae, I. (2013). Mixed-tenure neighbourhoods in London: policy myth or effective device to alleviate deprivation? *International Journal of Urban and Regional Research* 37 (2): 451–79.

Artioli, F. (2016). When administrative reforms produce territorial differentiation. How market-oriented policies transform military brownfield reconversion in France (1989–2012). *Environment and Planning C: Government and Policy* 34 (8): 1759–75.

Artioli, F. (2021). Sale of public land as a financing instrument. The unspoken political choices and distributional effects of land-based solutions. *Land Use Policy* 104: 105–99.

Atkinson, A. B., Rainwater, L. and Smeeding, T. M. (1995). *Income distribution in OECD countries: evidence from the Luxembourg Income Study.*

Atkinson, R. (2000). Measuring gentrification and displacement in Greater London. *Urban Studies* 37 (1): 149–65.

Baeten, G., Berg, L. D. and Lund Hansen, A. (2015). Introduction: Neoliberalism and post-welfare Nordic states in transition. *Geografiska Annaler: Series B, Human Geography* 97 (3): 209–12.

Baeten, G., Westin, S., Pull, E. and Molina, I. (2017). Pressure and violence: Housing renovation and displacement in Sweden. *Environment and Planning A: Economy and Space,* 49 (3): 631–51.

Balmer, I. and Bernet, T. (2015). Housing as a common resource? Decommodification and self-organization in housing. Examples from Germany and Switzerland. In: Dellenbaugh, M., Kip, M., Bieniok, M., Müller, A and Schwegmann, M. (Eds), *Urban Commons: Moving Beyond State and Market.* Basel: Birkhäuser.

Barker, V. (2013). Nordic Exceptionalism revisited: Explaining the paradox of a Janus-faced penal regime. *Theoretical Criminology* 17 (1): 5–25.

Beauregard, R. (1986). The chaos and complexity of gentrification. In: Smith, N. and Williams, P. (Eds), *Gentrification of the City.* Boston: Unwin Hyman.

Bell, D. (1973). *The Coming of Post-industrial Society.* New York: Basic Books.

Bengtsson, B. (2001). Housing as a social right: Implications for welfare state theory. *Scandinavian Political Studies* 24 (4): 255–75.

Bengtsson, B. and Ruonavaara, H. (2010). Introduction to the special issue: Path dependence in housing. *Housing, Theory and Society* 27 (3): 193–203.

Bernelius, V. (2013). *Eriytyvät kaupunkikoulut: Helsingin peruskoulujen oppilaspohjan erot, perheiden kouluvalinnat ja oppimistuloksiin liittyvät aluevaikutukset osana kaupungin eriytymiskehitystä.* Helsinki: Helsingin kaupungin tietokeskus.

Berry, M. and Huxley, M. (1992). Big Build: Property Capital, the State and Urban Change in Australia. *International Journal of Urban and Regional Research* 16 (1): 35–59.

Blakely, E. J. (2006). Fortress America separate and not equal. In: Platt, R. H. (Ed.), *The Humane Metropolis: People and Nature in the 21st-Century City.* Amherst: University of Massachusetts Press.

Blomgren, J., Hiilamo, H., Kangas, O., and Niemelä, M. (2014). Finland: Growing Inequality with Contested Consequences. In: Nolan, B. et al. (Eds), *Changing Inequalities and Societal Impacts in Rich Countries: Thirty Countries' Experiences.* Oxford: Oxford University Press.

Boddy, M. and Gray, F. (1979). Filtering theory, housing policy and the legitimation of inequality. *Policy & Politics,* 7 (1): 39–54.

Boone, L., Cournède, B. and Plouin, M. (2021). Finland's Zero Homeless Strategy: Lessons from a Success Story. *Ecoscope* 13 (12).

Borins, S. (1995). The New Public Management is here to stay. *Canadian Public Administration* 38: 122–32.

Brattbakk, I., and Hansen, T. (2004). Post-war large housing estates in Norway–Well-kept residential areas still stigmatised? *Journal of Housing and the Built Environment* 19: 311–32.

Bratu, C., Harjunen, O. and Saarimaa, T. (2021). City-wide effects of new housing supply: Evidence from moving chains. *VATT Institute for Economic Research Working Papers* 146.

Brenner, N. (2004). *New State Spaces: Urban Governance and the Rescaling of Statehood*. New York: Oxford University Press.

Brenner, N., Marcuse, P. and Mayer, M. (2009). Cities for people, not for profit. *City* (13) 2–3: 176–84.

Brenner, N. and Theodore, N. (2002). Cities and the Geographies of "Actually Existing Neoliberalism". *Antipode* 34 (3): 349–79.

Buitelaar, E. (2010). Window on the Netherlands: Cracks in the myth: Challenges to land policy in the Netherlands. *Tijdschrift voor economische en sociale geografie* 101(3): 349–56.

Buller, A. and Lawrence, M. (2022). *Owning the future: Power and property in an age of crisis*. London: Verso.

Burnazoğlu, M. (2023). *Inequalities Beyond the Average Man: The Political Economy of Identity-Based Stratification Mechanisms in Markets and Policy*. Doctoral dissertation, Utrecht University.

Butler, A. (2020). Toxic Toxteth: Understanding press stigmatization of Toxteth during the 1981 uprising. *Journalism*, 21 (4): 541–56.

Castells, M. (1977). *The Urban Question: A Marxist Approach*. Cambridge: The MIT Press.

Castells, M. (1983). *The City and the Grassroots: A Cross-cultural Theory of Urban Social Movements*. London: Arnold.

Cate, T. (2013). *An Encyclopedia of Keynesian Economics*. Cheltenham: Edward Elgar Publishing Limited.

Charlesworth, D., & Hyötyläinen, M. (2023). Housing cooperatives and the contradictions of Finnish land and housing policies. *International Journal of Housing Policy*, 1–22.

Chatterton, P. (2010). Seeking the urban common: Furthering the debate on spatial justice. *City* 14 (6): 625–8.

Childs, M. W. (1936). *Sweden: The middle way*. New Haven: Yale University Press.

Christophers, B. (2011). Revisiting the urbanization of capital. *Annals of the association of American geographers* 101(6): 1347–64.

Christophers, B. (2013). A monstrous hybrid: The political economy of housing in early twenty-first century Sweden. *New Political Economy* 18 (6): 885–911.

Christophers, B. (2017). The state and financialization of public land in the United Kingdom. *Antipode* 49 (1): 62–85.

Christophers, B. (2018). *The New Enclosure: The Appropriation of Public Land in Neoliberal Britain*. London: Verso.

Christophers, B. (2020). *Rentier Capitalism. Who Owns the Economy and Who Pays for It?* London: Verso.

Christophers, B. (2023). *Our Lives in Their Portfolios: Why Asset Managers Own the World*. London: Verso.

Christophers, B. and Whiteside, H. (2021). Commodifying Public Land in Canada and the United Kingdom. *Land Fictions: The Commodification of Land in City and Country* 44.

Clair, A., Reeves, A., McKee, M., and Stuckler, D. (2019). Constructing a housing precariousness measure for Europe. *Journal of European Social Policy*, 29: 1, 13–28.

Clapham, D. (2018). *Remaking housing policy: An international study*. London: Routledge.

Clapham, D. and Smith, S. J. (1990). Housing policy and 'special needs'. *Policy & Politics*, 18 (3): 193–205.

Clark, E. and Runesson, L. (1996). Municipal site leasehold in Sweden: A land policy instrument in Decay. *European Planning Studies* 4 (2): 203–16.

Clark, G. L. (1998). Pension fund capitalism: a causal analysis. *Geografiska Annaler: Series B, Human Geography* 80 (3): 139–57.

Dahlqvist, H. (2020). A critique of the grand narrative of the Swedish model. *Labor History* 61 (3–4): 247–66.

De Decker, P. and Pannecoucke, I. (2004). The creation of the incapable social tenant in Flanders, Belgium. An appraisal. *Journal of Housing and the Built Environment* 19 (3): 293–309.

De Soto, H. (2000). *The Mystery of Capital: Why Capitalism Triumphs in the West and Fails Everywhere Else.* New York: Basic Books.

Drucker, P. (1976). *The Unseen Revolution: How Pension Fund Capitalism Came to America.* London: Heinemann.

Dunleavy, P., Margetts, H., Bastow, S. and Tinkler, J. (2006). New public management is dead—long live digital-era governance. *Journal of Public Administration Research and Theory* 16 (3): 467–94.

Eerola, E., and Saarimaa, T. (2016). Kohtuuhintaisuuspolitiikka ei ole lääke asumisen kalleuteen. VATT POLICY BRIEF 3.

Elliott-Cooper, A., Hubbard, P., and Lees, L. (2020). Moving beyond Marcuse: Gentrification, displacement and the violence of un-homing. *Progress in Human Geography*, 44 (3): 492–509.

Engels, F. (1872). *The Housing Question.* Co-operative Publishing Society of Foreign Workers.

Eranti, V. (2014). Oma etu ja yhteinen hyvä paikallisessa kiistassa tilasta. *Sosiologia* 51 (1): 21–38.

Erikson, R., Hansen, E. J., Ringen, S. and Uusitalo, H. (1987). *The Scandinavian Model. Welfare States and Welfare Research.* London: M. E. Sharpe, Inc.

Esping-Andersen, G. (1990). *The Three Worlds of Welfare Capitalism.* Cambridge: Polity Press.

Fainstein, N. (1996). A Note on Interpreting American Poverty. In: Mingione, E. (Ed.), *Urban Poverty and the Underclass.* Oxford: Blackwell.

Fainstein, S. (2012). Land Value Capture and Justice. In: Ingram, G. K. and Hong, Y. H. (Eds), *Value Capture and Land Policies.* Cambridge: Lincoln Institute of Land Policy.

Falkenbach, H., Harjunen, O., Nokso-Koivisto, O., and Terviö, M. (2020). *Helsingin asuntotonttien luovutuksesta.* Helsinki: Unigrafia.

Fields, D. (2017). Urban struggles with financialization. *Geography Compass* 11, e12334.

Fitzpatrick, S. and Pawson, H. (2014). Ending security of tenure for social renters: Transitioning to 'ambulance service' social housing? *Housing Studies*, 29(5): 597–615.

Flusty, S. (2004). *De-Coca-Colonization: Making the Globe from the Inside Out.* London: Routledge.

Forrest, R. and Murie. A. (1983). Residualization and council housing: Aspects of the changing social relations of housing tenure. *Journal of Social Policy* 12 (4): 453–68.

Friedmann, J. (1986). The world city hypothesis. *Development and change* 17 (1): 69–83.

Friedmann, J. and Wolff, G. (1982). World city formation: an agenda for research and action. *International Journal of Urban and Regional Research* 6 (3): 309–44.

Friedrichs, J., Galster, G. and Musterd, S. (2003). Neighborhood effects on social opportunities: the European and American research and policy context. *Housing Studies* 18 (6): 797–806.

Fritzell, J. Bäckman, O. and Ritakallio V. M. (2012). Income inequality and poverty: do the Nordic countries still constitute a family of their own? In: Kvist, J. Fritzell, J. Hvinden, B. and Kangas, O. (Eds), *Changing Social Equality: The Nordic Welfare Model in the 21st Century.* Bristol: The Policy Press.

Gans, H. (1996). From 'Underclass' to 'Undercaste': Some Observations About the Future of the Post-Industrial Economy and its Major Victims. In: Mingione, E. (Ed.), *Urban Poverty and the Underclass.* Oxford: Blackwell.

George, H. (1879/1920). *Progress and Poverty.* New York: Doubleday, Page & Co.

Giddens, A. (1984). *The Constitution of Society. Outline of the Theory of Structuration.* Berkeley: University of California Press.

Glaeser, E. (2011). *Triumph of the City.* London: Macmillan.

Gotham, K. F. (2009). Creating liquidity out of spatial fixity: The secondary circuit of capital and the subprime mortgage crisis. *International Journal of Urban and Regional Research* 33 (2): 355–71.

Gotham, K. F. and Brumley, K. (2002). Using Space: Agency and Identity in a Public-Housing Development. *City & Community* 1 (3): 267–89.

Gourzis, K., Herod, A., and Gialis, S. (2019). Linking gentrification and labour market precarity in the contemporary city: A framework for analysis. *Antipode* 51 (5): 1436–55.

Gray, N. and Mooney, G. (2011). Glasgow's new urban frontier: 'Civilising' the population of 'Glasgow East'. *City* 15 (1): 4–24.

Gruening, G. (2001). Origin and theoretical basis of New Public Management. *International Public Management Journal* 4(1): 1–25.

Haatanen, P. (2017). *Suomen maalaisköyhälistö.* Helsinki: Into.

Haila, A. (1988). Land as a financial asset: the theory of urban rent as a mirror of economic transformation. *Antipode* 20 (2): 79–101.

Haila, A. (1990). The theory of land rent at the crossroads. *Environment and Planning D: Society and Space* 8 (3): 275–96.

Haila, A. (1999). The Singapore and Hong Kong property markets: lessons for the West from successful global cities. *European Planning Studies* 7 (2): 175–87.

Haila, A. (2004). Eurooppalainen kaupunki. *Tiede ja edistys* 29 (4): 287–95.

Haila, A. (2008). From Annankatu to Antinkatu: Contracts, Development Rights and Partnerships in Kamppi, Helsinki. *International Journal of Urban and Regional Research* 32 (4): 804–14.

Haila, A. (2015). Asuntopolitiikan kymmenen myyttiä. *Yhteiskuntapolitiikka* 80 (3): 283–91.

Haila, A. (2015). Ostajaressukat ja osaavat hinnoittelijat. In: Häkli, J., Vilkko, R. and Vähäkylä, L. (Eds), *Kaikki kotona: Asumisen uudet tuulet.* Helsinki: Gaudeamus.

Haila, A. (2016). *Urban land rent: Singapore as a property state.* Chichester: John Wiley & Sons.

Haila, A. (2021). Financialisation and Real Estate. In: Orum, A., Ruiz-Tagale, J. and Vicari-Haddock (Eds), *Companion to Urban and Regional Studies.* Oxford: Wiley.

Haila, A. and Le Galès, P. (2004). The coming of age of metropolitan governance in Helsinki? In: Heinelt, H. and Kubler, D. (Eds), *Metropolitan Governance – Capacity, Democracy and the Dynamics of Place.* New York: Routledge.

Hall, P. (1996). *Cities of Tomorrow*. Oxford: Blackwell.

Hall, T., and Vidén, S. (2005). The Million Homes Programme: a review of the great Swedish planning project. *Planning Perspectives* 20 (3): 301–28.

Halla, K. and Kyrö, M. (1979). Erityisryhmätutkimus. *Ministry of Social Affairs and Health, Research Department Publications* 12.

Hankonen, J. (1994). *Lähiöt ja tehokkuuden yhteiskunta: Suunnittelujärestelmän läpimurto suomalaisten asuntoalueiden rakentumisessa 1960-luvulla*. Tampere: Gaudeamus.

Hardin, G. (1968). The Tragedy of the Commons. *Science* 16 (3859): 1243–8.

Harjunen, O., Kortelainen, M. and Saarimaa, T. (2014). *Best Education Money Can Buy? Capitalization of School Quality in Finland*. Helsinki: VATT.

Harloe, M. (1995). *The people's home: Social rented housing in Europe and America*. Oxford: Blackwell.

Harvey, D. (1978). The urban process under capitalism: a framework for analysis. *International Journal of Urban and Regional Research* 2 (1–3): 101–31.

Harvey, D. (1989). From managerialism to entrepreneurialism: the transformation in urban governance in late capitalism. *Geografiska Annaler: Series B, Human Geography* 71 (1): 3–17.

Harvey, D. (2003). *The New Imperialism*. Oxford: Oxford University Press.

Harvey, D. (2005). *A Brief History of Neoliberalism*. Oxford: Oxford University Press.

Harvey, D. (2006). *Limits to Capital*. London: Verso.

Harvey, D. (2008). The Right to the City. *New Left Review* 53, September/October.

Harvey, D. (2009). *Social Justice and the City*. Athens: University of Georgia Press.

Harvey, D. (2014). *Seventeen Contradictions and the End of Capitalism*. Oxford: Oxford University Press.

Harvey, D. and Chatterjee, L. (1974). Absolute rent and the structuring of space by governmental and financial institutions. *Antipode* 6 (1): 22–36.

Häussermann, H. and Haila, A. (2005). The European City: A Conceptual Framework and Normative Project. In: Kazepov, Y. (Ed.), *Cities of Europe: Changing Contexts, Local Arrangements, and the Challenge to Urban Cohesion*. Oxford: Blackwell.

Hautajärvi, H., Heikonen, J., Kummala, P. and Tuomi, T. (2021). *Kenen kaupunki? Helsingin kaupunkisuunnittelu ja kulttuuriympäristö törmäyskurssilla*. Helsinki: Docomomo Suomi Finland ry, ICOMOSin Suomen osasto ry, Rakennustaiteen Seura ry ja Rakennusperintö-SAFA.

Haveri, A. (2015). Nordic local government: a success story, but will it last? *International Journal of Public Sector Management* 28 (2): 136–49.

Haveri, A. (2002). Uusi julkisjohtaminen kunnallishallinnon reformeissa. *Hallinnon tutkimus* 1: 4–19.

Hedman, N. (2022). *Finnish pension insurance system and its gender disparities*. Laurea University of Applied Sciences.

Helsingin kaupunki. (2017). *Selvitys syistä, miksi ara- ja välimuodon tavoitteita ei ole saavutettu sekä toimenpiteitä tavoitteisiin pääsemiseksi*. Kaupunginkanslia, talous- ja suunnitteluosasto.

Hietala, M., Kaleva, H., Kumpula, S. and Lahtinen, R. (2021). *Rajoituksista vapautuneet ARA-kohteet 2010–2020*. Asumisen rahoitus- ja kehittämiskeskuksen raportteja 1. Lahti: ARA.

Hilson, M. (2011). A consumers' international? The international cooperative alliance and cooperative internationalism, 1918–1939: A Nordic perspective. *International Review of Social History* 56 (2): 203–33.

Hochstenbach, C. (2017). State-led gentrification and the changing geography of market-oriented housing policies. *Housing, Theory and Society*, 34 (4): 399–419.

Hodkinson, S. and Essen, C. (2015). Grounding accumulation by dispossession in everyday life: The unjust geographies of urban regeneration under the private finance initiative. *International Journal of Law in the Built Environment* 7 (1): 72–91.

Hodkinson, S., Watt, P., and Mooney, G. (2013). Introduction: Neoliberal housing policy – time for a critical re-appraisal. *Critical Social Policy* 33 (1): 3–16.

Holgersen, S. and Baeten, G. (2017). Beyond a Liberal Critique of 'Trickle Down': Urban Planning in the City of Malmö. *IJURR* 40 (6): 1170–85.

Holt, R. (2018). *Global Cities – Which cities will be leading the global economy in 2035?* Oxford: Oxford Economics.

Hood, C. (1991). A public management for all seasons? *Public Administration* 69: 3–19.

Hughes, O. E. (2003). *Public Management and Administration: An Introduction.* New York: Palgrave.

Hyötyläinen, M. (2015). Uusliberaali kaupunkipolitiikka ja kuntien maankäyttö. *Yhteiskunta-politiikka* 80 (6): 625–34.

Hyötyläinen, M. (2016). The Poverty of Theory in Finnish Segregation Research. *Sosiologia* 53 (2): 105–21.

Hyötyläinen, M. (2020). "Not for Normal People": The Specialization of Social Rental Housing in Finland. *ACME: An International Journal for Critical Geographies*, 19 (2): 545–66.

Hyötyläinen, M. and Beauregard R. (2023). *The Political Economy of Land. Rent, Financialization and Resistance.* London: Routledge.

Hyötyläinen, M., and Haila, A. (2018). Entrepreneurial public real estate policy: The case of Eiranranta, Helsinki. *Geoforum* 89: 137–44.

Ilmavirta, T. (2008). Kaupunkiasuminen ja gentrifikaatio: Pasilan konepaja-alueen muu-toksen tarkastelua. In: Norvasuo, M. (Ed.) *Asuttaisiinko toisin? Kaupunkiasumisen uusia konsepteja kartoittamassa.* Helsinki: Yhdyskuntasuunnittelun tutkimus-ja koulutuskeskus.

Jäntti, M., Riihelä, M., Sullström, R., and Tuomala, M. (2010). Trends in Top Income Shares in Finland. In A. B. Atkinson, and T. Piketty (Eds), *Top Incomes: A Global Perspective.* Oxford: Oxford University Press.

James, L., Daniel, L., Bentley, R., and Baker, E. (2022). Housing inequality: A systematic scoping review. *Housing Studies*, ahead of print: 1–22.

Jessop, B. (1999). The Changing Governance of Welfare: Recent Trends in its Primary Functions, Scale, and Modes of Coordination. *Social Policy & Administration*, 33 (4), December 1999, 348–59.

Jessop, B. (2013). Revisiting the regulation approach: critical reflections on the contradic-tions, dilemmas, fixes and crisis dynamics of growth regimes. *Class & Capital* 37 (1): 5–24.

Jessop, B., Peck, J. and Tickell, A. (1999). Retooling the machine: economic crisis, state restructuring, and urban politics. In: Jonas, A. E. G. and Wilson, D. (Eds), *The Urban Growth Machine: Critical Perspectives Two Decades Later.* New York: State University of New York Press.

Jones, M. and Ward, K. (2002). Excavating the logic of British urban policy: neoliberal-ism as the 'crisis of crisis-management'. In: Brenner, N. and Theodore, N. (Eds), *Spaces of Neoliberalism.* Oxford: Blackwell Publishing.

Junnilainen, L. (2019). *Lähiökylä.* Tampere: Vastapaino.

Juntto, A. (1990). *Suomalainen Asuntopolitiikka: Topeliuksesta tulopolitiikkaan.* Tampere: Gaudeamus.

Juntto, A. (1992). Post-Industrial Housing Crisis: Finland as a Case Study. *Scandinavian Housing and Planning Research* 9 (2): 47–59.

Juntto, A., Viita, A., Toivanen, S., and Koro-Kanerva M. (2010). "Vuokra-asunto Helsingissä sijoituksena ja kotina. Vuokranantaja- ja vuokralaiskyselyn tuloksia." Suomen ympäristö 29/2010.

Jääskeläinen, L. and Syrjänen, O. (2010). *Maankäyttö- ja rakennuslaki selityksineen.* Helsinki: Rakennustieto Oy.

Kallin, H. and Slater, T. (2014). Activating territorial stigma: gentrifying marginality on Edinburgh's periphery. *Environment and Planning A* 46 (6): 1351–68.

Kangas, O. and Kvist, J. (2019). Nordic welfare states. In: Greve, B. (Ed.) *Routledge Handbook of the Welfare State.* New York: Routledge.

Karhula, A. (2015). Missä on Kallion gentrifikaatio? *Yhdyskuntasuunnittelu* 53 (4).

Karvonen, S., Kestilä, L. and Saikkonen, P. (2022). *Suomalaisten hyvinvointi 2022.* Terveyden ja hyvinvoinnin laitos.

Karvonen, S. and Kauppinen, T. (2009). Kuinka Suomi jakautuu 2000-luvulla? Hyvinvoinnin muuttuvat alue-erot. *Yhteiskuntapolitiikka* 74(5), 467–86.

Kauppinen, T., Kort teinen, M. and Vaattovaara, M. (2009). Pääkaupunkiseudun lamatyöttömien myöhemmät ansiotulot: iskikö lama kovemmin korkean työttömyyden alueilla? *Yhteiskuntapolitiikka* 74 (4): 358–74.

Keil, R. (2002). 'Common-sense' neoliberalism: progressive conservative urbanism in Toronto, Canada. In: Brenner, N. and Theodore, N. (Eds), *Spaces of Neoliberalism.* Oxford: Blackwell Publishing.

Kemppainen, T. (2017). *Disorder and insecurity in a residential context: a study focusing on Finnish suburban housing estates built in the 1960s and 1970s.* Helsinki: City of Helsinki Urban Research and Statistics.

Kemppainen, T., Lönnqvist, H., and Tuominen, M. (2014). Turvattomuus ei jakaudu tasan. Mitkä asuinalueen piirteet selittävät helsinkiläisten kokemaa turvattomuutta? *Yhteiskuntapolitiikka* 79 (1): 5–20.

Kervanto Nevanlinna, A. (2012). *Voimat jotka rakensivat Helsinkiä 1945-2010.* Helsinki: Otava.

Kettunen, P. (2012). Reinterpreting the historicity of the Nordic model. *Nordic Journal of Working Life Studies* 2 (4): 21–43.

Kettunen, H. and Ruonavaara, H. (2015). Discoursing deregulation: The case of the Finnish rental housing market. *International Journal of Housing Policy* 15 (2): 187–204.

Kildal, N. and Kuhnle, S. (2007). *Normative Foundations of the Welfare State: The Nordic Experience.* New York: Routledge.

Kirkness, P. and Tijé-Dra, A. (2017). (Eds) *Negative Neighbourhood Reputation and Place Attachment: The Production and Contestation of Territorial Stigma.* Oxon: Routledge.

Kohvakka, M. (2021). Justification work in a university merger: the case of the University of Eastern Finland. *European Journal of Higher Education* 11 (2): 197–215.

Kokkinen, J. (2008). Yhteiskuntavastuu palautettava valtion maapolitiikkaan. *Maankäyttö* 1.

Korhonen, E. (1997). Helsingin sosiaalisen vuokra-asumisen haasteet. In: Taipale, K. and Schulman, H. (Eds), *Koti Helsingissä. Urbaanin asumisen tulevaisuus.* Fagepaino: Helsinki.

Kortteinen, M., Lankinen, M. and Vaattovaara, M. (1999). Pääkaupunkiseudun kehitys 1990-luvulla: Kohti uudenlaista eriytymistä. *Yhteiskuntapolitiikka* 64 (5–6): 411–22.

Kortteinen, M., Tuominen, M. and Vaattovaara, M. (2005). Asumistoiveet, sosiaalinen epäjärjestys ja kaupunkisuunnittelu pääkaupunkiseudulla. *Yhteiskuntapolitiikka* 70 (2): 121–31.

Kortteinen, M. and Vaattovaara, M. (2000). Onko osa Helsingistä alikehityksen kierteessä? Yhteiskuntapolitiikka 65 (2): 115–24.

Kortteinen, M. and Vaattovaara, M. (2015). Segregaation aika. *Yhteiskuntapolitiikka* 80 (6): 562–74.

Koskela, H. (2009). *Pelkokierre.* Helsinki: Gaudeamus.

Koskela, K. (2008). *Naapuruston tulotason vaikutus koettuun hyvinvointiin pääkaupunkiseudun huonotuloisilla alueilla.* Pro gradu-tutkielma, Helsingin yliopisto.

Kröger, T. (2011). Retuning the Nordic welfare municipality: Central regulation of social care under change in Finland. *International Journal of Sociology and Social Policy* 31 (3/4): 148–59.

Kuisma, M. (2017). Oscillating meanings of the Nordic model: ideas and the welfare state in Finland and Sweden. *Critical Policy Studies* 11 (4): 433–54.

Kunnas, H. (2013). *Naapuruston vaikutus terveyskäyttäytymiseen pääkaupunkiseudun huonotuloisimmilla alueilla.* Pro gradu -tutkielma, Helsingin yliopisto.

Kuntaliitto. (2021). *Näkökulmia kaupunkien sosiaaliseen kestävyyteen.* Helsinki: Suomen Kuntaliitto.

Kuusela, H. and Ylönen, M. (2013). *Konsulttidemokratia: Miten valtiosta tehdään tyhmä ja tehoton.* Helsinki: Gaudeamus.

Kuusi, P. (1968). *60-luvun sosiaalipolitiikka.* Porvoo: Werner Söderström Oy.

Kvist, J. and Greve, B. (2011). Has the Nordic Welfare Model Been Transformed? *Social Policy & Administration* 45 (2): 146–60.

Kvist, J. and Fritzell, J. (2012). *Changing Social Equality: The Nordic Welfare Model in the 21st Century.* Bristol: Policy Press.

Larsen, T. S. (2014). Copenhagen's west end a 'paradise lost': the political production of territorial stigmatization in Denmark. *Environment and Planning A* 46 (6): 1386–402.

Larsen, T. S. and Delica, K. N. (2019). The production of territorial stigmatisation: A conceptual cartography. *City* 23 (4–5): 540–63.

Lawson, J. M. and Ruonavaara, H. (2019). *Land Policy for Affordable and Inclusive Housing: An International Review.* Smartland.

Lees, L. (2008). Gentrification and Social Mixing: Towards an Inclusive Urban Renaissance? *Urban Studies* 45 (12): 2449–70.

Lees, L., Shin, H. B. and López-Morales, E. (Eds). (2015). *Global Gentrifications: Uneven Development and Displacement.* Bristol: Policy Press.

Lees, L., Slater, T. and Wyly, E. (2008). *Gentrification.* New York: Routledge.

Lefebvre, H. (1991). *The Production of Space.* Oxford: Blackwell.

Lefebvre, H. (2003). *The Urban Revolution.* Minneapolis: University of Minnesota Press.

LeGales, P. (2002). *European Cities: Social Conflicts and Governance.* Oxford: Oxford University Press.

Lehtiö, S. (2004). Suomen pankkikriisin taustatekijät, luonne ja kriisinhoito erityisesti säästöpankeissa. *Kansantaloudellinen aikakauskirja* 100(2): 173–8.

Lehto, J. (2000). Different Cities in Different Welfare States. In: Bagnasco, A. and LeGalès, P. (Eds), *Cities in Contemporary Europe.* Cambridge: Cambridge University Press.

Levien, M. (2013). Regimes of dispossession: From steel towns to special economic zones. *Development and change* 44(2): 381–407.

Lewis, O. (1959). *Five families: Mexican case studies in the culture of poverty*. New York: Mentor Book.

Lilius, J. and Hirvonen, J. (2021). The changing position of housing estate neighbourhoods in the Helsinki metropolitan area. *Journal of Housing and the Built Environment* 2021. Published online 24 August 2021. Open access.

Listerborn, C. (2023). The new housing precariat: experiences of precarious housing in Malmö, Sweden. *Housing Studies*, 38:7, 1304–22.

Lobao, L., Martin, R., and Rodríguez-Pose, A. (2009). Rescaling the state: new modes of institutional–territorial organization. *Cambridge Journal of Regions, Economy and Society* 2 (1): 3–12.

Logan, J. R. and Molotch, H. L. (1987). *Urban Fortunes: The Political Economy of Place*. Berkeley: University of California Press.

Low, S., Donovan, G. T. and Gieseking, J. (2012). Shoestring democracy: gated condominiums and market-rate cooperatives in New York. *Journal of Urban Affairs* 34 (3): 279–96.

Macpherson, C. B. (1978). *Property, mainstream and critical positions*. Toronto: University of Toronto Press.

Madden, D. and Marcuse, P. (2016). *In Defence of Housing*. New York: Verso.

Makki, F. and Geisler, C. (2011). *Development by Dispossession: Land Grabbing as New Enclosures in Contemporary Ethiopia*. Paper presentation: International Conference on Global Land Grabbing. Institute of Development Studies, University of Sussex. April 6–8.

Marcuse, P. (1985). Gentrification, Abandonment, and Displacement: Connections, Causes, and Policy Responses in New York City. *Washington University Journal of Urban and Contemporary Law* 28: 195–240.

Marcuse, P. (1989). 'Dual City': a muddy metaphor for a quartered city. *International Journal of Urban and Regional Research* 13 (4): 697–708.

Marshall, T. H. (1987). *Citizenship and social class*. London: Pluto Press.

Marttinen, R. (2019). *Asuntojen hintojen ja vuokrien vuosijulkaisu 2019*. Helsingin kaupunginkanslia.

Marx, K. (1867/1990). *Capital Volume 1*. London: Penguin Classics.

Marx, K. (1939/1993). *Grundrisse: Foundations of the Critique of Political Economy (Rough Draft)*. Trans. Martin Nicolaus. London: Penguin Classics.

Marx, K. and Engels, F. (1881/1976). *Kirjeitä*. Suomennos: Koste, T. and Oittinen, V. Moskova: Kustannusliike Edistys.

Marx, K. and Engels, F. (2015/1888). *Manifesto of the Communist Party*. London: Penguin Classics.

Massey, D. S. and Denton, N. A. (1987). Trends in the residential segregation of Blacks, Hispanics, and Asians: 1970-1980. *American sociological review* 52 (6): 802–25.

Massey, D. S. and Denton, N. A. (1988). The Dimensions of Residential Segregation. *Social Forces* 67 (2): 281–315.

Massey, D. S. and Denton, N. A. (1993). *American Apartheid: Segregation and the Making of the Underclass*. Cambridge, MA: Harvard University Press.

Mazzucato, M. (2019). *The Value of Everything: Making and Taking in the Global Economy*. London: Penguin Books.

McKenzie, E. (1994). *Privatopia: Homeowner Associations and the Rise of Residential Private Government*. New Haven: Yale University Press

Meurman, O. I. (1947). *Asemakaavaoppi*. Helsinki: Otava.

Miller, H. L. (1962). On the "Chicago School of Economics". *Journal of Political Economy*, 70 (1): 64–9.

Mills, E. (1967). An aggregative model of resource allocation in a metropolitan area. *American Economic Review Papers and Proceedings* 57 (2): 197–210.

Mingione, E. (1996). *Urban Poverty and the Underclass*. Oxford: Blackwell.

Moisio, P. (2010). Tuloerojen, köyhyyden ja toimeentulo-ongelmien kehitys. In: Vaarama, M., Moisio, P. and Karvonen S. (Eds), *Suomalaisten hyvinvointi 2010*. Terveyden ja hyvinvoinnin laitos. Helsinki: Yliopistopaino.

Moisio, S. (2008). Towards Attractive and Cost-Efficient State Space: Political Geography of the Production of State Transformation in Finland. *World Political Science* 4 (3): 1–34.

Moisio, S. and Leppänen, L. (2007). Towards a Nordic competition state? Politico-economic transformation of statehood in Finland, 1965–2005. *Fennia-International Journal of Geography* 185 (2): 63–87.

Moisio, S. and Paasi, A. (2013). From geopolitical to geoeconomic? The changing political rationalities of state space. *Geopolitics* 18 (2): 267–83.

Mollenkopf, J. H. and Castells, M. (1991). *Dual City: Restructuring New York*. New York: Russell Sage Foundation.

Molotch, H. (1976). The City as a Growth Machine: Toward a Political Economy of Place. *American Journal of Sociology* 82 (2): 309–32.

Morris, A. (2015). *The Scholar Denied: W.E.B. Du Bois and The Birth of Modern Sociology*. Oakland: University of California Press.

Morris, L. (1996). Dangerous Classes: Neglected Aspects of the Underclass Debate. In: Mingione, E. (Ed.), *Urban Poverty and the Underclass*. Oxford: Blackwell.

Muth, R. (1969). *Cities and Housing*. Chicago: University of Chicago Press.

Myrdal, G. (1963). *Challenge to Affluence*. New York: Pantheon.

Mäkinen, E. (2000). *Maankäyttösopimus ja hyvä hallinto*. Tampere: Finnpublishers Oy.

Mäntysalo, R. and Nyman, K. (2001). *Kaavoitus – suunnittelua? Suunnittelun patologioita maankäyttö- ja rakennuslain sovelluksissa*. Julkaisu A 30 Arkkitehtuurin osasto. Oulun yliopisto.

Mösgen, A., Rosol, M., and Schipper, S. (2019). State-led gentrification in previously 'un-gentrifiable' areas: Examples from Vancouver/Canada and Frankfurt/Germany. *European Urban and Regional Studies* 26 (4): 419–33.

Nevalainen, J. (2004). Kaupungista puhumisen tavat vallankäytön välineenä. *Yhdyskuntasuunnittelu* 42: 3–4.

Newman, K. and Wyly, E. K. (2006). The right to stay put, revisited: Gentrification and resistance to displacement in New York City. *Urban studies* 43 (1): 23–57.

Nijman, J. and Wei, Y. D. (2020). Urban inequalities in the 21st century economy. *Applied geography* 117 (102188): 1–8.

Nurmi, E. (2005). *Maasta se suurikin ponnistaa. Helsingin kaupungin kiinteistövirasto 75 vuotta*. Porvoo: WS Bookwell.

Nygaard, K. (2021). Finland: Arsenal. *The Journal of Financial Crises* 3(2): 264–89.

Olsson, L. (2018). The neoliberalization of municipal land policy in Sweden. *International Journal of Urban and Regional Research* 42 (4): 633–50.

Osborne, D. E. and Gaebler, T. (1992). *Reinventing government: how the entrepreneurial spirit is transforming the public sector*. New York: Penguin.

Park, R. E. (1925). The City: Suggestions for the Investigation of Human Behavior in the Urban Environment. In: Park R. E., Burgess, E. W. and McKenzie, R. D. (Eds), *The City*. Chicago: The University of Chicago Press.

Park, R. E. (1926). The Urban Community as a Spacial Pattern and a Moral Order. In: Burgess, E. W. (Ed.), *The Urban Community*. Chicago: The University of Chicago Press.

Peck, J. (2002). Political economies of scale: Fast policy, interscalar relations, and neoliberal workfare. *Economic geography* 78 (3): 331–60.

Peck, J., Theodore, N. and Brenner, N. (2009). Neoliberal urbanism: models, moments, mutations. *SAIS Rev. Int. Affairs* 29 (1): 49–66.

Peck, J. and Theodore, N. (2007). Variegated capitalism. *Progress in human geography* 31 (6): 731–72.

Peck, J. and Theodore, N. (2001). Exporting workfare/importing welfare-to-work: exploring the politics of Third Way policy transfer. *Political geography* 20 (4): 427–60.

Peck, J. and Tickell, A. (2002). Neoliberalizing space. *Antipode* 34 (3): 380–404.

Pemberton, S., Fahmy, E., Sutton, E., and Bell, K. (2016). Navigating the stigmatised identities of poverty in austere times: Resisting and responding to narratives of personal failure. *Critical Social Policy* 36 (1): 21–37.

Perhiö, T. (2017). *Aluerakentaminen paikallisena asuntopoliittisena ratkaisuna Turussa 1963–1967*. Master's thesis: University of Helsinki, Faculty of Social Sciences, Department of Political and Economic Studies.

Piketty, T. (2013). *Capital in the Twenty First Century*. Harvard: The Belknap Press.

Preteceille, E. (2000). Segregation, class and politics in large cities. In: Bagnasco, A. and Le Galès, P. (Eds), *Cities in Contemporary Europe*. Cambridge: Cambridge University Press.

Rajavuori, A. (2022). *Eriarvoisuuden tila Suomessa 2022*. Kalevi Sorsa Säätiö.

Rasinkangas, J. (2013). *Sosiaalinen eriytyminen turun kaupunkiseudulla. Tutkimus asumisen alueellisista muutoksista ja asumispreferensseistä*. Turku: Siirtolaisuusinstituutti.

Richardson, H. W. (1977). *The New Urban Economics and Alternatives*. London: Pion Limited.

Righard, E., Johansson, M. and Salonen, T. (2015). *Social Transformations in Scandinavian Cities. Nordic Perspectives on Urban Marginalization and Social Sustainability*. Lund: Nordic Academic Press.

Rintala, T. (1995). *Medikalisaatio ja sosiaali- ja terveydenhuollon palvelujärjestelmän rakentuminen 1946-1991*. Stakes 54. Saarijärvi: Gummerus.

Roivainen, I. (1999). *Sokeripala metsän keskellä. Lähiö sanomalehden konstruktiona*. Helsinki: Helsingin kaupungin tietokeskus

Rolnik, R. (2013). Late neoliberalism: The financialization of homeownership and housing rights. *International Journal of Urban and Regional Research* 37 (3): 1058–66.

Rose, L. E. and Ståhlberg, K. (2005). The Nordic countries: Still the promised land? In: Denters, S. A. H, Denters, B. and Rose, L. E. (Eds), *Comparing Local Governance. Trends and Developments.* New York: Palgrave Macmillan.

Ruonavaara, H. (2017). Retrenchment and social housing: the case of Finland. *Critical Housing Analysis* 4 (2): 8.

Ruonavaara, H. (2005). How Divergent Housing Institutions Evolve: A Comparison of Swedish Tenant Co-operatives and Finnish Shareholders' Housing Companies. *Housing, Theory and Society* 22 (4): 213–36.

Ruonavaara, H., (1996). The home ideology and housing discourse in Finland 1900–1950. *Housing studies* 11 (1): 89–104.

Saikkonen, P., Hannikainen, K., Kauppinen, T., Rasinkangas, J., and Vaalavuo, M. (2018). *Sosiaalinen kestävyys: asuminen, segregaatio ja tuloerot kolmella kaupunkiseudulla.* Terveyden ja hyvinvoinnin laitos.

Sakizlioglu, N. B, and Uitermark, J. L. (2014). The symbolic politics of gentrification: The restructuring of stigmatized neighborhoods in Amsterdam and Istanbul. *Environment and Planning A: International Journal of Urban and Regional Research*, 46 (6), 1369–85.

Salo, R. and Mäntysalo, R. (2017). Path dependencies and defensive routines in Finnish city-regional land-use policy cooperation: case Ristikytö. *International Planning Studies* 22 (2): 128–44.

Sassen, S. (1991). *The Global City: New York, London, Tokyo.* Princeton: Princeton University Press.

Sassen, S. (2014). *Expulsions.* Harvard: Harvard University Press.

Savage, M. and Warde, A. (1993). *Urban Sociology, Capitalism and Modernity.* New York: Continuum.

Sayer, A. (1992). *Method in Social Science. A Realist Approach.* London: Routledge.

Sayer, A. (2015). *Why We Can't Afford the Rich.* Bristol: Policy Press.

Schwarze, T. (2022) Discursive practices of territorial stigmatization: how newspapers frame violence and crime in a Chicago community. *Urban Geography*, 43 (9): 1415–36.

Silagi, M. (1994). Henry George and Europe. Trans. S. Faulkner. *American Journal of Economics and Sociology* 53 (4): 491–501.

Sipilä, J. (2006). Äiti, koti ja isänmaa kilpailuvaltiossa. *Yhteiskuntapolitiikka* 71 (4): 411–15.

Skifter Andersen, H. (1995). Explanations of urban decay and renewal on the housing market – what can Europe learn from American research? *Netherlands Journal of Housing and the Built Environment*, 10: 65–85.

Skifter Andersen, H. (1998). Gentrification or social renewal? Effects of public supported housing renewal in Denmark. *Scandinavian Housing and Planning Research*, 15(3): 111–28.

Skifter Andersen, H. (2002). Excluded Places: The Interaction between Segregation, Urban Decay and Deprived Neighborhoods. *Housing, Theory and Society* 19 (3–4): 153–69.

Skifter Andersen, H. (2003). *Urban sores: On the interaction between segregation, urban decay, and deprived neighborhoods.* Ashgate: Aldershot.

Skifter Andersen, H. (2019). *Ethnic Spatial Segregation in European Cities.* New York: Routledge.

Slater, T. (2013). Your life chances affect where you live: A critique of the 'cottage industry' of neighborhood effects research. *International Journal of Urban and Regional Research* 37 (2): 367–87.

Slater, T. (2015). Territorial Stigmatization: Symbolic Defamation and the Contemporary Metropolis. In: Hannigan, J. and G. Richrads (Eds), *The Handbook of New Urban Studies.* London: Sage.

Slater, T. (2021). *Shaking up the City: Reframing Urban Inequalities.* Berkeley: University of California Press.

Slater, T. and Anderson, N. (2012). The reputational ghetto: territorial stigmatisation in St Paul's, Bristol. *Transactions of the Institute of British Geographers* 37 (4): 530–46.

Smets, P. and Salman, T. (2008). Countering Urban Segregation: Theoretical and Policy Innovations from around the Globe. *Urban Studies* 45 (7): 1307–32.

Smith, N. (1979). Toward a theory of gentrification: a back to the city movement by capital, not people. *Journal of the American Planning Association* 45 (4): 538–48.

Smith, N. (1982). Gentrification and uneven development. *Economic Geography* 58 (2): 139–55.

Smith, N. (2002). New globalism, new urbanism: gentrification as global urban strategy. *Antipode* 34 (3): 427–50.

Smith, N. (2008). *Uneven Development: Nature, Capital, and the Production of Space*. Athens: The University of Georgia Press.

Soederberg, S. (2018). The rental housing question: Exploitation, eviction and erasures. *Geoforum* 89: 114–23.

Stewart, M. (2002). Deprivation, the Roma and 'the underclass'. In: Hann, C. M. (Ed.), *Post-socialism: Ideals, Ideologies and Practices in Eurasia*. London: Routledge.

Stjernberg, M. (2019). *Concrete Suburbia: Suburban Housing Estates and Socio-spatial Differentiation in Finland*. Department of Geosciences and Geography A 77.

Swyngedouw, E., Moulaert, F. and Rodriguez, A. (2002). Neoliberal urbanization in Europe: large-scale urban development projects and the new urban policy. *Antipode* 34 (3): 542–77.

Swyngedouw, E. and Kaïka, M. (2003). The making of 'glocal' urban modernities. *City* 7 (1): 5–21.

Taipale, I. (1982). *Asunnottomuus ja alkoholi. Sosiaalilääketieteellinen tutkimus Helsingistä vuosilta 1937-1977*. Alkoholitutkimussäätiön julkaisuja. Jyväskylä: Gummerus.

Tammaru, T., van Ham, M., Marcińczak, S. and Musterd, S. (2015). *Socio-Economic Segregation in European Capital Cities: East Meets West*. New York: Routledge.

Teernstra, A. B. and Van Gent, W. P. (2012). Puzzling patterns in neighborhood change: Upgrading and downgrading in highly regulated urban housing markets. *Urban Geography*, 33 (1): 91–119.

Temmes, M. (1998). Finland and new public management. *International Review of Administrative Sciences* 64 (3): 441–56.

Teresa, B. F. (2016). Managing fictitious capital: The legal geography of investment and political struggle in rental housing in New York City. *Environment and Planning A* 48 (3): 465–84.

Thurber, A., Krings, A., Martinez, L. S., and Ohmer, M. (2021). Resisting gentrification: The theoretical and practice contributions of social work. *Journal of Social Work* 21 (1): 26–45.

Tranøy, B. S., Stamsø, M. A., and Hjertaker, I. (2020). Equality as a driver of inequality? Universalistic welfare, generalised creditworthiness and financialised housing markets. *West European Politics* 43 (2): 390–411.

Tulla, S. (1999). Securitisation and Finance for Social Housing in Finland. *Urban Studies* 36 (4): 647–56.

Turpeinen, O., Herranen, T. and Hoffman, K. (1997). *Helsingin historia vuodesta 1945*. Helsinki: Oy Edita Ab.

Turun kaupunki, Konsernihallinto. (2013). *Turun kaupunkiseudun asunto- ja maapoliittinen ohjelma 2014–2017*. Turun kaupungin tilastollinen vuosikirja.

Vaattovaara, M. (2002). Future Developments of Residential Differentiation in the Helsinki Metropolitan Area: Are We Following the European Model? *Yearbook of Population Research in Finland* 38: 107–23.

Vaattovaara, M. and Kortteinen, M. (2002). Beyond Polarisation versus Professionalisation? A Case Study of the Development of the Helsinki Region, Finland. *Urban Studies* 40 (11): 2127–45.

Vaattovaara, M. and Kortteinen, M. (2007). Eriytyykö Helsingin metropolialue? *Kvartti* 1: 46–62.

Vaattovaara, M. and Kortteinen, M. (2012). Segregaatiosta ja sen inhimillisestä ja yhteiskunnallisesta merkityksestä. *Talous & Yhteiskunta* 3: 60–66.

Van Aerschot, L., and Salminen, J. (2018). Hyvä, paha lähiö: nuoret ja asuinalueella syntyvä sosiaalinen pääoma. *Sosiologia*, 55(3).

Van der Wusten, H. and Musterd, S. (1998). Welfare state effects on inequality and segregation: Concluding remarks. In: Musterd, S. and Ostendorf, W. (Eds), *Urban Segregation and the Welfare State*. London: Routledge.

Van Gent, W. P. (2010). Housing policy as a lever for change? The politics of welfare, assets and tenure. *Housing Studies*, 25 (5): 735–53.

van Ham, M., Tammaru, T., Ubarevičienė, R. and Janssen, H. (2021). *Urban Socio-Economic Segregation and Income Inequality*. Cham: Springer.

Van Horn, R. and Mirowski, P. (2009). The rise of the Chicago School of Economics and the birth of neoliberalism. In: Mirowski, P. and Plehwe, D. (Eds), *The Road from Mont Pèlerin: The Making of the Neoliberal Thought Collective*. Cambridge, MA: Harvard University Press.

Veggeland, N. (2016). The Narrative of the Nordic Welfare State Model. In: Veggeland, N. (Ed.), *The Current Nordic Welfare State Model*. Nova Science Publishers, Inc.

Vesanen. (1991). *Hullunkirjoista talonkirjoihin. Selvitys laitos- ja avohoitopotilaiden asumisolosuhteista*. Sosiaali- ja terveyshallitus, Raportteja 42.

Vilkama, K. (2011). *Shared city or divided neighbourhoods? Residential segregation and selective migration of the native and immigrant populations in the Helsinki Metropolitan Area*. University of Helsinki.

Vilkama, K., Vaattovaara, M. and Dhalmann, H. (2013). Kantaväestön pakoa? Miksi maah- anmuuttajakeskittymistä muutetaan pois? "White Flight"? Why do people move out of immigrant-dense neighborhoods?" *Yhteiskuntapolitiikka* 78 (5): 485–97.

Virtanen, H. (2007). Monietnistyvät lähiöt – suomalaisten asuinalueiden etninen erilaistumiskehitys ja siihen vaikuttavat tekijät. *Yhdyskuntasuunnittelu* 45 (3): 6–19.

Virtanen, P. V. (2000). *Kunnan maapolitiikka*. Tampere: Rakennustieto Oy.

Wacquant, L. (1996). Red Belt, Black Belt: Racial Division, Class Inequality and the State in the French Urban Periphery and the American Ghetto. In: Mingione, E. (Ed), *Urban Poverty and the Underclass*. Oxford: Blackwell.

Wacquant, L. (2007) Territorial Stigmatization in the age of Advanced Marginality, *Thesis Eleven 9*, 66–77.

Wacquant, L. (2008). *Urban outcasts: A comparative sociology of advanced marginality*. Cambridge: Polity.

Wacquant, L., Slater, T. and Pereira, V. B. (2014). Territorial stigmatization in action. *Environment and Planning A* 46 (6): 1270–80.

Waris, H. (1962). *Suomalaisen yhteiskunnan sosiaalipolitiikka*. Porvoo: WSOY.

Watson, J. W. (1976). Land use and Adam Smith: A bicentennial note. *Scottish Geographical Magazine* 92 (2): 129–34.

Watt, P. (2009). Housing stock transfers, regeneration and state-led gentrification in London. *Urban Policy and Research*, 27 (3): 229–42.

Watt, P. (2020). Territorial stigmatisation and poor housing at a London 'Sink Estate'. *Social Inclusion*, 8 (1): 20–33.

Weber, R. (2002). Extracting value from the city: neoliberalism and urban redevelopment. In: Brenner, N. and Theodore, N. (Eds), *Spaces of Neoliberalism*. Oxford: Blackwell Publishing.

Whiteside, H. (2017). The Canada Infrastructure Bank: private finance as poor alternative. *Studies in Political Economy* 98 (2): 223–37.

Whiteside, H. (2019). The state's estate: Devaluing and revaluing 'surplus' public land in Canada. *Environment and Planning A: Economy and Space* 51 (2): 505–26.

Wollmann, H. (2004). Local government reforms in Great Britain, Sweden, Germany and France: between multi-function and single-purpose organisations. *Local Government Studies* 30 (4): 639–65.

Yliaska, V. (2017). Tehokkuustalouden lähihistoria. In: Eskelinen, T., Harjunen, H., Hirvonen, H., and Jokinen, E. (Ed): *Tehostamistalous*. Jyväskylä: SoPhi.

Yrigoy, I. (2020). The Role of Regulations in the Spanish Housing Dispossession Crisis: Towards Dispossession by Regulations? *Antipode* 52 (1): 316–36.

Zetterlund, H. (2022). *The Landed Municipality. The Underlying Rationales for Swedish Public Landownership and their Implications for Policy*. Uppsala: Geographica.

Zukin, S. (2011). Is there an urban sociology? Questions on a field and a vision. *Sociologica* 3.

Online resources

Act on Keva. https://www.keva.fi/globalassets/2-tiedostot/tama-on-keva--tiedostot/act-on-keva-1.7.2021.pdf (Accessed on 31.3.2022).

Act on Interest Subsidy for Rental Housing Loans and Right of Occupancy Housing Loans. https://www.finlex.fi/en/laki/kaannokset/2001/en20010604.pdf (Accessed on 01.12.2022).

Ahola, H. (2021). https://www.ara.fi/fi-FI/Tietopankki/ARAviesti/ARAviestin_ verkkoartikkelit/Vuokraasumisen_vuosikymmen(61589) (Accessed on 01.12.2022).

Amnesty International 31.5.2022. Covid-19: Pandemic restrictions magnified discrimination against most marginalized groups. https://www.amnesty.org/en/latest/news/2022/05/covid-19-pandemic-restrictions-magnified-discrimination-against-most-marginalized-groups/#:~:text=Marginalized%20groups%2C%20including%20LGBTI%2B%20people,today%20assessing%20the%20impact%20of (Accessed on 6.3.2023).

ARA 6.3.2023. Käyttö- ja luovutusrajoitukset. https://www.ara.fi/fi-FI/ARAasuntokanta/Kaytto_ja_luovutusrajoitukset (Accessed on 6.3.2023).

ARA 13.2.2020. Lyhytaikaisen korkotuen ARA-vuokra-asunnot https://www.ara.fi/fi-FI/ARAasuntokanta/Lyhytaikaisen_korkotuen_ARAvuokraasunnot (Accessed on 6.3.2023).

ARA. https://www.ara.fi/fi-FI/ARAasuntokanta/Kaytto_ja_luovutusrajoitukset (Accessed on 01.12.2022).

Boone et al. (2021). https://oecdecoscope.blog/2021/12/13/finlands-zero-homeless-strategy-lessons-from-a-success-story/ (Accessed on 29.3.2022).

Business Insider 3.2.2020. Bernie Sanders and AOC support the 'Nordic model'. https://markets.businessinsider.com/news/stocks/bernie-sanders-nordic-model-finland-american-dream-sanna-marin-2020-2-1028868627 (Accessed on 6.3.2023).

CNBC 5.1.2023. I'm a psychology expert in Finland, the No. 1 happiest country in the world—here are 3 things we never do. https://www.cnbc.com/2023/01/05/what-people-in-finland-happiest-country-in-world-never-do-according-to-psychologist.html#:~:text=For%20five%20years%20in%20a,possible%20life%20as%20a%200.%E2%80%9D (Accessed on 6.3.2023).

Constitution of Finland. https://www.finlex.fi/en/laki/kaannokset/1999/en19990731.pdf (Accessed on 28.3.2022).

Eiranranta housing profile 2016. http://openbuildings.com/buildings/eiranranta-housing-profile-4568 (Accessed on 28.10.2016).

Engels, F. (1872). *The Housing Question.* Co-operative Publishing Society of Foreign Workers. marxists.org (Accessed on 26.3.2022).

Financial Times 5.6.2017. Blackstone signs deal to buy Sponda of Finland. https://www.ft.com/content/013a9e0e-49d1-11e7-919a-1e14ce4af89b (Accessed on 6.3.2023).

The Finnish Environmental Administration. https://www.ymparisto.fi/en-us/housing/Housing_for_special_groups (Accessed on 01.12.2022).

The Finnish Landlord Association 2.11.2018. Oikeasti ihana asumistuki. https://vuokranantajat.fi/2018/11/oikeasti-ihana-asumistuki/ (Accessed on 6.3.2023).

Fortune 27.5.2020. On average, top CEOs make over $12.3 million. Can that continue after the coronavirus? https://fortune.com/2020/05/27/ceo-pay-average-coronavirus-lisa-su-bob-iger-reed-hastings-salary/ (Accessed on 6.3.2023).

The Guardian 21.6.2022. Covid vaccine figures lay bare global inequality as global target missed. https://www.theguardian.com/global-development/2022/jul/21/covid-vaccine-figures-lay-bare-global-inequality-as-global-target-missed (Accessed 6.3.2023).

Helsinki City Council minutes on real estate strategy. https://www.hel.fi/static/helsinki/valtuustoseminaari-2019/kiinteistostrategia.pdf (Accessed on 31.3.2022).

Helsingin kaupungin kiinteistöstrategia 2019. https://www.hel.fi/static/helsinki/valtuustoseminaari-2019/kiinteistostrategia.pdf (Accessed on 6.3.2023).

Helsingin kaupunginvaltuusto 2.2.2022. Asuntotonttien sekä asumista palvelevien tonttien maanvuokrauksen yleiset periaatteet. https://dev.hel.fi/paatokset/asia/hel-2016-012511/kvsto-2022-2/ (Accessed on 6.3.2023).

Helsingin Sanomat:

6.9.1999. Luokkayhteiskunnan mukainen aluejako palaa pääkaupunkiseudulle https://www.hs.fi/kaupunki/art-2000003825329.html (Accessed on 7.1.2023).

25.8.2000. Sato, VVO ja YH ajavat alas valtion tukemaa vuokra-asuntojen tuotantoa pääkaupunkiseudulla. https://www.hs.fi/kaupunki/art-2000003906411.html (Accessed on 6.3.2023).

29.9.2006. Maahanmuuttajat ovat keskittymässä samoihin kaupungin vuokrataloihin https://www.hs.fi/kaupunki/art-2000004428682.html (Accessed on 7.1.2023).

29.4.2011. Suomen kieli hiipuu lähiöissä – Maahanmuuttajien keskittymiä syntyy pääkaupunkiseudulle https://www.hs.fi/kaupunki/art-2000004803493.html (Accessed on 7.1.2023).

29.11.2011. Kiuru: Asuinalueiden eriytyminen luultua pahempi ongelma https://www. hs.fi/kotimaa/art-2000002512417.html (Accessed on 7.1.2023).

25.10.2013. Tutkija: Lähiöiden eriytymiskierre pysäytetään työtä luomalla − Monet ongelmalähiöt ovat omia eristyneitä ja sulkeutuneita saarekkeita. https://www.hs.fi/ kaupunki/art-2000002683606.html (Accessed on 7.1.2023).

27.10.2013. Maahanmuuttajien suuri määrä on jo syy muuttaa pois lähiöstä https://www. hs.fi/paakirjoitukset/art-2000002683924.html (Accessed on 7.1.2023).

30.10.2013. "Valkoinen pako" on totta, ja asiasta pitää pystyä puhumaan https://www. hs.fi/kotimaa/art-2000002684660.html (Accessed on 7.1.2023).

27.11.2013. Eriytyminen kiihtyy kaupunkien lähiöissä https://www.hs.fi/paakirjoitukset/ art-2000002691971.html (Accessed on 7.1.2023).

10.12.2015. Huono-osaisuus näkyy, kun tarkastelee yksittäisiä kortteleita https://www. hs.fi/kaupunki/art-2000002871910.html (Accessed on 7.1.2023).

12.12.2015. Joiltain asuinalueilta muutetaan turvattomuuden takia − Katso, mistä ja minne helsinkiläiset haluavat muuttaa (https://www.hs.fi/kaupunki/art-2000002872365.html (Accessed on 7.1.2023).

10.12.2015. Asuinalueiden väliset erot vahvistuvat yhä Helsingissä − "kansakunta on vaarassa haljeta" https://www.hs.fi/kaupunki/art-2000002871909.html (Accessed on 7.1.2023).

22.11.2018. Ensimmäistä kertaa Helsingissä: Kirjasto avattiin Laajasalon uudessa kauppakeskuksessa https://www.hs.fi/kaupunki/art-2000005907651.html (Accessed on 6.3.2023).

6.7.2019. Hallitus haluaa hillitä vuokrien nousua. https://www.hs.fi/paivanlehti/06072019/ art-2000006165156.html (Accessed on 6.3.2023).

20.10.2020. Helsinki haluaa vuokratonteista markkinahinnan: Uusi malli nostaisi asumisen hintaa monilla alueilla. https://www.hs.fi/kaupunki/art-2000006676107.html (Accessed on 6.2.2023).

10.2.2021. Jopa satojen eurojen vuokrankorotukset uhkaavat lukuisia Helsingin vuokra-asukkaita. https://www.hs.fi/kaupunki/art-2000007793494.html (Accessed on 6.2.2023).

6.8.2021. Pormestari Vartiainen palkkasi Helsinkiin historian ensimmäisen pääekonomistin. https://www.hs.fi/kaupunki/art-2000008176068.html?fbclid=IwAR2r39Vu P8Gq46x9wPne13TYQbmddnaO-YcbEvSLUMJb51vHRtbIlBti_KU. (Accessed on 6.3.2023).

19.9.2021. Juhana Vartiainen haluaa palkita työn¬¬tekijöitä suoritusten perusteella. https://www.hs.fi/kaupunki/art-2000008260167.html (Accessed on 6.3.2023).

21.2.2022. Asuntojen hinnat nousivat useilla Helsingin alueilla räjähdysmäisesti vain yhdessä vuodessa. https://www.hs.fi/kaupunki/art-2000008618055.html (Accessed on 6.3.2023).

Helsingin vasemmisto 11.2.2022. Helsingin maapolitiikka, tonttivuokrat ja asumisen hinta − mistä on kyse? https://www.helsinginvasemmisto.fi/helsingin-maapolitiikka-tonttivuokrat-ja-asumisen-hinta-mista-on-kyse/ (Accessed on 6.3.2023).

Helsinki 20. kaupunginosa, asemakaava. http://kartta.hel.fi/kaavapdf/10800.pdf (Accessed on 28.10.2016).

Kela. Social Insurance Institution of Finland. https://tietotarjotin.fi/tietopaketti/2699658/ tietopaketti-asumistuet?categories=asuminen (Accessed on 9.5.2023).

Kela. Social Insurance Institution of Finland. 2018. Research blog. http://tutkimusblogi. kela.fi/arkisto/4091 (Accessed on 7.8.2018).

Keva. Asukastoiminta Kevan kodeissa. https://vuokra-asunnot.keva.fi/asunnonhakija-ja-asukas/#question-27957 (Accessed on 6.3.2023).

Keva Investment Beliefs. https://www.keva.fi/globalassets/2-tiedostot/tama-on-keva--tiedostot/sijoitukset-talous-ja-raportointi/investment-beliefs.pdf (Accessed on 31.3.2022).

Keva Responsible Investment Beliefs. https://www.keva.fi/globalassets/2-tiedostot/tama-on-keva--tiedostot/sijoitukset-talous-ja-raportointi/responsible-investment-beliefs.pdf (Accessed on 31.3.2022).

KTI Benchmarking 2023. Finnish Property News. https://kti-kiinteistotieto-oy.creamailer.fi/email/63c15b99b63b1 (Accessed on 8.2.2023).

Lampi, P. (2013). "Mellunmäellä on rikas historia ja tulevaisuus" http://kaupunginosat.net/mellunmaki/forum/2-keskustelu/25-mellunmaella-on-rikas-historia-ja-tulevaisuus. (Accessed on 24.4.2013).

Land Policy Guidebook. https://www.kuntaliitto.fi/tilastot-ja-julkaisut/verkko-oppaat/maapolitiikan-opas (Accessed on 28.3.2022).

Länsiväylä 14.62017. "Asuntojen arvo laskee" – lapsiperheet vastustavat kehitysvammaisten nuorten tukiasuntolaa Kirkkonummella. https://www.lansivayla.fi/paikalliset/1733203 (Accessed on 6.3.2023).

Maanmittauslaitos. https://www.maanmittauslaitos.fi/tietoa-maanmittauslaitoksesta/organisaatio/tilastot#Pinta-alat-kunnittain (Accessed on 26.9.2023).

Maankäyttö- ja rakennuslaki. https://www.finlex.fi/fi/laki/ajantasa/1999/19990132 (Accessed on 31.3.2022).

The Ministry of the Environment 23.10.2013. Housing for special groups. https://www.ymparisto.fi/en-us/housing/Housing_for_special_groups (Accessed on 6.3.2023).

Ministry of Finance tasks and objectives – https://vm.fi/en/task-and-objectives (Accessed on 31.3.2022).

Mölsä, Seppo. 2016. Reilut 50 vuotta sitten Mauno Koivisto ja Armas Puolimatka synnyttivät lähiöiden laatikkoarkkitehtuurin. Rakennuslehti 30.5. https://www.rakennuslehti.fi/2016/05/50-vuotta-sitten-mauno-koivisto-ja-armas-puolimatka-synnyttivat-lahioiden-laatikkoarkkitehtuurin/ (Accessed on 10.3.2022).

Montalva Barba, M. A. (2022). To move forward, we must look back: White supremacy at the base of urban studies. *Urban Studies*, online only.

National Coalition Party 29.11.2022. Kokoomuksen vaihtoehtobudjetti 2023. https://www.kokoomus.fi/kokoomuksen-vaihtoehtobudjetti-2023-kestavan-tulevaisuuden-valintoja/ (Accessed on 6.3.2023).

Oulu Premises Centre. http://tilakeskus.ouka.fi/ (Accessed on 28.8.2015).

Politico (2020). politico.eu. Eight billionaires own the same as half the world. (Accessed on 30.5.2020).

Public Sector Pension Act. thttps://www.finlex.fi/fi/laki/ajantasa/2016/20160081 (Accessed on 31.3.2022).

Reuters 5.6.2017. Blackstone offers $2 billion for Finnish real estate firm Sponda https://www.reuters.com/article/us-sponda-m-a-blackstone-idUSKBN18W0NX (Accessed on 6.3.2023).

Senate Properties 2023. https://www.senaatti.fi/valtion-kiinteistot/ (Accessed on 6.3.2023).

Senate Station Properties Ltd 2023. www.senaatti.fi/asema-alueet/en/ (Accessed on 6.3.2023).

Soininvaara, O. 2020. https://www.soininvaara.fi/2020/09/22/kaupunkiymparisto-lautakunnan-lista-22-9-2020/ (Accessed on 31.3.2022)

Statistics Finland 24.3.2023. Number of people at risk of poverty or social exclusion was 894,000 in 2021. https://www.stat.fi/en/publication/cl8lp8xaorjoa0cw1txm8lzp9 (Accessed on 9.5.2013).

Statistics Finland 19.12.2022. Tuloerojen kehitys Suomessa – tuloerot kasvoivat vuonna 2021. https://www.stat.fi/julkaisu/clbks9mb7xzkn0bumw1pbcgc6 (Accessed on 9.5.2023).

Statistics Finland. (2022). Hedelmällisyyden kehitys – lapsiluku pienenee. https://tilastokoulu.stat.fi/verkkokoulu_v2.xql?page_type=sisalto&course_id=tkoulu_vaesto&lesson_id=12&subject_id=2 (Accessed on 26.3.2022).

STT 14.2.2022. Helsingissä valmistui jälleen yli 7000 uutta asuntoa vuonna 2021. https://www.sttinfo.fi/tiedote/helsingissa-valmistui-jalleen-yli-7000-uutta-asuntoa-vuonna-2021-rakentamisen-tahti-jatkuu-reippaana?publisherId=60590288&releaseId=69932426 (Accessed on 6.3.2023).

Tampere Premises Centre. http://www.tampere.fi/tilakeskus/kehityshankkeet/inka8722innovatiivisetkaupungit.html (Accessed on 28.8.2015).

Tampereen kaupungin tilastollinen vuosikirja. Tampereen kaupunki, Konsernihallinto, 2012-2013. https://www.tampere.fi/liitteet/t/XlT1oFvgS/Tampereen_kaupungin_tilastollinen_vuosikirja_2012-2013.pdf (Accessed on 31.3.2022).

Turun kaupungin asunto- ja maankäyttöohjelma vuosille 2009–2013. https://ah.turku.fi/jlk/2009/1105013x/Images/870637.pdf (Accessed on 31.3.2022).

The Washington Post 3.2.2020. Bernie Sanders is fan of the 'Nordic Model'. Finland's leader says it's the American Dream. https://www.washingtonpost.com/world/2020/02/03/bernie-sanders-is-fan-of-nordic-model-finlands-leader-says-its-american-dream/ (Accessed on 6.3.2023).

Waldron, R. (2021). Responding to housing precarity: the coping strategies of generation rent. *Housing Studies.* Online only.

YLE 25.3.1999. Kapiteelille 9 miljardin markan kiinteistöt. https://yle.fi/a/3-5129195 (Accessed on 21.12.2022).

YLE 4.6.2018. Helsinki korottaa vuokra-asuntojensa hintoja. https://yle.fi/a/3-10222023 (Accessed on 6.3.2018).

YLE 2.2.2022. Helsinki haluaa jatkossa vuokratonteistaan markkinahinnan. https://yle.fi/uutiset/3-12299534 (Accessed on 6.3.2023).

Appendix

Part I consists primarily of desktop studies. Chapter 1 is a literature review. Chapter 2 analyses segregation research publications, policy papers and news articles (particularly Finland's largest newspaper *Helsingin Sanomat*) between the years 1999 and 2015. The primary data used for the studies at the core of this book consist of interviews with representatives of state and municipal land and housing policy authorities in Finland. A total of 25 interviews in ten cities were conducted between 2013 and 2015 for a research project entitled Land Policy and Property Rights. The project was funded by the Academy of Finland, coordinated by Professor Anne Haila, and carried out at the University of Helsinki. The interviews were conducted to investigate what type of land policy is practised in cities, the goals and means of the land policy, and how various institutional changes have affected these goals and means; Chapter 4 is largely based on this study. The interviewed officials were chiefs of municipal real estate management, chiefs of municipal housing departments, and the cities' mayors or vice mayors. The interviewees were chosen to enable the comparison of different types of cities, such as cities that had large land banks and cities that did not, old cities and new cities, growing cities and dying industrial cities. The interviewees represent people with a long professional history of decision-making regarding municipal land policy and who are experts in their field. In the interviews, land policy authorities expressed their arguments in favour of chosen land use objectives and land management strategies. The interviews also illustrate how authorities speak about social housing; what kind of arguments they use to legitimate the targeting of the provision of social housing to distinct groups and how Finland's housing policy authorities interpret housing needs.

These interviews were complimented in 2018 by interviewing five former members of the City of Helsinki Real Estate Committee, to gain more insight on how the selling of municipal land – the topic of Chapter 5 – was justified. And in 2019 a real estate boss at the state real estate company Senate Properties was interviewed concerning the state's contemporary real estate policies. In addition to interviews with policy authorities, municipal land policy and land management strategy documents are used. Documents include municipal land use and housing programmes and statistical yearbooks (Helsinki 2008–17; Tampere

2013; Turku 2009–13, 2014–17), and Helsinki City Council and Real Estate Committee meeting minutes. These documents are used to illustrate the general strategies of the respective cities and to find out whether there were disagreements or conflicts about the new real estate policies such as selling of public land.

In Chapters 6 and 7 I draw on the findings of two studies which interviewed residents in Helsinki about their experiences of living in social housing, and in neighbourhoods known for their social housing. In Chapter 6 I refer to the findings of a study conducted in 2013 in an East Helsinki housing estate regarding residents' perceptions and experiences regarding the reputation of their neighbourhood and how housing tenure features in those perceptions. Altogether 14 residents representing homeowners, private renters and social housing tenants were interviewed. Chapter 7 introduces the case of Keva, a so-called non-profit housing association displacing 56 households in Helsinki and selling the social housing apartments on the private market. Tenants from four households were interviewed to learn about their experiences of dispossession in 2020. One of the displaced tenants was the author's earlier acquaintance and she acted as an initial informant. Unofficial discussions were had with her about the displacement and she went out of her way to provide an understanding of how the events unfolded from the tenants' perspective. As rapport already existed, the informant provided me an entry to conduct interviews with her former neighbours. These interviews were semi-structured and lasted from one to two hours. The small number of interviews is explained, on the one hand, by the difficulty of reaching displaced people after the fact. Gentrification scholars have noted how studying the displaced is to study the invisible (Atkinson 2000). Furthermore, as Baeten et al. (2017, 635) note, displaced "people are not necessarily willing to 'be interviewed' about their troublesome life trajectories". And on the other hand, as the interviews showed and as discussed in the book, the tenants were concerned about running into trouble with the landlord, which would explain the wariness to participate. But the people who did agree to talk to me about their painful experiences did so willingly, and cast a piercing light on how our system of housing provision failed miserably to secure their right to stay put in their neighbourhood and how policy worked instead as a mechanism in exacerbating urban inequality.

Both Keva's Portfolio Manager and Housing Secretary, who signed the letter regarding the termination of rental contracts, refused to be interviewed regarding Keva's perspective on the matter. The study has then relied on public documents, namely Keva's Annual and Interim Reports and Keva's documents regarding investment practices, called *Investment Beliefs* and *Responsible Investment Beliefs* (Keva 2017) to get an understanding of the logic of their operation as a landlord. Furthermore, a desktop study has been conducted on the transformations in Finland's housing finance, housing policies and the Finnish pension sector and how it has permeated the housing sector.

All interviews with residents were discussions in informal settings in which the author provided a safe and anonymous setting for the residents to recount their experiences and opinions. All interviewees – both residents and officials – are treated as anonymous and any detailed personal information that might identify them is undisclosed. 25 project interviews were conducted by Juha Laukkanen and transcribed by me. I also carried out, transcribed and analysed all interviews with REC members, state real estate company representative and residents.

Index

EU representative:
Easy Access System Europe
Mustamäe tee 50, 10621 Tallinn, Estonia
Gpsr.requests@easproject.com